Class, Race and Education under Neoliberal Capitalism

Class, Race and Education under Neoliberal Capitalism

Edited by

Dave Hill

CLASS, RACE AND EDUCATION UNDER NEOLIBERAL CAPITALISM
Edited by Dave Hill

First Published in India 2017

ISBN 978-93-5002-462-1

Published by
AAKAR BOOKS
28 E Pocket IV, Mayur Vihar Phase I, Delhi 110 091
Phones: 011 2279 5505, 2279 5641
aakarbooks.gmail.com

Laser Typeset at
Arpit Printographers, Delhi 110 032

Printed at
Sapra Brothers, Delhi 110 092

Contents

Preface: Analysing and Resisting Neoliberal Capitalism in Eduction by Ravi Kumar 7
Foreword by Peter McLaren 13
Acknowledgements 19
Introduction 21

Part 1: Class and Race

1. Social Class and Education 31
Dave Hill
2. The Culturalization of Class and the Occluding of Class Consciousness: The Knowledge Industry in/of Education 54
Deborah Kelsh and Dave Hill
3. Culturalist and Materialist Explanations of Class and "Race": Critical Race Theory, Equivalence/Parallelist Theory, and Marxist Theory 95
Dave Hill

Part 2: Neoliberalism, Immiseration and Workers' Rights

4. Books, Banks and Bullets: Controlling Our Minds: The Global Project of Imperialistic and Militaristic Neoliberalism and its Effect on Education Policy 143
Dave Hill
5. Globalization and its Educational Discontents: Neoliberalization and its Impacts on Education Workers' Rights Pay and Conditions 173
Dave Hill

6. Emboungeoisment, Immiseration, Commodification—Marxism Revisited: A Critique of Education in Capitalist Systems 210
Nigel M. Greaves, Dave Hill, and Alpesh Maisuria

7. Immiseration Capitalism, Activism and Education: Resistance, Revolt and Revenge 238
Dave Hill

Preface

Analysing and Resisting Neoliberal Capitalism in Eduction

Ravi Kumar

Educational discourse getting limited to reactions to policy decisions of state and not transcending the disciplinary boundaries produces serious ramifications. One such ramification is the absence of any effort to construct a much needed holistic analysis of the situation and secondly, the failure to suggest how to get out of such a situation. It raises many eyebrows when you use words like resistance and subversion in academia and it largely reflects the way internalization of education as an ideological state apparatus has happened and the way teachers have become facilitators of rule of capital rather than teacher-transformers. Because transformation is not merely about changing lives of individuals through giving them education; it is more about questions like can lives be changed with a degree from schools? Is it not about the question of education and employment embedded in the larger context of the system?

Questions like the one asked above are uncomfortable ones and the educational discourse in India is yet to come out of its shortcomings to analyse how neoliberalism impacts education since it fails to address such questions. The effort is sparse and mostly from those who have been a critique of the changes in educational policy in the context of state withdrawal. It is important to contextualize such policy changes within the trajectory of development of capitalism and works of Dave Hill does precisely that. Dave Hill through his works on contemporary capitalism, its workings and education as located within it demonstrates the vicarious pleasure that owners of capital derive out of dehumanizing our existence because it allows them to maximize surplus accumulation through making education into a business. The beauty of his work lies in not merely analysing the dynamics but going beyond it to the realm of resisting this attack on education and society in general.

Neoliberalism is not a mode of production, it is rather a stage in development of capitalism, a stage that has its own characteristics, which though relies on the same old order and intent of maximizing surplus accumulation but uses more violent, aggressive and unabashedly dehumanizing traits. It is, as it is, only a new avatar of capitalism. What must become amply clear is that in order to get rid of it one will have to get rid of the capitalist order itself. In other words, neoliberalism is not so much an issue as capitalism is. This needs emphasis because unless it is realized the danger is always to prioritize one stage/form of capitalism as relatively better and more human over the other stage/form. This prioritization, then, would allow us to get out of the rut created by rule of capital and, therefore, we will be restrained and ambushed by capital wherever it would find us hampering its march towards accumulating surplus.

As a new stage neoliberalism works at three levels: (1) as a politico-economic ideology; (2) as/through state; and (3) as a cultural instrument that makes everybody a part of its programme. It demolishes democracy (and even liberal bourgeois democracy) and shows how democracy becomes an instrument in the hands of private capital in a very *overt* manner. Because of its new character, it has managed to take control of our everyday lives and all spheres of our existence. In this sense it has invaded our personal lives making us machinations of the grand order called capitalism. As Bourdieu says:

> The neoliberal programme draws its social power from the political and economic power of those whose interests it expresses: stockholders, financial operators, industrialists, conservative or social-democratic politicians who have been converted to the reassuring layoffs of laissez-faire, high-level financial officials eager to impose policies advocating their own extinction because, unlike the managers of firms, they run no risk of having eventually to pay the consequences. Neoliberalism tends on the whole to favour severing the economy from social realities and thereby constructing, in reality, an economic system conforming to its description in pure theory, that is a sort of logical machine that presents itself as a chain of constraints regulating economic agents (Bourdieu, 1998).

There is in a certain sense internalization of what the capital wants within us. This internalization lets us participate in the programme of capital, i.e. to optimize surplus extraction through various means. We start living the dream of private capital as it becomes our own dream. The better life in this sense becomes how capital defines 'better'. For instance, we bask in the glory of how good the workplace or its ethics is; how caring the bosses are; or how good it is of the boss to give us gadgets that we may not afford. We do not realize while basking in this glory that capital has undone the great fight that the workers fought for eight-hour work or the fight to have our own time to think and become part of a collective. We take pride in effectively working for endless hours and getting away from anything collective. The ways of working of capital at this stage are new, vicious and callous.

> In this way, a Darwinian world emerges—it is the struggle of all against all at all levels of the hierarchy, which finds support through everyone clinging to their job and organization under conditions of insecurity, suffering, and stress. Without a doubt, the practical establishment of this world of struggle would not succeed so completely without the complicity of all the *precarious arrangements* that produce insecurity and of the existence of a *reserve army of employees rendered docile by these social processes that make their situations precarious*, as well as by the permanent threat of unemployment. This reserve army exists at all levels of the hierarchy, even at the higher levels, especially among managers. The ultimate foundation of this entire economic order placed under the sign of freedom is in effect the *structural violence* of unemployment, of the insecurity of job tenure and the menace of layoff that it implies. The condition of the "harmonious" functioning of the individualist micro-economic model is a mass phenomenon, the existence of a reserve army of the unemployed.
>
> This structural violence also weighs on what is called the labour contract (wisely rationalized and rendered unreal by the "theory of contracts"). Organizational discourse has never talked as much of trust, cooperation, loyalty, and organizational culture as in an era when adherence to the organization is obtained at each moment by eliminating all temporal guarantees of employment (three-quarters of hires are for fixed duration, the proportion of temporary employees keeps rising, employment "at will" and the right to fire an individual tend to be freed from any restriction) (Bourdieu, 1998).

Neoliberalism, hence, does not leave any field untouched. It does away with the idea of public itself, takes away freedom of speech, subverts any idea of collective, democracy and dissent and transforms everything human into a well calculated and measured instrument subservient to its needs. "National and global capitalisms wish to cut public expenditure and have generally succeeded in doing so. They do this because public services are expensive. Cuts in public expenditure serve to reduce taxes on profits, which in turn increases profits from capital accumulation. Additionally, the capitalist class globally have: (a) a business agenda for education that centres on socially producing labour power (people's capacity to labour) for capitalist enterprises; (b) a business agenda in education that centres on setting business "free" in education for profit making; and (c) a business agenda *for* education corporations that allows edubusinesses to profit from national international privatizing activities" (Kumar and Hill, 2009, p. 2). It is here that education becomes important for it. In the Indian context what this meant was,

> **First**, the state must abdicate its constitutional obligation towards education of the masses in general and school-based elementary education in particular, become dependent on international aid for even primary education and work through NGOs, religious bodies and corporate houses. **Second**, the people neither have a human right as enshrined in the UN Charter nor a Fundamental Right to receiving free elementary education of equitable quality as implied by the 86th Amendment. **Third**, education is a commodity that can be marketed in the global market. It follows, therefore, that the education system—from the pre-school stage to higher education—must be, as rapidly as possible, privatized and commercialized. This central thesis has originated from the highest echelons of the global market economy and the Indian Parliament, along with India Inc., has unfortunately acquiesced without any critical scrutiny whatsoever, purportedly in the larger "national interest" (Sadgopal, 2008).

Historically, it got translated into the following on the ground:

- *Trivialization* of the goals of education, e.g. confusing education with merely literacy (e.g. National Literacy Mission of the 1990s) or skills (the 11th Plan attempts to equate education with market skills).
- *Fragmentation* of knowledge into marketable competencies, as was done in Minimum Levels of Learning (MLLs) during the early 1990s.
- *Alienation* of knowledge from its social ethos and material base, a phenomenon that has prevailed since independence but has been exacerbated several-fold in recent years by rapidly growing dependence on information technology in schools, particularly expensive private schools.
- *Increasingly* dominant role of the global market forces in determination of the character of knowledge (e.g. computer companies designing syllabi, textbooks and learning softwares).
- *Institutionalization* of economic, technological and socio-cultural hegemony of the international instruments in the formulation of curriculum, as evident in the space being given to the World Bank, UN agencies, corporate houses and their

foundations, foreign universities and externally funded researches and projects in decision-making (e.g. the Karnataka state government's move in 2007 to build SIEMAT under the control of Wipro Ltd. which was forestalled owing to public outcry).

- *Introduction* of parallel and hierarchical educational streams for different social segments, as discussed above.
- *Marginalization* of poor children and youth as well as the backward regions through competitive screening and a discriminatory system of institutional assessment and accreditation (e.g. Pratham's assessment of reading, writing and computing skills of grade V children in ASER Reports of 2006 and 2007 or NAAC's standard criteria for categorizing colleges/ universities); and
- *Attrition* of the state-supported and democratic structures for educational planning, finance allocation and management, as exemplified by the introduction of the idea of School Vouchers in the 11th Plan, though none of the seven CABE committees had recommended it in 2005 (Sadgopal, 2008).

Neoliberalism in education is about turning learning experiences into mechanical skill development processes shorn of any critical insight. It seeks to paralyze mental abilities to imagine alternatives and hope for better futures. This is the reason why in every discourse on education one finds emphasis on skill development at its core. Education is meant to destabilize the pillars of inequality and foster a thought process that democratizes our existence through a dialogic process of learning. The neoliberal, on the other hand, is fearful of this kind of education because it does not want subversive minds to develop. It does not want one to even think that there can be an alternative to capitalism. By doing this it stunts intellectual growth of students in schools and colleges and universities; it destroys the idea of equality based on gender or class or caste. Any resistance to neoliberalism in general and neoliberal education in particular will have to locate itself within the context of developing an education system, creating a pedagogical and curricular framework that becomes an antithesis to the existing system.

This book by Dave Hill will fill the much needed expansion of discourse on neoliberalism and education. It brings the perspective from a wider angle because of its approach of revolutionary critical pedagogy and its geographical location from where it began. Indian educational discourse will have to expand itself to critically reflect on the developments in the country and this will be of great help.

References

Bourdieu, Pierre (1998). Utopia of Endless Exploitation: The Essence of Neoliberalism, Le Monde Diplomtique, available at http://mondediplo.com/1998/12/08bourdieu (Accessed on July 12, 2004).

Kumar, Ravi and Hill, Dave (2009). 'Introduction: Neoliberal Capitalism and Education' in Hill, Dave and Kumar, Ravi (eds.) *Global Neoliberalism and Education and its Consequences*, Routledge: New York and London.

Sadgopal, Anil (2008). Common School System and the Future of India, Radical Notes, available at http://radicalnotes.com/2008/02/28/common-school-system-and-the-future-of-india/ (accessed on March 7, 2007)

Foreword

Peter McLaren

Few educators have been more of an inspiration to teachers and the education activists that inhabit inner-cities worldwide than Dave Hill. Nor to my knowledge is there another single educator who has given more sustained ballast to the socialist movement in education worldwide, largely due to his tireless efforts at building international networks of critical educators for the purpose of moving forward a transnational socialist agenda. This is no mean feat, especially at a time when there is a full frontal assault on municipal services, government programmes that serve working class youth, and the system of public education.

Capitalist globalization is teaching us that workers of other nations are the enemy rather than the transnational corporations that divide and weaken all workers. A brutal market-based initiative funded by private foundations, powered by high octane doses of novelist Ayn Rand's *The Fountainhead*, and her 'greed-is-good' philosophy, and fanatically inspired by University of Chicago economist Milton Friedman's economic theory (epitomized in books such as *Capitalism and Freedom)*, have—thanks largely to a billion dollar public relations campaign that allows them to survive their graft-ridden attempts to privatize public education—forced many public schools into receivership.

Those who are not 'creamed' into the high echelon ranks of the educational system—those with limited proficiency in English, who scramble for survival in working class neighbourhoods, or who have special needs—are left to scavenge through the debris of what is left of public education after the shock-and-awe effects of neoliberal market orthodoxy which has created self-perpetuating mechanisms of educational success for the ruling class and their confederacy of patrons and immiseration education for the rest.

It is precisely at this historical conjuncture that Dave Hill has emerged as one of public education's most ardent and fearless defenders. And while his scholarly work and activism has emerged out of the field of critical educational studies, where it has been forged as much in the crucible of working class struggle as it has in the heady salons of the university professoriat, it has applications elsewhere, including the realm of Marxist theory and revolutionary socialist praxis. It is here that Dave Hill, from a London East End family emerges as a critical polymath, as someone who over the years has been ideologically steeled by working the shop floor, by serving as a trade union representative, by teaching prisoners, adult education tutors and Vietnamese refugees in immigrant camps, by serving his working class constituents with fearless tenacity as an elected councillor of the Labour Party, by teaching at the comprehensive school level and in higher educational institutions throughout England where he worked with mature and non-standard entry students as well as students from privileged backgrounds, and by forging his perspectives on global politics as a part-time photo-journalist for some various left presses in Britain, covering elections in Portugal, Spain and France for *New Socialist*, *Labour Weekly* and *Tribune*.

While Dave Hill is more at home working with students from his London East End roots, organizing picket lines, setting up independent research units consisting of top education scholars, or editing *the Journal of Critical Education Policy Studies* (one of the widest circulation English language online refereed education policy journals, with a million free downloads since 2003), or engaging in strategic planning with his comrades in Socialist Resistance, left Unity, and the Trade Unionist and Socialist Coalition than he is lecturing to elite audiences in conferences on educational reform where he is in high demand worldwide as a keynote speaker, he never loses sight of his guiding star—which illuminates a democratic alternative to a society ruled by capital's value form. This forging of a democratic socialist alternative is not an exclusionary movement on Hill's part. In fact, he partners in critical solidarity with liberal, democratic-participative groups who work under the banner of social justice with a view to deepening their understanding of and appreciation of Marxist analysis.

This was the case in my own meeting with Dave Hill in the mid-1980s in Oxford Ohio. Dave Hill never gave up on this fledgling critical educator who was raised academically in the tradition of Foucault, Derrida, and existential phenomenology, marinated with the anarchist works of the Beat poets and literature born in the heat of the civil rights movement.

Over time, largely through an engagement with the works of Marx, I began to appreciate more and more the work of Hill and his colleagues—Glenn Rikowski, Mike Cole and Paula Allman. And over time alliances were made—largely through the leadership of Dave Hill—that now have an international reach, bringing together North American, Latin American, European and Southeast Asian educational workers. This book is very much a product of that union, but its centrepiece is the sturdiness of a Marxist theory co-developed by Hill that has weathered countless crises, not least of which has been the overpopulation of postmodern scholarship in our educational theorizing. His work has galvanized teachers, scholars and workers of every stripe to adopt a Marxist analysis of class into their work. I have served on the barricades with Dave in England, Ireland, Greece and Turkey.

During a break at an education conference in Limerick, Dave attended an urgent meeting about the €100 (£83) flat-rate household charge that every Irish homeowner was required to pay as part of a government 'austerity' measure. Dave stood on a chair amidst a raucous crowd of protestors that had gathered in a hotel meeting room and gave a vintage impromptu speech, a lesson on political extemporization of the kind that has made him famous, as he sliced through the rhetoric of the Fine Gael-Labour coalition, comparing the house tax to Margaret Thatcher's poll tax, with a tongue as sharp as the razor with which Jack the Ripper wielded with such ferocity in the same dark streets where Dave and his brothers roamed as children, the streets where their father, a cabinet-maker, had laboured for years, cutting flat stock with a double bevel mitre saw, chasing after job after job. Afterwards, in a local pub over a pint of plain, where locals were slagging each other and acting the maggot, Dave Hill was approached and thanked for his comradeship and solidarity. I have seen that happen many times in several places.

I remember vividly Dave taking me on a tour of Syntagma Square in Athens, not far from the underground passage where Dave, his comrade Kostas Skordoulis, and a handful of workers from the 4th International were trapped by a phalanx of baton-wielding riot police, who pounded them mercilessly with canister after canister of tear gas, knowing that there was no place for the gas to escape, except into the burning lungs of Dave and his comrades. Dave would have to forgo his speeches for a time after his ordeal, to give his lungs time to repair the ravages of the chlorobenzylidene malononitrile. The following year I met Dave in Ankara, Turkey, where we were tear-gassed while participating in a protest rally. The haze left by the gas was so thick that we became separated in the melee. My crumpled body, felled by a wave of riot police, was dragged from the street by a waiter from a nearby restaurant and hidden in a back room until the police left the area. Shortly after returning to the streets, I found Dave and another comrade searching for me. They were already preparing to join the next round of protests.

Dave is what we refer to in the United States as a scholar-activist. His presence, whether in person or through his many publications, is respected in international conferences on Marxist and critical education worldwide, although he is acutely aware of the higher status accorded to those groups and organizations known as BANA—Britain, North America and Australasia. Dave's own perspective is democratic revolutionary Marxist, where he adopts a classical Marxist social class analysis (i.e. using a binary analysis of class), contesting other approaches that diminish both the importance and urgency of class-based exploitation, the defining feature of capitalism, the capital-labour relation. The 'activist' side of Dave Hill urges us to go beyond critique into socialist reconstruction, and additionally, to go beyond social democratic reformism into revolutionary anti-capitalist Marxism. It is here that Dave Hill parts company with many academic Marxists, whose commitment to Marxism remains antiseptically cleaved from the interests of the wider polity and too often remains trapped at the level of academic brinkmanship, forging esoteric enclaves in university departments for the purposes of producing arcane works that speak mainly or only to those interested in debating footnotes. Dave Hill has been producing articles, chapters, pamphlets, blogs and books and collabouratively publishing on socialist education for over twenty-five years, with most of the work available online for increased accessibility.

Hill pays close attention to the existence of horizontal (for example, unskilled manual, white collar lower level management and supervisory, professional strata) and vertical segmentation (on the basis of gender, "race" for example) within the working class, which is that class of people who sell their labour power but his fundamental focus is the transcendence of the capital/labour relation altogether. In addition, he rejects Weberian inspired/lifestyle classifications used in official government statistics with respect to identifying patterns and processes of privilege and underprivilege within the capitalist state, maintaining that such classifications 'hide' the capitalist class, hide the relations of production—the source of Marxist definitions of class, and serve to segment and divide the working class—that class of workers (and dependents) who sell their labour-power for a wage and who are condemned to suffering and protracted agony as a result of the built-in crises endemic to capitalism.

That both Dave Hill and I have been criticized as Marxist educators by right-wing pandits in both our countries should not be surprising, especially in the context of the resurgent neo-Confederate ideologies percolating throughout the United States. But certain factions of the educational left have also attacked us for the failings of our supposed Marxist 'orthodoxy' and in Dave's case this is most readily explained by his trenchant criticisms of neo-Marxism, revisionist Marxism, reformist Marxism, identitarianism and postmodernism.

Clearly, it is not academic or theoretical disputes within Marxist educational theory or the desire to detoxify the liberal reformism that has taken hold of so much of the educational left that drives Dave Hill's project for a democratic socialist alternative to immiseration capitalism. For Hill, the struggle for socialism is also a moral imperative. Consequently, this book reflects outrage at the morbid, obsessional fear and hatred of the working class by the capitalist class and the puritanical zeal that fuels their rationalizations as to why the price paid for the comfort of the rich must be in the currency of human tragedy: the tears of the poor. Now that the multinational corporations have integrated East Asia into networks of integrated production, the overall process of capitalist globalization has been intensified, sternly decreeing all of us to become agents of mass consumption. The moral opprobrium heaped by Hill on the capitalist class is entirely justified, as we increasingly inhabit a world where the poor are terminally disempowered and disenfranchised, where we are witnessing an exponential increase in joblessness, anxiety, suicides, early deaths, chronic ill-health, homelessness, hunger, and hopelessness. Neoliberal capitalist policies, Hill writes, are deliberately causing immiseration. Not one to waffle or apologize, Hill calls it like it is: class genocide.

As a revolutionary Marxist educator, Hill is quick to appreciate the potential role of teachers in the struggle for socialism. Since they are connected with the social production of labour power, acting, in fact, as intellectual guardians of the labourers responsible for a glorious capitalist future, teachers are deemed dangerous by the sentinels of the capitalist hegemony. The state wishes to guard against forms of pedagogy whose criteria might hinder the reproduction of certain forms of labour-power necessary to grease the wheels of capitalist production and to ensure that those applying the grease are covered in chalk dust and not tainted by theory, and thus less likely to ask questions. State education wishes to restock such teachers. For such teachers will not be a threat to the new and ominous possibilities we face under the current capitalist threat, including new forms of authoritarian rule, and the rise of fascism and military dictatorships. To the extent that liberating one's own words becomes a basis for liberating one's deeds, the Marxist approach to socialist democracy argued in this book is urgently needed for understanding both the perils and the promises affecting human life at a time of capitalist retrenchment and reconstitution. And for working towards an alternative to the capitalist organization of human affairs.

Class, Race and Education under Neoliberal Capitalism, affords activists and educators a special opportunity to find some of the most influential works on Marxist education to date in a single volume. It is in this sense that this collection by Dave Hill has the potential to become a 'quilting point' for progressive educators worldwide to enter into serious dialogue with Marxist critique in order to advance the necessary socialist re-ordering and reconstruction of the economy, society and polity built on the imperatives of economic equality and social justice for all.

Acknowledgements

Permission sought and obtained for the reproduction of each of these chapters and articles.

Chapter 1 was first published as Hill, D. (1999) Social Class and Education. In D. Matheson and I. Grosvenor (eds.) *An Introduction to the Study of Education*. pp. 84-102. London: David Fulton.

Chapter 2 was first published as Kelsh, D. and Hill, D. (2006) The Culturalization of Class and the Occluding of Class Consciousness: The Knowledge Industry in/of Education. *Journal for Critical Education Policy Study,* 4(1). March. Online at http://www.jceps.com/index.php?pageID=article&articleID= 59.

Chapter 3 was first published as Hill, D. (2009) Culturalist and Materialist Explanations of Class and 'Race': Critical Race Theory, Equivalence/Parallelist Theory and Marxist Theory. *Cultural Logic: An Electronic Journal of Marxist Theory and Practice.* Online at http://clogic.eserver.org/2009/2009//////////htm/l.

Chapter 4 was first published as Hill, D. (2004) Books, Banks and Bullets: Controlling Our Minds—The Global Project of Imperialistic and Militaristic Neo-liberalism and its Effect on Education Policy. *Policy Futures in Education,* 2, 3-4, pp. 504-522 (Theme: Marxist Futures in Education). Online at http://www.wwwords.co.uk/pdf/viewpdf/asp?j=pfie&vol=2&issue=3&year=2004&article=6Hill_PFIE_2_34_web&id=81.158.104.245.

Chapter 5 was first published as Hill, D. (2005) Globalisation and its educational discontents: Neoliberalisation and its impacts on education workers' rights, pay, and conditions. *International Studies in the Sociology of Education* 15(3), pp. 257-288.

Chapte 6 was first published as Greaves, N.M. Hill, D. and Maisuria, A. (2007) Embourgeoisment, Immiseration, Commodification—Marxism Revisited: A Critique of Education in Capitalist System. *Journal for*

Critical Education Policy Studies, 4(1). May. Online at http://jceps.com/pring.php?articleID=83.

Chapter 7 was first published as Hill, D. (2012) Immiseration Capitalism, Activism and Education: Resistance, Revolt and Revenge. *Journal for Critical Education Policy Studies,* 10(2). October Online at http://www.jceps.com/index.php?pageID=article& article ID=259.

Introduction

Marxist Theory

With the onset of Austerity Capitalism and Immiseration Capitalism, and with the increasing commodification, marketization, privatization and commercialization of society, and of education, Marxist theory and analysis and Marxist education theory have taken on a new urgency. An urgency in both understanding what is going on— and in informing, playing a part in—the resistance, informing activism within the education arenas, and in the wider society. In this volume, there is more than critique— there is a call for anger and analysis, a call to action, a demand for theoretically informed practice in the different arenas of Resistance.

This need for Marxist analysis—and organization and activism—is particularly pronounced in the face of the ever more widely apparent 'class war from above', which various chapters in this volume expose, in which bankers and the transnational and national capitalist class gets ever richer, while for billions globally, and millions in each of the 'advanced capitalist economies of 'The West', the living standards, the conditions of labour, the quality and provision of public and formerly public institutions and services—and the basic material conditions of life themselves—are diminished, depleted and degraded. We are now, in much of the advanced, late capitalist industrialized world, in an era of intensified class struggle, intensified (gendered and 'raced') social class stratification. And intensified resistance.

What I try to do in this collection of essays, written from a classic Marxist analysis, is to lay bare how the capitalist class and their sometimes unwitting, sometimes unwilling, helpmates in the knowledge industry/academia, and in other areas of cultural reproduction such as the media, use the ideological (and repressive) state apparatuses, such as education, to divide, disarm and demoralize critical, Marxist analysis and activism along, for example, lines of social class strata and of 'race'.

Immiseration Capitalism in the Era of Austerity

As Saad-Filho notes,

> In essence, neoliberalism is based on the systematic use of state power, under the ideological guise of 'non-intervention', to impose a hegemonic project of recomposition of the rule of capital at five levels: domestic resource allocation, international economic integration, the reproduction of the state, ideology, and the reproduction of the working class. (Saad-Filho, 2011)

Immiseration Capitalism is the intensification of neoliberal capitalism. Its impacts are increased, intensified, human suffering and despair—sheer fear for many, nagging ever-present anxiety for others over where the next meal is coming from, how to clothe a growing child, is, for many, immense. Many, globally, are falling into absolute immiseration, not simply the relative immiseration of much of the post (second) world war period.

> In recent decades there has been across the Capitalist world, the progression of '*relative* immiseration', with the wealth of the working class growing far more slowly than that of the Capitalist class. But what we are seeing now, most spectacularly of all in Greece, but also in countries such as Britain, Ireland and the USA, is the progression of '*absolute* immiseration', with an absolute deterioration of income, wealth and living conditions- and mass impoverishment. (Hill, 2012. See also Hill 2006)

The term 'Immiseration Capitalism' draws on Marx's concept of immiseration in Volume 1 of *Capital.* (Malott and Hill, 2013). As Marx put it:

> Accumulation of wealth at one pole ... is at the same time accumulation of misery, the torment of labour, slavery, ignorance, brutalization and moral degradation at the other pole, i.e. on the side of the class that produces its own product as capital. (1976/1867:799)

These changes in the material conditions of hundreds of millions of workers—workers from middle as well as lower strata, together with social/cultural degradation— degrading of the social and welfare state, slashing of welfare and social benefits, —are only too evident. The poor are dying younger. Formerly affluent manual workers, supervisors, professional workers now scavenge for food in rubbish bins and wait in line at soup kitchens, millions of jobless youth see their hopes—of employment, housing, family life—sundered, while those in work are forced to work harder and longer for less and less, under poorer and poorer conditions.

Widespread changes in class and political consciousness, explosive revulsion at immiseration capitalism, at impoverishment, at the growing and stark inequalities between 'haves' and 'have-nots', between the capitalist economic social class and the capitalist political class—overwhelmingly their subservient servants—on one side, and the 99 per cent on the other are on multitudinous lips and minds. The corollary to this intensification of immiseration, of capitalist exploitation, is the intensification of resistance. Resistance that is visibly expressed in the rebellions, riots and flames on the streets of Athens, Ankara, London, (in these first three, I participated), Lisbon, Istanbul, Rio de Janeiro, Sofia, with millions demonstrating and taking part in general strikes, in 'Occupy'/ *Indignado* movements, in student, worker, environmentalist and community protests. In the words of Karl Marx and Friedrich Engels' (1848),

> Society as a whole is more and more splitting up into two great hostile camps, into two great classes directly facing each other: Bourgeoisie and Proletariat'. (Marx and Engels, 1848/1960:109)

Alongside the revulsion, this growing anger and resistance, there is something else- something immensely dangerous to the capitalist class. That is, a gradually developing understanding that the logic of Capital demands that it, capitalism, cannot be adequately reformed, but that it must be replaced. A revolutionary perspective that insists on the primacy of changing capitalist relations of production. 'And this 'revolutionary doing' is to expose—in the act of transcending—the dictatorship of abstract labour (and abstract time) as the root of class exploitation and human immiseration' (Hill et al., 2013). This Marxist 'revolutionary doing', is the development of class consciousness, of the understanding and the will to political action with a socialist, a Marxist perspective.

Capitalism and Class

It is important to make clear that neoliberalism is simply the latest stage of capitalism. This book is written as a critique not just of neoliberal capitalism as it has developed since the 1970s since the Thatcher-Reagan era. And not just a critique of the current phase of that era, since 2007-2008, of 'Immiseration' or 'Austerity Capitalism'. This book is, in essence, a critique of capitalism itself, of capitalist economic relations, of capitalist social relations, of the Capital-Labour relation. All capitalism, Capitalism itself, is based on, characterized by, defined by, the Capital Labour relation—the exploitation of the labour power of workers by the capitalist class.

We Marxists, and critical educators in general, seek to serve and advance the interests of the working class. We, as teachers, as educators, are working class, too, we sell our labour power to capitalists and to the apparatuses of the capitalist state, such as schools and universities. We have to challenge the dominant ideology, the hegemony of the ruling class, the bourgeoisie, the capitalist class. We are in a battle for dominance of our ideas; there are "culture wars" between different ways of looking at/interpreting the world. We have to contest the currently hegemonic control of ideas by the capitalist state, schools, media, and their allies in the religions. If we sit and do nothing, if their ideas are not contested, then capitalism will continue to rule, to demean, to divide, to impoverish us, and the planet.

Resistance and Programme

At certain times in history, and in certain locations, the disjunction—the gap, the difference—between the material conditions of workers' existence on the one hand, our daily lived experience, and, on the other hand, what the newspapers and the media and the imam and the priest and the rabbi say/preach, that gap becomes so stark, so obvious, that workers' subjective consciousness changes. At this moment—now—in some countries in the world, the gap between the "official" ideology that "we are all in together" and that "there is no alternative" (to austerity), or, in schools and universities faced by commodification and managerialism and (pre)-privatization—that gap becomes so large that the ruling party, and the ruling capitalist class, and capitalism itself, loses legitimacy. And so, as in Greece now, and in Portugal, in Spain, in Turkey and Brazil, and in other countries such as Britain, we Marxists are necessary. Necessary in leading and developing changes in consciousness, a change in class consciousness, and in playing a leading role in organizing for the replacement of capitalism.

The resistance cannot be aimless, cannot be inchoate. There has to be consideration of, discussion of, understanding of 'programme', of aims, of where we want to go, beyond 'heaving them (those in power) out'.

In 1938, in *The Transitional Programme*, Trotsky addresses the types of programmes moving the discussion beyond *minimum programme* (minimum acceptable reforms, such as those to protect and improve existing rights and entitlements, such as rights at work, social and political rights)) and *maximum programme* (socialist revolution, with the type of society ultimately envisaged by Marx, a socialist non-capitalist/post-capitalist society) that were advanced by the late 19th and early 20th century on class not as an abstract category but instead as a lived experience" (p. 117). The politics of cultural forms and practices, then, are grounded in experience, which Apple frames as containing a "truth" beyond the explanatory reach of class as relation to property in a system of production.

What this does, however, is posit experience, as Young (2006) has argued in a critique of Patricia Hill Collins' work, as "the limit text of the real" (p. 2). Young explains why this is problematic:

> experience is a highly mediated frame of understanding. Though it is true that a person of colour experiences oppression, this experience is not self-explanatory and, therefore, it needs to be situated in relation to other social practices. Experience seems local but it is, like all cultural and political practices, interrelated to other practices and experiences. Thus its explanation come from its "outside." Theory, specifically Marxist theory, provides an explanation of this outside by reading the meaning of all experiences as determined by the economic realities of class. (p. 2)

Similarly, Gimenez (2001) has argued that while experience is "illuminating" because it gives us access to "how people describe their understanding of their lives,"

> Experience in itself, however, is suspect because, dialectically, it is a unity of opposites; it is, at the same time, unique, personal, insightful and revealing and, at the same time, thoroughly social, partial, mystifying, itself the product of historical forces about which individuals may know little or nothing about. (p. 30)

In other words, experience is not the limit text of the truth, because it is a description, and "description... no matter how thorough, has meaning only within a specific theoretical context" (Gimenez, 2001, p. 29). And the theories that people have to understand experience, even to frame the description of experience, are heavily mediated by the interests of the capitalist class, which privileges those theories that accord with its aim: more profit for itself. In other words, theory that is "out there" to use to frame or explain experience is *put* "out there" by the capitalist class.

Apple knows this. He himself writes that "Grasping what [current developments in the marketization of the world] means is made harder in daily life for all of us because of the dominant forms of interpretation that are now made available or *not* made easily available in education and in the media" (2006, p. 16).

What Apple wants to get at by examining experience is "possibilities that exist for altering dominant relations" (1986, p. 24). However, this is a *limited programme*. It can only result in small changes at local sites, changes that, because they take place within the framework of capitalism, can succeed only in securing gains that (a) take away from the resources of another group at another site, given the limited resources the capitalist class allots to and divides among the proletariat; or (b) can easily be taken away in another local struggle where the group who serves the interests of the capitalist class are advantaged in some way or another. Moreover, it conveniently forgets that these "possibilities" are likely those formulated out of theories that the capitalist class has put out there. Still, Apple valorizes the experiential and in doing so, serves the interests of the capitalist class.

Apple's triptych formulation aligns with that of Anderson and Collins' (1998) formulation of the "matrix of domination" that understands "race, class, and gender as different but interrelated axes of social structure" (p. 3). In this widely accepted and used framework, race, class, and gender are understood as "interlocking categories of experience that affect all aspects of human life; thus, they simultaneously structure the experiences of all people in this society. At any moment, race, class, or gender may feel more salient or meaningful in a given person's life, but they are overlapping and cumulative in their effect on people's experience" (p. 3).

Gimenez (2001) refers to this as the theory of *intersectionality*: "an account of the multiplicity of locations effecting individuals [sic] experiences, or as a study of the patterned variations in the identities individuals claim for themselves regardless of those locations." She critiques it because it "cannot explain either the sources of inequalities or their reproduction over time" (p. 29). Insofar as Apple posits a triptych formulation, his framework has the same limit.

Furthermore, though, the triptych framework undermines itself. As Young argues in his critique of Collins,

> If race, class, gender, and the accompanying ideological apparatuses are interlocking systems of oppression, as Collins suggests, then the experiential is not the site for the "true" but rather the site for the articulation of dominant ideology. On what basis, then, could the experiential provide grounds for an historical understanding of the structures that make experience itself possible as experience? (2006, p. 2)

The triptych framework Apple currently uses, in which "it is from the experience of attempting to create a new, more democratic politics of school life that we can learn what is possible" (1993, p. 41), ignores that such experiences are ideological in the sense, as explained above, that ideology involves an attempt to make sense of cultural contradictions rooted in the relations of exploitation by covering them over and re-narrating them in terms of some "differences" that, while the differences appear at the level of culture to be natural, are not, but rather socially constructed. This is the place to say that social differences are, by ideology, naturalized as inevitable, rather that interrogated and critiqued as socially constructed (Ebert, 1996, p. 8).

It is important to note that Apple's (and Collins') triptych formulation of race, class, and gender does not enable understanding of the relations between these three formations. In the triptych formulation, they are unified only at the level of experience, and even there each may not be acknowledged. In contrast, the Marxist theory of class does provide an integrated and transformative understanding of the three.

In the Marxist theory of the social, as opposed to that of the revisionist left, individual differences and differences within individuals are valorized under capitalism only to be curtailed by being pressed into the service of "the specific end and aim, the sum and substance, of capitalist production": "the production of surplus-value [profit]" (Marx, 1867/1967a, p. 298). Individual differences are not under capitalism brought out so as to allow human capacities to be developed for their own sake and for the benefit of all, but in order to be shaped so that they can be used to enrich the capitalist class by being developed as labour-power. As Marx and Engels argued, "differences of age and sex have no longer any distinctive social validity for the working class. All are instruments of labour, more or less expensive to use, according to their age and sex" (1848/1985, p. 88).

In other words, the core opposition between labour and capital that structures all production practices is used by the capitalist class for one purpose: "production of surplus-value [profit]," which as Marx explains is "the absolute law" of the capitalist mode of production (Marx, 1867/1967a, p. 618). The capitalist class, in its quest for ever more surplus-value, seizes upon any opposition that, owing to historical developments preceding or within capitalism, enables the production of more surplus-value. As Marx argues, the "division of labour seizes upon, not only the economic, but every other sphere of society and everywhere lays the foundation of that all engrossing system of specializing and sorting men" (1867/1967a, p. 354). These socially constructed and ideologically naturalized and enforced oppositions—those involved in race, gender, sexuality, age, ability, and so forth—are folded in to the core opposition of labour and capital. In *Capital* Volume 1, in the chapter on "The Working Day," Marx in fact shows how and explains why gender and age were folded into class.

This is to say that, in capitalism, race *is* class, gender *is* class, ability *is* class. This is *not* to argue that race, gender, ability, and so forth are not heavily mediated by cultural practices informed by ideology. They are. And those cultural practices informed by ideology have devastating effects on individuals and social groups. As McLaren and Scatamburlod'Annibale (2004) have argued, "An historical materialist approach ...acknowledges the 'material' force of ideologies—particularly racist ideologies." However, as they go on to explain, such an approach acknowledges ideologies also as forces that "assign separate cultural and/or biological essences to different segments of the population which, in turn, serve to reinforce and rationalize existing relations of power" (p. 186).

In other words, cultural practices informed by ideology enable the reproduction of race, gender, ability, and so forth *as* class. From the vantage point of classical Marxism, then, Apple, in his separation of race, gender, and class into separate "dynamics" does not serve the interests of the proletariat as a whole, and in fact, works to shore up ideological understandings that reproduce inequity.

Marxism does not valorize the proliferation of differences said to be actually existing, since to do so would be to contribute to the reduction of persons to "instruments of labour." Rather, through ideology critique Marxism produces revolutionary knowledges which are capable of explaining and transforming the exploitative social relations of wage labour. These relations require that some qualities be ideologically apprehended as constituting identities—age, sexuality, gender...—in order to supply the differences which can be hierarchized into strata in the workforce and then used to explain away the hierarchization as "naturally" following from (naturalized) difference.

The Knowledge Industry in/of Education: Professional Ideologues and the Dismissal of the Vanguard

What the dominant ideology needs most to secure in order to reproduce the social relations of production in capitalism is the subject who understands herself to be "free" and therefore understands the sale of her own labour-power on the market to be the practice of freedom rather than the effect of "the dull compulsion of economic relations" (Marx, 1867/1967a, p. 737). All knowledges which attempt to inculcate the subject as "free" must involve a double move: the cause of all inequity—the fact that the binary class relations of exploitation emerge from the historical development of private ownership of what is socially produced, specifically, the means of production —must be occluded, and a cultural space must be opened in which the individual or group has agency, and therefore believes he or she is free within the given mode of production and that knowledge of class is therefore no longer necessary. This is a tactic used by the knowledge industry. Morton (1990) has theorized it as the practice of "set[ting] the limits of the horizon surveyed in such a way as to occlude the 'troublesome,' while claiming to open up issues to the full spectrum of 'reasonable' views" (p. 57).

Apple, in using a Weberian-based theory of class, and other writers such as Allman (for a critique, see Kelsh, 2006) , in rejecting the centrality of property to the concept of class, both engage in this practice of opening up issues to the full spectrum of "reasonable" views: a wide variety of classes. They disappear the "troublesome": class as that which is determined by the social (property) relations of production. In this way, they open a space for individual or group agency.

Apple in particular, by pluralizing the Marxist concept of property from the vantage point of "market situation," makes it possible for everyone to be an "owner" of something and have a degree of power and therefore agency or "freedom." His Weberian-based theory of class, that is, is deployed both as an alibi to explain away inequitable access to resources (rather than to explain the cause of it), and as that which opens the space for the agency of the subject: one can, by apprehending the social from the vantage point of the market, believe that the exercise of agency consists in the rational calculation of the most effective means to realize the life chances allowed by the market situation. Because this is a "freedom" which masks that persons who do not own the means of production are compelled to sell their labour-power, it is a "freedom" which protects the regime of wage-labour from question.

As we will explain, a Weberian-based theory of class, such as that used by Michael W. Apple, does not contradict the interests of the capitalist class because such a theory of class can ultimately be used to reproduce a "liberal" view of the subject as "free man" who "is the cause, and not the effect, of social meanings" (Zavarzadeh and Morton, 1991, p. 1).

The understanding of class underpinning Apple's works, in which everyone is regarded as an "owner" of something or other and can imagine based on that ownership of "possessions" that she has a degree of power and therefore agency or "freedom," aligns with the Bush Administration's theme of the "Ownership Society," the "unifying theme on domestic policy as put forth in President Bush's [Second] Inaugural Address" (Rosenbaum, p. 20). It is also in alignment with themes Margaret Thatcher has often used, as, for example, when she argued that

> Private ownership—of companies, of homes, of property of every kind—goes far deeper than mere efficiency. All of us in politics have dreams. It is

> part of mine to give power and responsibility back to people, to restore to individuals and families the sense and feeling of independence. The great reform of the last century was to make more and more people voters. The great reform of our time is to make more and more people owners (Thatcher, 1986).

As explained in the USA in the *Economic Report of the President* (2005), "When used in economics, the term resource refers not just to natural resources, such as land or clean air, but to anything of value, such as skills. A property right refers broadly to the arrangements society uses to assign people control over resources" (p. 118). As in the Weberian understanding of class, "property" in the understanding of the Bush Administration refers to any tangible or intangible entity an individual can be said to possess and bring to the "market." As explained in the "Overview" of the Economic Report, "Property rights have a variety of names, including deeds, titles, permits, vouchers, allowances, or accounts" ("Overview"). Thus in the framework of the Ownership Society, "property" includes homes, health savings accounts, social security savings accounts (Office of the Press Secretary, 2004), and school vouchers (Rosen, 2005).

On the basis of this very broad and Weberian-based understanding of property, David Boaz, executive vice president of The Cato Institute, claims that "increasing numbers of Americans are becoming capitalists—people who own a share of productive businesses through stocks or mutual funds" (n.d., para. 6). Yes, notes Robert Reich, "It's true that more than half of American households now own stocks in corporations. But for most, it's just a few thousand dollars worth. And the total value of their current portfolio is less than they invested" (2004, para. 4).

However, all these people are not capitalists insofar as the "property" they own does *not* enable them to live off the labour-power of others, and does *not*, for example, enable themto incorporate in a country where labour-power is cheaper and command that labour-power in the interest of appropriating ever more surplus-value. Instead, most live in fear of losing health care, seeing their retirement accounts wiped out, or watching as a chief executive engages in such risky (market) behavior (for the purpose of more profit for the few) that thousands of dollars invested in stocks evaporate. It is the ability to critique the bourgeois class interests of notions such as the "Ownership Society" that is lost when the concept of property is either erased, as it is in Allman (for a critique, see Kelsh, 2006), or pluralized, as it is in Apple.

Indeed, Apple's works in particular not only removes the capitalist class from view, but provide alibis for the capitalist class. He describes what he calls the "professional and managerial new middle class" (2006; see also 1992, pp. 134-136, 140-142):

This fraction of the professional new middle class gains its own mobility within the state and within the economy based on the use of technical expertise. These are people with backgrounds in management and efficiency techniques who provide the technical and 'professional' support for accountability, measurement, 'product control,' and assessment that is required by the proponents of neoliberal politics of marketization and neoconservative policies of tighter central control in education. (2006, p. 48)

By advancing an understanding of class in which there is no capitalist class, Apple takes the focus off of the capitalist class and puts it on this class fraction. An example of the way this alibi for the capitalist class becomes taken up is evident in the "Manifesto" of the students occupying the Sussex University Library:

We are here because the standards at Sussex University are falling. We believe that the recent cuts to the library epitomize the problems facing students at this university. We believe that we are entitled to a high level of education and that large seminars and few resources, either academic or material, are not going to achieve this. We regret that this action may inconvenience library staff and we stress that this action is in opposition to the library cutbacks and redundancies perpetrated by university senior management. We demand more transparency from the university and that it calls an emergency council meeting, open to all students, during term. We want to show the university the extent and level of discontent among students and we wish to show our complete support for the aims of the sort Sout campaign [the general campaign against the cuts at the University of Sussex], as well as the staff in all their industrial action... From Bogota to Paris, our struggle at Sussex University is global. (Personal communication, Marx SIG, March 10, 2006)

In the view of the students, the cause of inequitable distribution of resources is "university senior management." The students' focus is not on the capitalist class, and this may block the development of their class consciousness. What is necessary to explain is *why* university senior management made such decisions, and to implicate their decisions in the totality of capitalist practices.

This is *not* to argue that the student action and statement are not important. They are important, as are tens of thousands of other local, sectional, trade-based, and community-based issues, as we noted in the

Introduction. And in such conditions class consciousness can develop. However, class consciousness cannot develop without the theory that, as Marx notes in his Afterword to the Second German Edition of *Capital* Volume 1, "represents the class whose vocation in history is the overthrow of the capitalist mode of production and the final abolition of all classes—the proletariat" (1867/1967a, p. 16). It is this very theory that Apple, in all his works, denies to the proletariat, and which we are working to make available.

It is also necessary to note that there is nothing "new" about the "middle class" fraction Apple describes here. As Apple is well aware (1992, p. 127), classical Marxism theorizes that "the class which has the means of material production at its disposal, has control at the same time over the means of mental production, so that thereby, generally speaking, the ideas of those who lack the means of mental production are subject to it" (Marx and Engels, 1965/1989, p. 64). But as Apple himself explains, "These ideas," (i.e. the ideas of the capitalist class) "were under constant threat, however. They needed constant attention because hegemonic control was not guaranteed. Because of the class conflicts also generated out of, and causing, changes in that mode of production, there always existed the possibility of different ideological tendencies which could subvert the dominant ones" (1992, p. 127).

What one of us (Kelsh, 1998, Part I, section II and Part II, section VIII) has theorized as the class fraction of knowledge workers constituting the knowledge industry is a class fraction that arises from the material circumstances Apple summarizes above. The concept of the knowledge industry follows Marx and Engels' understanding of management of the ruling ideas by "its active, conceptive ideologists, who make the perfecting of the illusion of the class about itself their chief source of livelihood" (1965/1989, p. 65). The knowledge industry, which opposes the organization of all workers into a proletariat class-conscious movement, is not a "new" fraction but a fraction that has a material basis in the relations of production and becomes quite prominent during prolonged periods of crisis in capitalism, which themselves occur more and more as the contradictions of capitalism intensify.

As the contradictions of capitalism intensify, it becomes necessary for the bourgeoisie to revolutionize the means of production to increase profit. It also becomes necessary for Capital to manufacture knowledges that ease workers through the shifts in the relations of production that the revolutionizing of the means entails. In other words, outsourcing, downsizing, intensification of work—all of these require that knowledge workers (academics, media commentators, publishers, and so forth) manufacture and disseminate knowledges that update the ruling ideology and *naturalize* it.

The understanding of the social put forth by Apple, where neither the economic, the political, nor the cultural sphere is determinant (1993, p. 25), and instead determination by any "sphere" is seen to be "historically contingent" (1993, p. 5), advances a view of the social in which local analyses are the only ones possible. In such a framework, it becomes impossible, as Ebert argues, "to connect the mediated [cultural practices] to other social practices, and consequently the inquiry into and analysis of the mediations, themselves, takes the place of knowledge of the social totality in which mediations are relays of underlying connections" (1996, pp. 42-43).

For historical materialists, however, "*cultural and ideological practices are not autonomous* but are instead primary sites for reproducing the meanings and subjectivities supporting the unequal gender, sexual, and race divisions of labour, and thus a main arena for the struggle against economic exploitation as well as cultural oppression" (Ebert, 1996, pp. 42-43, emphasis added). The work of the knowledge industry (those knowledge workers who update the ruling ideology and naturalize it) is to augment ideology rather than critique it and expose it as a site of class struggle[4].

It is the work of the knowledge industry to augment ideology, and this is not "new." Augmenting ideology is the central practice of the knowledge industry which Marx does not name but nevertheless critiques in the Afterword to the Second German Edition of *Capital:* "in France and in England the bourgeoisie had conquered political power. Thenceforth, the class struggle, practically as well as theoretically, took on more and more outspoken and threatening forms. It sounded the knell of scientific bourgeois economy. It was thenceforth no longer a question, whether this theorem or that was true, but whether it was useful to capital or harmful, expedient or inexpedient, politically dangerous or not. In place of disinterested inquirers, there were hired prize-fighters; in place of genuine scientific research, the bad conscience and the evil intent of apologetic" (1867/1967a, p. 15).

These prize- fighters—today they are "academostars"—manufactured the "reactionary socialism," "conservative, or bourgeois socialism," and "critical-utopian socialism and communism" critiqued in *The Communist Manifesto* by Marx and Engels (pp. 106-118). Those who, as Marx argues in the Afterword to the Second German Edition of *Capital*, "still claimed some scientific standing and aspired to be something more than mere sophists and sycophants of the ruling class, tried to harmonize the Political Economy of capital with the claims, no longer to be ignored, of the proletariat. Hence, a shallow syncretism, of which John Stuart Mill is the best representative" (p.15). In *Imperialism,* Lenin later theorized this fraction as a "stratum of bourgeoisified workers" who are "the real *agents of the bourgeoisie in the labour movement,* the labour lieutenants of the capitalist class, real channels of reformism and chauvinism" (1939, p. 14).

All of this points out that Apple, in his claim that "binary working class/ruling class models neglect the crucial role played by the middle stratum" (1992, p. 134), is working as a part of the knowledge industry and manufacturing a claim. This relates directly to the second point we would like to makeabout this "professional and managerial new middle class." It is that Michael W. Apple himself, along with the many others who truncate, dismiss, trivialize, and otherwise evacuate the Marxist concept of class of its core transformative concepts, are a part of this fraction.

In distorting in order to dismiss classical Marxism, and in substituting a Weberian-based theory of class for the Marxist theory of class, they engage in the very "product control" Apple discusses as the work of this "new" class fraction. As he notes, "managerial discourse provides 'subject positions' through which people can imagine themselves and their institutions in different ways" (2006, p. 25). That is *precisely what Apple does*, and his discourses are ideological in that they seek to enable individuals to solve in the theoretical imaginary contradictions rooted in the social relations of production.

It is the work of the vanguard, which opposes the "fraction of the professional new middle class" Apple advocates, to make transformative theory available to the proletariat (as we are attempting to do here). The vanguard is theorized by Marx and Engels in *The Communist Manifesto:*

> In times when the class struggle nears the decisive hour, the process of dissolution going on within the ruling class, in fact within the whole range of old society, assumes such a violent, glaring character, that a small section of the ruling class cuts itself adrift, and joins the revolutionary class, the class that holds the future in its hands. Just as, therefore, at an earlier period, a section of the nobility went over to the bourgeoisie, so now a portion of the bourgeoisie goes over to the proletariat, and in particular, a portion of the bourgeois ideologists, who have raised themselves to the level of comprehending theoretically the historical movement as a whole. (p. 91)

Apple forthrightly opposes the vanguard (2006, p. 81). Thus, while the capitalist class has its spokespersons, the proletariat does not! This is the case especially when one considers that all Apple offers as a role for those who oppose the "fraction of the professional new middle class" is what he refers to as a secretarial role: he wants a group to "act as secretaries for some of our colleagues in education and for the activists in multiple communities, making public their partial, but still successful, resistances to the regime of regulation that we are currently experiencing" (2006, p. 122).

His service to the capitalist class is in full view here, as he deflects attention from the capitalist class and the regime of wage-labour and replaces it with the "regime of regulation," and offers only the dissemination of local experiences, which, as we have already argued, simply reiterates dominant discourses.

By discrediting and erasing the Marxist concept of class, Apple and others deny workers the access to revolutionary theory that is necessary for the development of class consciousness. As Lenin argued, "without a revolutionary theory there can be no revolutionary movement" (1902/1969, p. 25). In doing so, revisionist left theorists manufacture a knowledge that contributes to the production of subjects who are unable to understand their own position in the social (property) relations of production.

The Assimilation of the Left into the Service of Capitalist Interests

In the context of critiquing Apple as a member of this "professional and managerial new middle class," it is quite telling to note the following argument he makes about this "class": "Members of this fraction of the upwardly mobile professional and managerial new middle class do not necessarily believe in the ideological positions that underpin all aspects of the conservative alliance. In fact, in other aspects of their lives they may be considerably more moderate and even 'liberal' politically." Yet they do this work of management because "their own mobility *depends* on the expansion of both such expertise and the professional ideologies of control, measurement, and efficiency that accompany it" (2005, p. 387; 2006, p. 105).

This needs to be read in relation to Apple's reliance on and advocacy of Erik Olin Wright's work. Apple draws heavily on his work, and at the 2005 AERA convention in Montreal, advocated use of Wright's theory of class (Kelsh and Hill, notes, April 14, 2005).

Wright's formulation of class across his many works is a Weberian-based one that is useful to look at closely for several reasons. In addition to the fact that his ongoing work on class is highly influential in the social sciences, he has participated in some of the crucial debates surrounding "new class" theories such as the 1979 debate over Barbara and John Ehrenreich's formulation of "the professional managerial class" anthologized in *Between Labor and Capital* (Walker, 1979). Wright is well-read in classical Marxist theory, having spent much of his professional career debating in a number of texts the "problems of the conceptual foundation of Marxist theory" with colleagues whose work now forms the core of what is known as "analytical Marxism" (Wright, Levine and Sober, 1992, pp. 2-7).

Moreover, Wright knows well that the classical Marxist concept of class is centered on relation to property and that one class has because the other does not: as he says, "the welfare of the rich causally depends on the deprivations of the poor—the rich are rich *because* the poor are poor; and that the welfare of the rich depends upon the *effort* of the poor" (Wright, 1989, p. 8; original emphases). He has furthermore revised his previous theory of "contradictory class locations," which was central to the debate over the Ehrenreich's theorization, in order to put exploitation rather than domination at its centre (1989, pp. 12-14). Finally, he explicitly rejects the Weberian definitions of class because they are "'market-based' definitions, whereas Marxist definitions were 'production-based'" (1989, p. 13). And yet, in his book *The Debate on Classes* (1989), he reproduces a Weberian theory of class to which he adheres in subsequent texts (for example, *Class Counts*, 1997).

"Organization," Wright argues, "is a productive resource in its own right"; it is a "productive asset," a form of property which he conceives to be "independent of the expenditure of labour power, the use of means of production, or the skills of the producer" (1989, p. 16). Through this move, in which organization capacity or "knowledge" is severed from both the question of "organization (knowledge) for what purpose" and the material conditions of possibility that allow some forms of organization to surface and not others, Wright further pluralizes an already pluralized understanding of property (insofar as he already accepts Roemer's understanding of "skill" as property).

Thus for Wright, class is not constituted in the relations of production as Marx understands them, but in culture on the market, as Weber understands it. Wright's theory in the end is not fundamentally different from Lyotard's theorization of postmodernism in which it is accepted that "knowledge has become the principle force of production over the last few decades" (1989, p.5), and this despite Wright's ostensible return to the concept of exploitation. Because he pluralizes property, Wright's "exploitation" is still "domination" in the way that Anthony Giddens, following Weber, formulates it in relation to his understanding of "power" as "the capacity of actors to secure outcomes where the realization of these outcomes depends upon the agency of others" (1979, p.93). This is a Weberian theory of power—"power" is "the chance of a man or a number of men to realize their own will in a social action even against the resistance of others who are participating in the action" (Weber, 1914/1968, p. 926).

Wright's is a theory of class that substitutes domination for exploitation and puts it at the centre of social life. Domination presupposes that power comes from the individual, from his or her "will". As such, it is a concept that cuts the relation between one's capacity to secure outcomes in one's favour, and the stolen labour-power of the proletariat that the capitalist class uses to enable one to secure outcomes in one's favour. As Weber writes, "the structure of dominancy and its unfolding is decisive in determining the form of social action and its orientation toward a 'goal.' Indeed, domination has played the decisive role particularly in the economically most important social structures of the past and present, viz. the manor on the one hand, and the large-scale capitalistic enterprise on the other " (1914/1968, p. 941). Power is here entirely separable from property and labour-power such that formulations and discussions of class can address power in local senses only, manufacturing and promulgating power as an issue of individual "will," "imagination," "hope," "commitment," or "competition," cut off from the social relations of production and thereby masking them.

Knowledge workers never stand outside the contradictions of capitalism and are subject to them, open to assimilation into the knowledge industry whose proposals for "reform" play into the occlusion of class and class interests that are beneficial to the bourgeoisie. As Angela Davis (1997) has recently argued, while militant activists who achieve positions of power in the state apparatus "truly believe that they will be able to bring about radical transformations from and within new positions of state power,"

> under such conditions transformation is conceptualized very differently. The formulation of radical prison work as leading towards the reduction of prison populations and the abolition of jails and prisons as the primary means of addressing social problems such as crime, unemployment, undereducation, etc. recedes and is replaced with the goal of creating better, more progressive jails and prisons. I am not suggesting that we should not use whatever political arenas are available to us. However, once one becomes integrated into state

> structures, it becomes increasingly difficulty to think about ways of developing radical oppositional practices. (pp. 307-309)

Wright's comments in his Preface to *Classes* (1985) speak to this assimilation, as he discusses how he has "become integrated into a nexus of rewards that is very alluring," and how he "do[es] not know" "whether or not... the work [on classes] has benefited or suffered from the particular conditions under which it was produced" (p. 3).

In relying on Wright's theorization of class, Apple himself is assimilated into this "nexus of rewards."

Acknowledging the capitalist class interestedness of his position, however, is not something that, using his theory of the social, he would be obligated to do, or even recognize—the Weberian-derived understanding of class he uses is not relational, and thus provides Apple with an alibi for not accounting for his own theoretical position and its effects on the social totality.

Conclusion: For Class and Class Consciousness

The Weberian theory of class is dominant, and in schools as elsewhere, promotes intra-class competition. That is, it has a tendency to exacerbate divisions and antagonisms between students at different socio-economic levels, as Brantlinger's (1993; 2003) work, which also uses a Weberian class framework, illustrates. These divisions and antagonisms can function as major obstacles to student agency and educational achievement at all socio-economic levels. The reproduction and circulation of a Weberian-derived understanding of class is also anti-pedagogical because it professes that there are differences, but cannot explain why. The logical extension of it encourages the use among students and others of one's will and domination to obtain attributes—grades, favours—that enable one to get ahead within the system, and without ever questioning it. If one does not obtain such attributes that enable one to "get ahead," the only reason within this logic for not doing so is not having tried hard enough.

Assuming a Weberian-derived theory of class creates problems for critiques of capitalism's role in socioeconomic inequity related to schools. Critical commentary tends to take the focus off the capitalist class and place "blame" on "upper/middle class" discursive practices, and it does so one-sidedly, that is, without explaining the historical and ideological reasons why these strata of the proletariat engage in such discursive practices. Such one-sided blaming is a vulgarized form of critique that is not pedagogical and thus not enabling of "middle" class development of capacity for historical materialist critique and thus class consciousness as part of the proletariat. This anti-pedagogical blaming functions as an exorcism of guilt and contradicts the explicit aim of such texts: to change the practices of these strata from those that enforce the existing order to those that work to expose and change it. Such texts thus occlude the theoretical means to expose and change the existing order, as well as the more necessary object of critique: the capitalist class and property relations.

Owing to this relay where focus is shifted from the capitalist class and property relations to the middle strata practices severed from relation to property relations, the "cause" of socioeconomic inequity and exploitation in schools is shifted from production practices to cultural practices, specifically to discursive practices. This happens because the upper/middle strata do not hold economic power and are seen, following Apple, Allman, Wright, and others to hold only organizational power that appears not to be rooted in the social relations of production—unless one focuses on the Marxist theory of property and class. Ultimately, the shift in focus away from class understood in terms of the Marxist theory of property is a practice on the part of knowledge workers that blocks development of knowledge-producing critique of capitalist class practices. It thus blocks the development of class consciousness necessary to intervene in and abolish the cause of socio-economic inequity: private ownership by the few of the means of production.

It has been our aim in this essay to critique the revisionist left that represents itself as producing the most useful analyses, and to critique it in order to expose the limits of its analyses, together with their implication in the support of capitalist class practices of exploitation. We hold that to most effectively contest the right, and the capitalist class whose interests the right serves, the left must play a part—for example in local, national and global campaigns, and in sectional and particularistic movements — in building the Marxist understanding of social class, class consciousness, and class struggle, rather than occluding, in their culturalization of class, these understandings that are necessary to replace capitalism with socialism.

Notes

1. In order to enable access on the part of the reader to fundamental texts of classical Marxism and set them in chronological relation to one another and such other texts as those of Weber, we provide in-text citations and references that include both the original date of publication, as well as the publication date of the editions we have used.
2. The limited purpose of capitalism gives rise to numerous other inversions in

the material conditions—the exploitative social relations of production—in which all persons live, for example: "past labour [capital], dominates living labour" (1894/1967c, p. 45);"it is not the workman that employs the instruments of labour, but the instruments of labour that employ the workman" (1867/1967a, p. 423); "in manufacture, in order to make the collective labourer, and through him capital, rich in social productive power, each labourer must be made poor in individual productive powers" (1867/1967a, p. 361); machinery, "the most powerful instrument for shortening labour-time, becomes the most unfailing means for placing every moment of the labourer's time and that of his family, at the disposal of the capitalist for the purpose of expanding the value of his capital" (1867/1967a, p. 408); ... "property turns out to be the right, on the part of the capitalist, to appropriate the unpaid labour of others or its product, and to be the impossibility, on the part of the labourer, of appropriating his own product" (1867/1967a, p. 584). Overall, Marx argues, "capital... becomes a very mystic being since all of labour's social productive forces appear to be due to capital, rather than labour as such, and seem to issue from the womb of capital itself. Relations under which value is originally produced are pushed completely into the background" (1894/1967c, p. 827).

3. We acknowledge that Michael W. Apple has for several decades kept issues of inequity at the forefront of educational theory and research, and alive in the minds of individuals. Such work is necessary. However, insofar as his work is descriptive rather than explanatory with reference to causality, it does not go far enough. Now—with unprecedented ravages to the environment, health, education, academic freedom, and so forth resulting from the practices of the capitalist class—now is the "untimely time" to move forward and foreground capitalist class society and the contradiction between the classes as the cause that must be abolished. It is time for what Marx referred to as "the ruthless criticism of everything existing," which as Marx notes is "ruthless in two senses: The criticism must not be afraid of its own conclusions, nor of conflict with the powers that be" (1843/1978, p. 13). It is in the interests of socially necessary societal development that we take up Marx's call for such criticism.
4. What happens when the knowledge industry and other ideological state apparatuses do not carry out this function is analysed in Hill, 2004: "Books, banks and bullets: Controlling our minds—the global project of imperialistic and militaristic neoliberalism and its effect on education policy," *Policy Futures*, 2, pp. 3-4 (Theme: Marxist Futures in Education). http://www.wwwords.co.uk/pfie/content/pdfs/2/issue2_3.asp and in Hill, 2001: "State Theory and The Neo-Liberal Reconstruction of Schooling and Teacher Education: A Structuralist Neo-Marxist Critique of Postmodernist, Quasi-Postmodernist, and Culturalist Neo-Marxist Theory", *The British Journal of Sociology of Education,* 22, 1, pp.137-157.

References

Allman, P. (1999). *Revolutionary social transformation: Democratic hopes, political possibilities and critical education.* Westport, CT: Bergin & Garvey.

Anderson, M.L. and Collins, P.H. (1998). Introduction. In M.L. Anderson and P.H. Collins, (eds.), *Race, class, and gender: An anthology* (3rded.). (1-10). New York: Wordsworth Publishing Company.

Apple, M.W. (1979). *Ideology and curriculum.* New York: Routledge.

Apple, M.W. (1982). *Education and power.* Boston: Ark Paperbacks.

Apple, M.W. (1986). *Teachers and texts.* New York: Routledge & Kegan Paul.

Apple, M.W. (1992). Education, culture, and class power: Basil Bernstein and the neo-Marxist sociology of education. *Educational Theory, 42*(2), pp. 127-145.

Apple, M.W. (1993). *Official knowledge.* New York: Routledge.

Apple, M.W. (2003). *The state and the politics of knowledge.* New York: Routledge Falmer.

Apple, M.W. (2005). Audit cultures, commodification, and class and race strategies in education. *Policy Futures in Education, 3*(4), pp. 379-399.

Apple, M.W. (2006). *Educating the "right" way.* New York: Routledge.

Brantlinger, E.A. (1993). *The politics of social class in secondary school: Views of affluent and impoverished youth.* New York: Teachers College Press.

Brantlinger, E.A. (2003). *Dividing classes: How the middle class negotiates and rationalizes school advantage.* New York: Routledge Falmer.

Breen, R. (2001). A Weberian approach to class analysis. Retrieved February 20, 2005 fromhttp://www.ssc.wisc.edu/~wright/Chapter%202%20—%20Breen%20Jan%202004.pdf.

Boaz, D. (n.d.). Defining an ownership society. Retrieved April 1, 2005 from http://www.cato.org/cgi -bin/scripts/printtech.cgi/special/ownership_society/boaz.html.

Davis, A. (1997). Angela Davis: Reflections on race, class, and gender in the USA. In L. Lowe and D. Lloyd (eds.), *The politics of culture in the shadow of capitalism* (pp. 303-323). Durham: Duke University Press.

Dumenil, G. and Levy, D. (2004). *Capital resurgent: Roots of the neoliberal revolution.* London: Harvard University Press.

Ebert, T. (1996). *Ludic feminism and after: Postmodernism, desire, and labour in late capitalism.* Ann Arbor: The University of Michigan Press.

Engels, F. (1975). *Anti-Duhring.* Moscow: Progress Publishers.

Engels, F. (1890/1987). Letter to Bloch. In H. Selsam and H. Martel (eds.), *Reader in Marxist philosophy* (pp. 204-206). New York: International Publishers.

Farahmandpur, R. (2004). Essay review: A Marxist critique of Michael Apple's neo-Marxist approach to educational reform. *Journal of Critical Education Policy Studies, 2*(1). Retrieved February 1, 2006 from http://www.jceps.com.

Fussell, P. (1983). *Class.* New York: Ballantine Books.

Giddens, A. (1979). *Central problems in social theory.* Berkeley: University of California Press.

Gimenez, M. (2001). Marxism, and class, gender, and race: Rethinking the trilogy. *Race, Gender and Class, 8* (2), pp. 23-33.

Hall, S. (1992). Cultural studies and its theoretical legacies. In L. Grossberg, et al. (eds.), *Cultural studies* (pp. 277-285). New York: Routledge.

Harvey, D. (2005) *A brief history of neoliberalism.* Oxford: Oxford University Press.

Hill, D. (1999). Social class. In D. Matheson and I. Grosvenor (eds.), *An Introduction to the Study of Education.* London: David Fulton.

Hill, D. (2001). State Theory and The Neo-Liberal Reconstruction of Schooling and Teacher Education: A Structuralist Neo-Marxist Critique of Postmodernist, Quasi-Postmodernist, and Culturalist Neo-Marxist Theory, *The British Journal of Sociology of Education.* 22, 1, pp. 137-157.

Hill, D. (2004). Books, banks and bullets: Controlling our minds—the global project of imperialistic and militaristic neoliberalism and its effect on education policy. *Policy Futures*, 2, pp. 3-4 (Theme: Marxist Futures in Education). Online at: http://www.wwwords.co.uk/pfie/content/pdfs/2/issue2_3.asp Neoliberalisation and its impacts on education workers' rights, pay and conditions. April 9, 2006.

Hill, D. and Cole, M. (2001). Social class. In D. Hill and M. Cole (eds.), *Schooling and Equality: Fact, Concept and Policy*. London: Kogan Page.

Kelsh, D. (1998). Desire and class: The knowledge industry in the wake of poststructuralism. *Cultural Logic (1)*2.http://eserver.org/clogic/.

Kelsh, D. (2001). (D)evolutionary socialism and the containment of class: For a red theory of class. *The Red Critique: Marxist Theory Critique Pedagogy, 1(1),* 9-13. Retrieved February 20, 2005 from http://www.redcritique.org.

Kelsh, D. (2006). Review: Erasing class by erasing property: A Marxist critique of Paula Allman's *Critical education against global capitalism* and *Revolutionary social transformation.*

Kelsh, D. and Hill, D. (2005). Notes, Michael W. Apple, "What Role Can Education Play in Changing Society?" AERA Convention, Friday afternoon, April 14, 2005.

Larrain, J. (1996). Stuart Hall and the Marxist concept of ideology. In D. Morley, and K. Chen (eds.), *Stuart Hall: Critical dialogues in cultural studies* (pp. 47-70). New York: Routledge.

Lenin, V.I. (1916/1939). *Imperialism.* New York: International Publishers.

Lenin, V.I. (1902/1969). *What is to be done?* New York: International Publishers.

Lubienski, S.T. (2003). Celebrating diversity and denying disparities: A critical assessment. *Educational Researcher, 32,* 30-38.

Luxemburg, R. (1899/1970). Reform or revolution. *Rosa Luxemburg speaks.* NY: Pathfinder.

Lyotard, J.F. (1989). *The postmodern condition: A report on knowledge.* (G. Bennington and B. Massumi, Trans.). Minneapolis: University of Minnesota Press.

Marx, K. (1843/1978). Letter to Kreuznach, September, 1843: For a ruthless criticism of everything existing. In R. Tucker (ed.), *The Marx-Engels reader.* Second edition. 12-15. New York: W.W. Norton & Company.

Marx, K. (1859/1989). *A contribution to the critique of political economy.* (S.W. Ryazanskaya, Trans.). Maurice Dobb (ed.), New York: International Publishers.

Marx, K. (1867/1967a). *Capital: A critique of political economy (Vol. 1: The process of capitalist production).* (Samuel Moore and Edward Aveling, Trans.). Frederick Engels (ed.), New York: International Publishers.

Marx, K. (1885/1967b). *Capital: A critique of political economy (Vol. 2: The process of circulation of capital).* Frederick Engels (ed.), New York: International Publishers.

Marx, K. (1891/1938). *Critique of the Gotha Programme.*New York: International Publishers.

Marx, K. (1894/1967c). *Capital: A critique of political economy (Vol. 3: The process of capitalist production as a whole).* Frederick Engels (ed.), New York: International Publishers.

Marx, K. (1953/1993). *Grundrisse: Foundations of the critique of political economy (rough draft).* (Martin Nicolaus, Trans.). New York: Penguin Books.

Marx, K. (1995). From "Results of the Immediate Process of Production." In D. McLellan (ed.), *Karl Marx, Capital, An abridged edition* (pp. 383-400). New York: Oxford University Press.

Marx, K. and Engels, F. (1848/1985). *The Communist manifesto.* New York: Penguin Books.

Marx, K. and Engels, F. (1965/1989). *The German ideology: Part one.* C.J. Arthur (ed.), New York: International Publishers.

McLaren, P., and Scatamburlod'Annibale, V. (2004). Class dismissed? Historical materialism and the politics of "difference." *Educational Philosophy and Theory,* 36 (2), 183-199.

Morton, D. (1990). Texts of limits, the limits of texts, and the containment of politics in contemporary critical theory. *Diacritics,* 20(1), 57-75.

Nealon, J., and Giroux, S.S. (2003). Differences. In J. Nealon, and S. Giroux (eds.), *The theory toolbox: Critical concepts for the humanities, arts, and social sciences.* 157-206. New York: Rowman & Littlefield Publishers, Inc.

Office for National Statistics. (2000). *Living in Britain 2000.* Retrieved December 1, 2005 from http://www.statistics.gov.uk.

Office of the Press Secretary. (June 17, 2004). Fact sheet: America's ownership society: Expanding opportunities. Retrieved April 1, 2005 from http://www.whitehouse.gov/news/releases/2004/08.

Reich, R. (2004). What ownership society? Retrieved April 1, 2005 from http://www.tompaine.com/print/what_ownership_society.php.

Rikowski, G. (2001). *After the manuscript broke off: Thoughts on Marx, social class and education.* A paper prepared for the British Sociological Association Education Study Group Meeting, King's College London, June 23, 2001. Retrieved February 25, 2006 from http://www.leeds.ac.uk/educol/documents/00001931.htm.

Rosen, H.S. (2005). The ownership society. Retrieved April 1, 2005 from http://www.whitehouse.gov/cea/ownership-society-20050301.pdf.

Rosenbaum, D.E. (2005, January 16). Bush to return to "Ownership Society" theme in push for social security changes. *The New York Times,* p. 20.

Thatcher, M. (1986). Speech at Lord Mayor's Banquet. Retrieved February 23, 2006 from http://www.margaretthatcher.org/Speeches/displaydocument.asp?docid=106512&doctype=1.

US Department of Labour, Bureau of Labour Statistics. Productivity. Retrieved March 28, 2005 from http://www/bls.gov/bls/glossary.htm#L.

Weber, M. (1914/1968). *Economy and society: An outline of interpretive sociology,* 2 Vols. (E. Fischoff, H. Gerth, A.M. Henderson, F. Kolegar, C.W. Mills, T. Parsons, et al., Trans.). New York: Bedminster Press, 1968.

Wright, E.O. (1979). Intellectuals and the class structure of capitalist society. In P. Walker (ed.), *Between labour and capital* (pp. 191-212). Boston: South End Press.

Wright, E.O. (1985). *Classes*. London: Verso.

Wright, E.O. (1989). A general framework for the analysis of class structure. In E.O. Wright (ed.), *The Debate on Classes,* (pp. 3-43). London: Verso.

Wright, E.O. (1997). *Class counts: Comparative studies in class analysis.* Cambridge: Cambridge University Press.

Wright, E.O., Levine, A. and Sober, E. (1992). *Reconstructing Marxism.* New York: Verso.

Young, R. (2006). Putting materialism back into race theory: Towards a transformative theory of race. *The Red Critique: Marxist Theory Critique Pedagogy, 11*. Retrieved February 22, 2006 from http://www.redcritique.org.

Zavarzadeh, M. (1995). Post-ality: The (dis)simulations of Cybercapitalism. *Transformation, 1,* 1-75.

Zavarzadeh, M. and Morton, D. (1991). Theory pedagogy politics: The crisis of "the subject" in the humanities. In D. Morton and M. Zavarzadeh (eds.), *Texts for change* (pp. 1-32). Urbana and Chicago: University of Illinois Press.

3

Culturalist and Materialist Explanations of Class and "Race": Critical Race Theory, Equivalence/ Parallelist Theory, and Marxist Theory

Dave Hill

Summary

In this essay I examine the interconnections between "race"[1] *and social class, with some reference to caste, in schooling and society.*

I need to state that this is a panoptic paper that attempts to bring together, to link, empirical and theoretical data and conceptual analyses across a number of areas: These are: firstly, culturalist and materialist issues and analyses of "race," caste, and class oppression, particularly in Britain, the USA and India; secondly, South Asian, other Black and Minority Ethnic groups (BME) and White working class labour market and educational experience in Britain; thirdly, Marxist, revisionist socialist, and social democratic educational and political analysis; and, finally, neoliberal and neoconservative policy and its impacts. In particular, this chapter attempts to compare BME oppression and exploitation in the UK and, tangentially, in the USA, with caste oppression and exploitation in India and also as it manifests itself in Britain. Both are examined through a materialist, class perspective: a Marxist analysis. Panoptic approaches can have value: a bringing together, an interrelating, of different aspects and areas of analysis, enabling, potentially, wider social theorizing. They potentially enable a wider understanding, or facilitate a wider evaluation of an overarching theory, such as Marxism, as it analyses a variety of linked issues. In this paper, the issues above are linked in terms of Marxist analysis of capitalism, class oppression, and the implications of such analysis for the politics of resistance. A hazard with panoptic papers is that they can be dense, heavily referenced and footnoted. But this is to enable pursuit of further study/reading across a number of fields. In addition, a key strength of the panoptic approach is that it is multidisciplinary, enabling analysis, synthesis and evaluation across a number of disciplines.

In this article, I critique three forms of analysis/theorizing of "race," caste, and class oppression:

1. Critical Race Theory, a theory that sees "race" as the most significant form of oppression, rather than social class. This theory originated in the USA (where its main theorists include Bell, e.g. 1992, 2004; Mills, e.g. 1997, 2003; Delgado, 1995; and Delgado and Stefanic, 2000, 2001). It has been recently (pretty much since Gillborn, 2005) imported into Britain by writers such as David Gillborn (2005, 2006a, b, 2008a, b, 2009a, b, c), John Preston (2007), and Namita Chakrabarty (e.g. Chakrabarty and Preston, 2008);

2. "Parallelist" or "Equivalence" theories, widespread in the USA, and, for example, espoused by Michael W. Apple (Apple and Weiss, 1983; Apple, 1988, 1993, 1996, 1999, 2001). These argue that there is an equivalence or parallelism, between "race," class and gender as forms of structural oppression in society; and

3. Caste Analysis, theories salient in India (and other South Asian countries such as Pakistan, Nepal), but present in Indian (and some other South Asian) heritage/Diasporic communities, for example in Britain, that the dominant form of oppression is caste oppression, of Dalits ("Untouchables") by (high-caste) Brahmins and other castes (for sustained critiques in India, see Quadri and Kumar, 2003; Iliah, 2005; Kumar and Kumar, 2005, Murali Krishna, 2007; Kumar, 2010, and, in the UK, Borbas et al., 2006).

I critique these from empirical and theoretical/analytical perspectives, concluding that the salient forms of discrimination, oppression and inequality in the classroom, as in the economy and society, whether in the UK, USA or India, or elsewhere, are those relating to ("raced" and gendered and caste-divided) social class.

While recognizing the power of subjective identities and consciousness, and while not being dismissive of racism as intrinsic to global capital's agenda, I suggest that these forms and processes of ("race," gender, caste) marginalization and inequality are functional for the capitalist system of exploitation, which uses schooling and formal education and other agencies of the state to reproduce the existing patterns and forms of educational, social, and economic inequalities.

They are functional in a number of ways: they occlude class consciousness and impede the development of the working class movement by dividing the working class; they lend themselves to the creation of bourgeois groups among immigrant-descended/black/caste groups which have a self-interest in perpetuating the capitalist system of exploitation; and they facilitate the extraction of surplus value by sustaining pools of marginalized cheap labour.

Part 1: "Race," Class, and Capital

In this section, I examine the interconnections between "race" and social class, with some reference to caste and gender, in schooling, society, and economy in the UK, in particular relating to the two million children and adults in Britain who are of South Asian heritage.

Education policy relating to ethnic diversity in Britain springs (though not unproblematically, or in an unmediated fashion) from capitalist ruling-class demands for capital accumulation and profit, as does wider policy (Hill, 2001, 2007a, b, c, d). This is classic Marxist analysis. Education policy is linked to wider "race" policy in society, for example labour/employment law, welfare rights law, settlement/immigration rights and laws, and economic and fiscal policy.

These "race policies" and education policies can be analysed, variously (and sometimes in combination), as (i) racist (or caste) supremacist or (ii) assimilationist/monoculturalist, or (iii) multiculturalist/celebrating cultural diversity; (iv) integrationist, recognizing (some of) the diversity of "race" and ethnic cultures, but within (in Britain) an affirmation of "Britishness"; or (iv) anti-racist/critical policy for equality. These types of "race" policy all have a class dimension.[2]

How is this so? It is because these policies have impacts on the extents to which policy serves to include and empower, or exclude and disempower, sections and strata of the ("raced" and gendered and caste divided) working class. Thus some education and other policies are clearly class hegemomic and class supremacist I'm happy with supremacist, but if you prefer, use hegemonic, why not use both? as well as "race" or caste supremacist, other education and cultural policies accept aspects of working class cultures and/or ethnic minority cultures, and other policies—egalitarian policies —attempt either a reformist meritocratic or slightly redistributive set of policies (social democratic policies).

The classical Marxist analysis I am suggesting here is that social class is the primary explanation for economic, political, cultural and ideological change. Social class, though manifestly layered into strata, and manifestly structured along lines of "race"/ethnicity, gender, and caste, for example, is the essential form of capitalist exploitation and oppression, and it is the dominant form of capitalist exploitation and oppression.

Kelsh and Hill (2006) (see also Kelsh, 2001) argue that it is

> necessary to bring the Marxist concept of class back into educational theory, research, and practice. It has the explanatory power to analyse the structure of ownership and power in capitalist social relations and thus to point to ways of restructuring society so that public needs take priority over private profit.

Such an analysis is developed powerfully in Kelsh's most recent publication, Kelsh, Hill, and Macrine (2009). As Banfield (2009a) notes,

> When class is treated as an analytic category all signs of life are lost in the dizzy heights of abstraction. The gritty realities of class disappear when it is seen as an idea (theory, perspective, a social scientific category) and not, what it really is: a social relation. (See also Banfield, 2009b.)

Marxist analysis suggests that we live in a capitalist society and economy in which the capitalists—those who own the banks, factories, media, corporations, businesses, that is, the means of production—profit from exploiting the workers. Capitalists exploit workers' labour power—the labour power of men and women workers, workers from different, ethnic groups and religions, and those from different castes. Capitalism appropriates surplus value from the labour of the ("raced" and gendered and caste-divided) working class (see, for example, Marx, 1867/1996, explained in the Appendix to Chapter 8 of Cole 2009 for an explanation, and also the explanation in Faivre, 2009).

The capitalist system—with a tiny minority of people owning the means of production—oppresses and exploits the working class. This, indeed, constitutes the essence of capitalism: the extraction of surplus value—and profit—from workers by capitalist employers. These capitalists may be white, black, men, women, (high caste) Brahmin, or ("untouchable") Dalit. In India as well as in Britain, there are millionaire men, women, Brahmin, and Dalit capitalists—and politicians.

Marxist analysis also suggests that *class conflict*, which is an essential feature of capitalist society, will result in an overthrow of capitalism given the right circumstances. There has been considerable debate, historically, in different countries over whether this can, or will, be achieved either by*revolutionary* force or by *evolutionary* measures and steps for example through the evolutionary, reformist measures of social democracy). Important examples of such debates between protagonists of revolutionary socialism and those of evolutionary socialism/social democracy are the late 19th century debates in Germany over "Revisionism" associated with the revisionist Eduard Bernstein (e.g. in 1899, his *The Prerequisites for Socialism and the Tasks of Social Democracy*—see Tudor and Tudor, 1988) on the one hand, and on the other hand, orthodox revolutionary Marxist critics of revisionism such as Rosa Luxemburg (for example, in *Reform and Revolution*, in 1899/1900).

Today such debates are carried on between revolutionary socialists/ Marxists such as the various Trotskyite groups, parties and internationals on the one hand, and social democratic parties and internationals on the other. As for where the former communist parties stood, a historical transition was made in the 1970s and 1980s by various communist parties and leaders when they foreswore revolution and adopted gradualist social democracy.[3] These arguments and conflicts take place within many leftist revolutions. Today, for example, in Venezuela, Trotskyites argue for a revolutionary rupture with capitalism, while others urge caution, an accommodation with capitalism and capitalists. (See Gonzalez, 2007; ISG, 2007; Esteban et al., 2008; Fuentes, 2009.) And Trotskyite, revolutionary, anti-capitalist groups and parties have persistent major problems working within larger left formations, united fronts and popular fronts. Thus PSOL at first joined the PT government in Brazil but left in 2004 in protest at (Brazilian President) Lula's neoliberal pro-capitalist policies, and in 2007 Sinistra Critica pulled out of the broader left Rifondazione Comunista. There is considerable current debate within the Trostskyite movement and internationals over the incompatibility of socialist revolution with social democratic broader parties. (See, for example, Bensaid, 2009.)[4] Historically, and indeed in current times, it is, of course the armed/police forces of the capitalist state that shoot first—and where the local capitalist state is not powerful enough in the balance of class forces in any particular site, then in come the United States cavalry, acting on behalf of transnational capital and its national capital—on behalf of the international capitalist system itself. (See, for example, Brosio, 1994.)

And yet there are denials, by postmodernists and other theorists of complexity and hybridity and postmodernists and post-ists of various stripes, that we no longer live in a period of metanarratives, such as mass capitalism, social class, working class, or, indeed, "woman" or "black."[5]For many theorists since the 1980s, history is at an end, the class war is over, and we all exalt in the infinite complexity and hybridity of subjective individualist consumerism. It is interesting, and rarely remarked upon, that arguments about "the death of class" are not advanced regarding the capitalist class. Despite their horizontal and vertical cleavages (Dumenil and Levy, 2004), they appear to know very well who they are. Nobody is denying capitalist class consciousness.

Opposition to the rule of capital and its policies (either its wider policies, or specific policy) is weakened when the working class is divided, by "race," caste, religion, tribe, or by other factors.

When I say "divided," I am using it here as an active verb, to mean that the capitalist class divides the working class, for example by its ideological state apparatuses—its media, its formally or informally segregated school systems. This is "divide and rule." Examples of schooling systems perpetuating such divisions are in apartheid South Africa, Arab-Jew segregated schooling in Israel, Protestant-Catholic religiously segregated Northern Ireland, and parts of the USA—in particular its inner cities, and, indeed, parts of Britain, where, in some inner-city working class schools, more than 90 per cent of the pupils are from minority ethnic groups.[6]In many of the cities of the USA and Britain the ethnic division is localized. But such segregation and division is overwhelmingly a class stratification. It is rarely the millionaire and capitalist minorities who live in the ghetto, or poor minorities or whites who live in "millionaires row."

Part 2: South Asians in Britain: "Race," Class and the Labour Market in Britain

It is obvious to note that some workers, such as legal and "illegal" immigrants, and ex-colonialized and ex-imperialized populations (as well as white, non-colonized East Europeans) are exploited far more than others. Various groups are "racialized,"[7] or xeno-racialized,[8] a process by which they are ascribed particular social and ability characteristics, sometimes demonized and vilified, into particular labour market, housing market and education market situations.

Abbas (2007) notes, in relation to South Asians,[9] that "ethnic minority immigrants were ... placed at the bottom of the labour market, disdained by the host community, and systematically ethnicised and racialized in the sphere of capital accumulation" (p. 3), and that the "ethnic penalty" experienced by first generations has largely translated to second generations (p. 4).

There are different typical class locations and positions within the labour market (and education attainment tables) for the different ethnic groups. Pakistanis and Bangladeshis (i.e. British Pakistanis and British Bangladeshis and those who have immigrated from Pakistan and

Bangladesh) have similar labour market circumstances and in general greater disadvantage than other ethnic groups. These Pakistani and Bangladeshi men have the lowest economic activity rates of all populations, and high unemployment rates. Forty-four per cent of all Bangladeshi men and 18 per cent of Pakistani men aged 25 and over were employed part-time. This compared to 5 per cent of White British (Abbas, 2007).

Of all ethnic minorities, Indian men (British Indian and those immigrated from India and other countries) have employment rates that are, on average, most similar to White Britons. As a population in Britain they are considerably more middle class than Bangladeshis and Pakistanis. The Indian population has relatively high levels of qualifications. Nonetheless, Indians have significantly worse outcomes in the labour market compared to White Britons with similar qualifications (Simpson et al., 2001; see also, Abbas, 2007).

Educational Attainment: "Race," Class, and Gender in England and Wales

With respect to educational achievement in England and Wales, Gillborn and Mirza (2000) show very clearly that it is the difference between social classes in attainment that is the fundamental and stark feature of the education system in England and Wales, rather than "race" or gender.

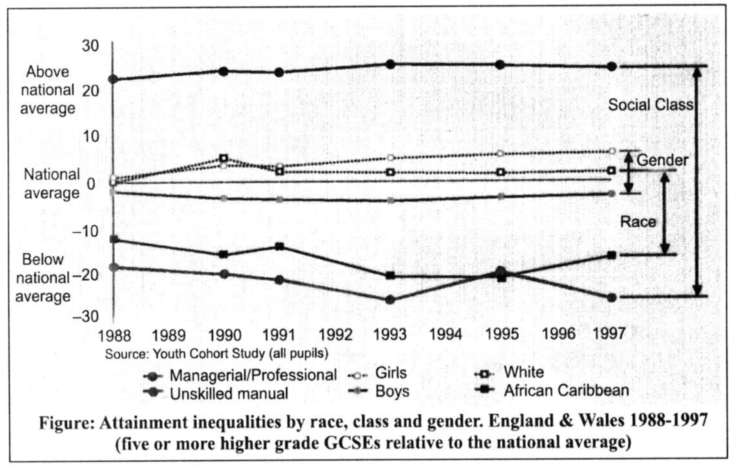

Figure: Attainment inequalities by race, class and gender. England & Wales 1988-1997 (five or more higher grade GCSEs relative to the national average)

Gillborn & Mirza, 2000, p. 22

In their analysis of attainment inequalities by class, "race," and gender

1988-97 (five or more higher grade GCSEs—General Certificates of Education—the exam taken by virtually all sixteen year olds in England and Wales—relative to the national average) the gender difference between girls and boys is half that relating to "race" (comparing white students with African Caribbean). This in turn is less than half of the social class difference—the difference between children of managerial professional parentage, on the one hand, and children from unskilled manual working-class homes (Gillborn and Mirza, 2000:22). Gillborn and Mirza's study concerns a study of all social strata/social class groups.

Strand (2007, p. 13) points out that

> In terms of national data, the Youth Cohort Study (YCS) has historically provided the best estimate of national figures for attainment at school leaving age by ethnicity. A representative sample of approximately 30,000 pupils is surveyed approximately every two years. Analysis of examination results at age 16 for 1992, 1994, 1996, 1998, 2000 and 2002 shows a consistent picture of Indian pupils gaining higher examination scores than White British pupils, while Black, Bangladeshi and Pakistani pupils consistently achieve lower examination scores than White British. In the last published results for GCSE examinations for 2006 (DfES, 2007), 80% of Chinese pupils, 72% of Indian and 69% of Mixed White and Asian pupils achieved the benchmark of five or more GCSE A*-C grades, compared to 58% of White British pupils. This level of success was achieved by 57% of Bangladeshi pupils, 51% of Black African and Pakistani pupils, 45% of Black Caribbean pupils and just 10% of Gypsy/Roma pupils.

This data does not show an overall pattern of White supremacy. Indians do better as an ethnic group than Whites, so do Mixed White and Asian students.[10] This (YCS) data cited by Strand (2007), like that of Gillborn and Mirza (2000) above, concerns a sample of all social strata/social class groups.

Dehal (2006) refers specifically to the educational attainments of "the poor"—the poorest strata of the working class, those who are entitled to and claim Free School meals (FSM). Dehal points out that the impact of economic disadvantage does differ significantly across "BME" (Black and Minority Ethnic) groups. He concludes that "economic disadvantage is the key driver of ethnic disparity." In other words, economic poverty is the most important factor in low levels of academic/school attainment.

In the first figure/picture below ("Economic disadvantage is the key driver of ethnic disparity"), the left-hand chart shows this clearly (as does the Gillborn and Mirza chart above). The right-hand chart shows the proportions of school students in each of eight ethnic groups who do receive FSM, who are in the poorest 14% of the population in England and Wales.

The second figure below ("but its impact does differ substantially across BME groups") shows that the different ethnic groups among these "poorest" 14% of children at state schools do perform differently to each other. Other than Gypsy/Roma, Whites do worst.

Figure 1: Economic Disadvantage is the key driver of Ethnic disparity...

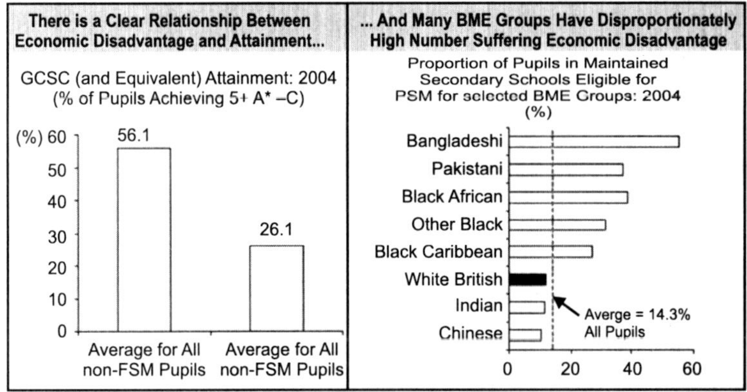

Figure 2: ...But its impact does differ Substantially Across BME Groups

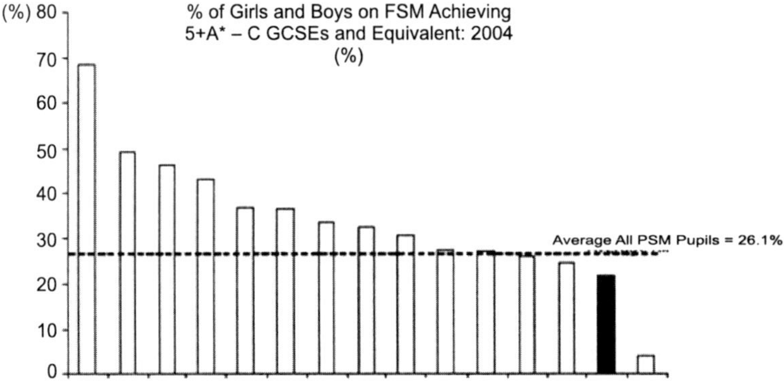

Dehal's (2006) conclusion is that there is a specific "race" factor involved. Some ethnic groups of 15-16 year-olds in receipt of free school meals—such as White and African-Caribbean and Roma children—do perform/attain more poorly than the average for all 15-16 year-old children in receipt of free school meals, and considerably more poorly than the Chinese and Indian group of such children. Strand (2007, p. 32) also shows figures for Free School meals—a crude marker of poverty—in relation to various ethnic groups in England and Wales. (On p. 29 of Strand's text there is data on the socio-economic class composition of each ethnic group, in Table 5 and Figure 3 on that page.)

Gillborn and Mirza's (2000) conclusion from their own data is that

> social class and gender differences are ... associated with differences in attainment but neither can account for persistent underlying ethnic inequalities: comparing like with like, African-Caribbean, Pakistani and Bangladeshi pupils do not enjoy equal opportunities. (p. 27).

However, the "race" effect, the effect of being part of a particular ethnic group, and thereby 'winning' or 'losing' from the "race" effect,, has less impact on achievement and under-achievement than does social class. Class analysis is more reliable as a measure of achievement/ underachievement, than "race" analysis. Demie and Tong (2007), and Demie et al. (2007) provide a detailed analysis at the level of one ethnically diverse London Borough, Lambeth. In Lambeth, one sizeable White group, the Portuguese, does significantly worse on standard scores of attainment at various age levels than do other groups, for example.

Strand's (2007) data and analysis suggest that in terms of "raw score" at Key Stage 3 (age 14) test results in England and Wales, the "gaps" for KS3 results are that

> [t]he social class gap was largest with a 10 point gap between pupils from higher managerial and professional families and those where the main parent was long-term unemployed. The maternal education gap was also large with a nine used above point gap between pupils with mothers qualified to degree level or higher and those with mothers with no educational qualifications. These compare to an ethnic gap of three points. The gender gap was just 0.8 points, with boys scoring lower than girls. (2007, p. 6)

A summary of Strand's work (Strand, 2008a) shows that

> White British working class pupils (both boys and girls) and Black Caribbean boys were the lowest performing groups at age 16 and made the least progress during secondary school. In particular White British working class pupils show a marked decline in attainment in the last two years of secondary school. Pupils from most minority ethnic groups made good progress during secondary school and showed greater resilience to deprivation relative to their deprived White British peers.

With respect to non-working class school students, Strand (2008a) notes that "Black Caribbean and Black African pupils from more advantaged homes underachieved in relation to their White British peers."

To turn to BME groups who are *not* Black Caribbean or Black African, with specific respect to the education of South Asians in Birmingham, England, Abbas (2007) carried out a theoretical and empirical study of the ways in which different South Asian groups, Bangladeshi, Indian, and Pakistani, achieve entry into the selective education system—that is, entry to either the paid for/privately purchased private school places, or entry to the (free) grammar schools.

His findings are that certain working class South Asian parents possess strong middle class attitudes towards selective education, irrespective of their ability to facilitate it as a function of their financial, cultural, or social capital. Middle class South Asians were not only highly motivated but also possessed the economic, social, and cultural capital to ensure successful selective school entry.

To conclude this section, Abbas' conclusion, like those of the studies above, is that, "in general, social class status was the strongest factor in the likelihood of gaining entry into selective schools" (Abbas, 2007, p. 75).[11] Abbas, while asserting the salience of social class factors in educational attainment, also, like Dehal and like Gillborn and Mirza above, draws attention to what he sees as culturally specific attitudes to education.

Part 3: Three Critiques of Marxist Analysis: (1) Revisionist Socialist/Gender/"Race"/Class Parallelism; (2) Critical Race Theory; (3) Caste Analysis

Marxist analysis, crucially concerning the objective salience of social class (objective as contrasted with subjective consciousness/awareness of social class), is of course, contested, particularly in the USA, not only on the right but also by radical (denoted as "left liberal" or "revisionist socialist" by Kelsh and Hill, 2006) scholars such as Michael W. Apple. It is also contested by Critical Race Theorists (and, indeed, by others/other theories) who see "race" oppression as the salient structural and policy form of oppression (such as Paul, 2001). It is also contested by those in India who prioritize caste analysis and caste suffering/oppression and caste politics as the fundamental form of oppression.

I now wish to address these three types of non-Marxist, indeed, in essence, anti-Marxist analyses and theories.

The first, Critical Race Theory, sees "race" as the fundamental form of social, economic, and political oppression.[12]

The second perspective asserts either a parallelist or tryptarchic analysis of "race," social class, and gender oppression (Apple's broad view, and that of many others in the USA, such as Lois Weiss).[13]

The third contestation of Marxist analysis is caste analysis, predominantly in India, but throughout the Indian, Pakistani, and Nepali diasporas.[14]

Critical Race Theory

Critical Race Theory, imported from radical analysis in the USA, is propounded in the UK primarily by David Gillborn and by John Preston and Namita Chakrabarty. To repeat, there is full agreement with Gillborn (and great appreciation of his substantial corpus of work over a twenty-year period) on the ubiquity of racism, how it plays out within schools and the education system, its impacts, the salience of "race" as the ever-present, or most present, *subjective* feelings and consciousness among most in BME (Black and Minority Ethnic) groups in Britain ("people of colour," in the USA) concerning their daily awareness of personal and institutional discrimination and oppression. His latest book, *Racism and Education: Coincidence or Conspiracy?* (2008), extends this to education policy, showing the racist nature and effects of New Labour government education policy in England and Wales, in particular regarding assessment and exclusion from schools. But the pre-eminent focus of this book, and his recent articles setting out Critical Race Theory, is the pre-eminence of "race" rather than social class as a form of structural oppression. Accompanying it is an attack on class analysis.

Gillborn (2008) is right about underachievement by Blacks (Black Caribbean and Black African school students) in England and Wales. However, to repeat the points made above in relation to Dehal's data and analysis, most of this underachievement is related to class location—Black Caribbeans are, with Bangladeshis, Pakistanis and Traveller/Roma, the most heavily working class of any ethnic group. When class location—as measured by those claiming and in receipt of Free School Meal (FSM)—is accounted, the all minority ethnic groups other than Gypsy Roma/travellers perform better than whites.

Regarding more privileged groups in society, Strand (2008b) points out that (at age 16) "White British pupils from high SEC" (Socio-Economic Class) "homes are one of the highest attaining ethnic groups, while White British pupils living in disadvantaged circumstances are the lowest attaining group" (p. 2). Gillborn (e.g. pp. 54-56), too, draws attention to this, showing that with regard to non-FSM students (for example, at age

16 in their national GCSE assessments) that white students perform better than (most) other ethnic groups.

To repeat, and, as shown by the final Dehal table above, the poor white working class (as measured by FSM), being in receipt of free school meals, performs less well than the working class of nearly all other ethnic groups. Most BME groups do better than whites, once allowance has been made/controlled for class location as measured by FSM.

It seems that Gillborn's own statistics (in Gillborn and Mirza, 2000) and other empirical data I present or refer to in this paper (see also Independent Working Class Association, 2005) lend compelling support to a Marxist critique of "race" salience theories in general (such as, currently, Critical Race Theory) offered, for example, by Cole, Maisuria, Miles and Sivanandan, and the Institute of Race Relations that he founded, in Britain,[15] and in the USA by the *Red Critique* journal, for example, Young, 2006. In his work on Critical Race Theory, Gillborn in most cases ignores and in other cases belittles the class dimension, a class dimension that, ironically, his own statistics of 2000 (Gillborn and Mirza, 2000) draw attention to.

Gillborn (in his Chapter 3, 2008, p. 45) does refer to the relative importance of and intersections between, inequalities based on "race," class, and gender. He does, as have I, following Strand and Dehal (Dehal, 2006; Strand, 2007, 2008a, b) above, note that "economic background is not equally important for all students." On p. 46 he criticizes an "exclusive focus on class." On p. 69 Gillborn notes that "the data certainly confirms that social class background is associated with gross inequalities of achievement at the extremes of the class spectrum." He repeats: "However, class does not appear to be equally significant for all groups." He then adds, importantly for his argument (i.e. an argument that seeks to avoid concentrating on data concerning the poorest strata in society), "the growing emphasis on FSM students projects a view of failing Whites that ignores 5 out of 6 students who do not receive FSM."

But contemporary and recent Marxist work, including my own work, does not have an exclusive focus on class. As this article, and an accompanying article (Hill, 2009), I hope, makes clear, we adhere to a notion of "raced" and gendered class, in which some (but not all) minority ethnic groups are racialized or xeno-racialized (explained below) and suffer a "race penalty" in, for example, teacher labelling and expectation, treatment by agencies of the state, such as the police, housing, judiciary, health services and in employment. Gillborn gives specific recognition to the analysis that social class is "raced" and gendered (e.g. p. 46), but gives relatively little—in fact very substantially less—explicit (other than implicit) recognition that "race" is classed (and gendered). While his work is not silent on social class disadvantage and social class based oppression, his treatment of social class analysis is dismissive and his treatment of social class underachievement in education and society, extraordinarily subdued. In Hill (2009), *Race and Class in Britain: a Critique of the Statistical Basis for Critical Race Theory in Britain: and Some Political Implications*, I also critique what I regard and analyse as the misuse of statistics in arguments put forward by some Critical Race Theorists in Britain showing that "Race" "trumps" Class in terms of underachievement at 16+ exams in England and Wales.[16] Accepting the urgent need for anti-racist awareness, policy and activism—from the classroom to the street[17]—I welcome the anti-racism that CRT promulgates and analyses while criticizing its over-emphasis on "white supremacy" and its statistical misrepresentations.

The Marxist Concept of Racialisation

A number of critiques of CRT appear very convincing. These critiques and their concepts draw attention to CRTS's empirical, theoretical and political failings. These critiques (in Britain) include: Miles' thesis of racialization (Miles, 1987, 1989, 1993); Sivanandan's theory of xeno-racism (2001, and, in Fekete, 2001); Cole's thesis of xeno-racialization (e.g. Cole 2008a, b, 2009); and Cole's critique of dangers of aspects of Critical Whiteness Studies (Cole, 2008a, p. 124; Cole, 2008b, 2009).

Cole (2007, p. 124) continues his discussion of racialisation, referring to Miles (1987, p. 75). Cole makes it clear that, like racism, racialization is not limited to skin colour: "the characteristics signified vary historically and, although there have usually been visible somatic features, other non-visible (alleged and real) biological features have also been identified." Cole (2007, p. 124) adds "cultural" to Miles "biological" (features) and includes culturally specific appurtenances, for example recognizing that "people are sometimes racialized on grounds of clothing (e.g. the hijab)."

Cole (2004a, b; also see Cole 2006, 2007a, b, 2008a, b, 2009) has introduced the concept of xeno-racialization (developing Sivanandan's discussion of xenoracism) to describe the process whereby refugees, economic migrants, and asylum-seekers (often white) become racialized. Sivanandan defines xenoracism as follows:

> It is a racism that is not just directed at those with darker skins, from the former colonial territories, but at the newer categories of the displaced, the dispossessed and the uprooted... It is a racism, that is, that cannot be colour-

> coded, directed as it is at poor whites as well, and is therefore passed off as xenophobia, a "natural" fear of strangers. But in the way it denigrates and reifies people before segregating and/or expelling them, it is a xenophobia that bears all the marks of the old racism. It is racism in substance, but "xeno" in form. It is a racism that is meted out to impoverished strangers even if they are white. It is xeno-racism. (Sivanandan, 2001; also cited in Fekete, 2001 p. 26)

Critical Race Theory and White Supremacy

One of two major tenets of CRT that Cole (2008a, b, 2009; see also Cole and Maisuria (2007, 2009)) critically examine is CRT's "idea that the concept of *white supremacy* better expresses oppression in contemporary societies based on 'race' than does the concept of *racism*." Cole and Maisuria (and Cole) argue that Critical Race Theory "homogenizes all white people together in positions of class power and privilege, which, of course, is factually incorrect, both with respect to social class inequality in general, and, as will be shown in later in this paper, with reference to xeno-racialization." Cole and Maisuria (2007) continue, "it is certainly not white people as a whole who are in this hegemonic position, nor white people as a whole who benefit from current education policy, or any other legislation. Indeed the white working class, as part of the working class in general, consistently fares badly in the education system."

Cole (2008a) notes that, in focusing on issues of colour and being divorced from matters related to capitalist requirements with respect to the labour market, CRT is ill-equipped to analyse the discourse of xeno-racism and processes of xeno-racialization.

McGary (1999:91) points out that "Black people have been used in ways that white people have not." Young's (2001) comment (with which Cole, Maisuria and I would concur) is that McGary's "observation may be true, but it does not mean that whites have not also been 'used.'" Young continues, "yes, whites may be 'used' differently, but they are still 'used' because that is the logic of exploitative regimes— people are 'used,' that is to say, their labour is commodified and exchanged for profit."

Young continues, in his critique of McGary, that such a view

> disconnects black alienation from other social relations; hence, it ultimately reifies race, and, in doing so, suppresses materialist inquiries into the class logic of race. That is to say, the meaning of race is not to be found within its own internal dynamics but rather in dialectical relation to and as an ideological justification of the exploitative wage-labour economy.

Critical Race Theory, and other similar theories of "race" salience, such as (Molefi Kete Asante, and of Paul Gilroy (2001), critiqued in Young, 2006) are understandable, as Leonardo (2004) notes, in the USA, as a salient subjective lens and understanding/analysis of felt (and indeed, of course, actual and widespread) oppression. As Leonardo (2004), Young (2006), Cole and Maisuria (2007), and Cole (2008b) note, Critical Race Theory, just as earlier theories such as that of Fanon and Negritude, do draw into the limelight, do expose and represent black experience, humiliation, oppression, racism. But they collude, just as much as race equivalence theorists such as Michael W. Apple, in super-elevating subjective consciousness of one aspect of identity and thereby occluding the ("raced" and gendered) class-essential nature of capitalism and the labour-capital relation. As such it seeks social democratic reformism, the winning of equal rights and opportunities—within a capitalist (albeit reformed) economy and society. As Young (2006) puts it,

> unlike many commentators who engage race matters, I do not isolate these social sites and view race as a local problem, which would lead to reformist measures along the lines of either legal reform or a cultural-ideological battle to win the hearts and minds of people and thus keep the existing socio-economic arrangements intact ... the eradication of race oppression also requires a totalizing political project: the transformation of existing capitalism – a system which produces difference (the racial/gender division of labour) and accompanying ideological narratives that justify the resulting social inequality. Hence, my project articulates a transformative theory of race—a theory that reclaims revolutionary class politics in the interests of contributing towards a post-racist society.

Critical Race Theory seems analytically flawed, to be based on the category error of assigning "race" as the primary form of oppression in capitalist society, and to be substantially situationally specific to the USA, with its horrific experience and legacy of slavery. It also seems to me to be a form of left radical United States imperialist hegemonizing, that is, of USA-based academics projecting on to other countries those experiences and analyses and policy perspectives that derive most specifically from the USA experience of slavery and its contemporary effects. I am very much aware of the existence and horrors of racism in, for example, Britain and Europe in general.[18] Notwithstanding those horrors, the Critical Race Theory analysis would appear to have less significance and applicability in, for example, Western and Eastern Europe, or, for example, India, Pakistan, and Nepal, than in the USA.

The Equivalence or Parallelist Theory of "Race" Class and Gender

Many of the points I make above in Critical Race Theory seem to me to be of equal value in relation to "Equivalence" or "Parallelist" theory (e.g. of Michael W. Apple).

Apple criticizes class analysts for ignoring "race," gender, and sexuality. He suggests that we need a much more nuanced and complex picture of class relations and class projects to understand what is happening in relation to "racial dynamics" as well as those involving gender.[19] Like Leonardo (2004) he sees shortcomings in classical Marxist analysis of class, "race," gender. Leonardo sees strengths in both class analysis, with its emphasis on objective analysis, and CRT (and, presumably, other theories and analyses that prioritize "race" experience and awareness and oppression). Apple doesn't.

Apple's accusation is that classical Marxists "privilege" class and marginalize "race," gender, and sexuality. *But the concept of class, the existence of class, the awareness of class, is itself sometimes buried beneath, hidden by, suffocated, displaced, in the recent (though not the early) work of Michael W. Apple.*

As Kelsh and Hill (2006) critique,

> What is masked from workers, because the capitalist class and its agents work to augment ideology in place of knowledge, is that some workers are poor not because other workers are wealthy, but because the capitalist class exploits all workers, and then divides and hierarchizes them, according to capitalist class needs for extracting ever more surplus value (profit).

Kelsh and Hill argue that "the Marxist concept of class, because it connects inequitable social relations and explains them as both connected and rooted in the social relations of production, enables class consciousness and the knowledges necessary to replace capitalism with socialism." They continue, "the Marxist concept of class, however, has been emptied of its explanatory power by theorists in the field of education as elsewhere who have converted it into a term that simply describes, and cannot explain the root causes of, strata of the population and the inequities among them."

The African-American scholar of the 1940s, Oliver Cromwell Cox argued that "making sense of the meaning of race and the character of race relations in American life requires an understanding of the dynamics of capitalism as a social system and its specific history in this country" (Reed, 2001). Cox's main book, *Caste, Class, and Race* (1948, reprinted in 2001), argued against the "caste school of race relations." He did this on the grounds that "it abstracted racial stratification in the United States from its origins and foundation in the evolution of American capitalism." He criticized those who compared racial stratification in the USA with the caste system in India for treating "racial hierarchy as if it were a timeless, natural form of social organization." As Reed (2001) notes, "the caste approach to the study of American race relations has not been in vogue for several decades; other equally misleading metaphors have long since supplanted it."

As Reed (2001) notes,

> Cox's critique of the caste school was linked to his broader view of the inadequacy and wrong-headedness of attitudinal or other idealist approaches to the discussion of racial inequality. He emphatically rejected primordialist notions of racial antipathy or ethnocentrism as explanations of racial stratification. He insisted that racism and race prejudice emerged from the class dynamics of capitalism and its colonial and imperial programmes ... , race was most fundamentally an artefact of capitalist labour dynamics, a relation that originated in slavery. "Sometimes, probably because of its very obviousness," he observed, "it is not realized that the slave trade was simply a way of recruiting labour for the purpose of exploiting the great natural resources of America." This perspective led to one of Cox's most interesting and provocative insights, that "racial exploitation is merely one aspect of the problem of the proletarianization of labour, regardless of the colour of the labourer. Hence racial antagonism is essentially political-class conflict." We should not make too much of the adverbs "simply" and "merely." Seeing race as a category that emerges from capitalist labour relations does not necessarily deny or minimize the importance of racial oppression and injustice or the need to fight against racism directly.
>
> Cox did not dismiss racism among working class whites. He argued that "the observed overt competitive antagonism is produced and carefully maintained by the exploiters of both the poor whites and the Negroes." He recognized that elite whites defined the matrix within which non-elite whites crafted their political agency, and he emphasized the ruling class foundations of racism as part of his critique of the liberal scholars of race relations who theorized race relations without regard to capitalist political economy and class dynamics. (Reed, 2001)

More recently Young (2006) has also criticized scholars who theorize race relations without regard to capitalist political economy and class dynamics, arguing "social alienation is an historical effect and its explanation does not reside in the experience itself; therefore, it needs explanation and such an explanation emerges from the transpersonal space of concepts."

And, Young criticizes views such as that of McGary (1999) that "it is possible for African-Americans to combat or overcome ... alienation ... without overthrowing capitalism." Young criticizes this as a "pro-capitalist" position: "Here, we see the ideological connection between the superstructure (philosophy) and the base (capitalism). Philosophy provides ideological support for capitalism, and, in this instance, we can also see how philosophy carries out class politics at the level of theory" (Althusser, 1971, p. 18).[20] Similar criticism, of pro-capitalism (albeit of a radical reformist, social democratic variety), of failing to locate racism within the labour-capital relation, within capitalist political economy and class dynamics, can be levelled at the work of Michael W. Apple.[21]

Caste Analysis

I would wish to advance a similar critique of the hegemony and the caste system in India, and among Indian-heritage people in Britain. There is no denying the material reality and form, the murderous and tragic consequences of the caste system currently and historically, primarily for Dalits, the Untouchables, who are regarded as impure by higher caste Brahmins and others. Whole libraries have been written on caste oppression, lakes of tears have been shed and blood flown.[22]

In the British context, particularly worth noting is, Borbas, Haslam, and Sampla's 2006 report for the Dalit Solidarity Network, *No Escape: Caste Discrimination in the UK*. This draws similar attention to caste discrimination that exists in the Indian Diaspora, with over 300 million people worldwide suffering from caste-based discrimination and caste-like practices linked to untouchability (p. 4). Their report on caste discrimination in England, with an estimated 50,000 Dalits, gives evidence of job discrimination against Dalits and lower castes, for example, with higher castes rejecting or resenting taking orders from, being managed by, Dalits or lower caste Indians, and with the different castes and the Dalits all having different temples/gurdwaras/places of worship. In addition, inter-caste marriages are unusual. The authors (p. 7) note that "the rules of endogamy (marrying within the caste group) are still strictly followed."

When I raise the issue of caste discrimination in Britain or India, I often get the retort, "caste is a pre-capitalist social formation." And so it is, but caste lives today, in capitalism, with the emergence of economic elites, a capitalist class and class stratification in the Scheduled Castes, the Backward Castes, the Backward Tribes, and the Dalits.[23]

Indeed, it is these elites who benefit disproportionately from caste-based access to education. This is played out with the quota system for entry to universities. A quota of places is reserved for various groups within higher education and also within state employment. This is termed "reservation" in India and is protected/enforced as part of the Indian Constitution.

Capitalism has benefited from this caste politics/policy/legislation. Social class and the idea of class conflict has been put on backburner in India. Economic and social justice are no longer the justice achieved through class struggle but rather through the government reforms for certain castes. Kumar (2008a) notes that "such measures have been continuing for Scheduled Castes and Scheduled Tribes for decades and it came for the Backward Castes (BCs) in jobs with the Mandal Commission (with the National Front Government during 1989) and in higher education institutions with the government passing a law and the Supreme Court upholding it."

There is no denying that caste repression has been there in Indian society throughout (and, of course, before) capitalism in India. However its "social" content and "economic" content has often been seen in disjunction, which leads to flawed analysis. Rather than struggling specifically for "caste rights," the rights of Dalits and of Scheduled Castes, a Marxist approach and analysis is that the political struggle should be for Dalit rights or poor Backward Caste rights by virtue, not of their caste position, but by virtue of their social class position, as landles?

Emphasis on the "social," the subjective identity of caste, just as, with the pre-eminence accorded by some writers to the subjective identity of "race" in the USA, for example, is perpetuated through the ideological apparatuses used by the dominant and entrenched hegemonic interests to perpetuate the economic (and resultant social) inequalities that exist.

A class divided by caste, or divided by "race"—whether such divisions are inflamed by "saffron fascists" in India or by racists in the USA (or Britain), or whether they are perpetuated by reformist "reservation"/huge scale quota systems (valuable though, in part they might be)—serve to divide and perpetuate capitalist class rule. "The workers united will never be defeated," a phrase thundered out of a million voices on demonstrations and struggles in countries such as France, Portugal, Spain, and Britain at various times, is a phrase and concept and organizational aim understood well by those opposed to the development of working class consciousness.

As Ravi Kumar (2008c) notes,

> And now because of the host of measures/reforms an elite has emerged within the Dalits as well as the BCs (as indicated starkly in North India by political formations led by Mayawati in Uttar Pradesh, Mulayam Singh Yadav in Uttar Pradesh and Laloo Prasad Yadav in Bihar). They are now very much part of the plan of capitalist expansion. Nobody is talking about land reforms,

> minimum wages, gender equality (in fact the Women's Reservation Bill has been stuck in Parliament for ages because of objections made by the Backward Caste lobby), unemployment and growing disparity. And their support as well as close relationship with big industrial houses shows how much they care for the uplifting of even their own caste people, people from the same caste.

Ashwani Kumar (2008) gives the example from Rajasthan: "There are many lower caste people who have economically reached the upper class but do not want to give up the benefits associated with having a Scheduled Caste or Tribe certificate," and he gives the example of the Meena tribe, many of whose members are top government officials, but whose offspring continue to reap the benefits of "reservation." Similarly, Ravi Kumar 2008c (Chapter 9) analyses the enormous inequity within the *jatis* (sub-castes) with an elite emerging among them which manipulates the caste identity and consolidates it for its own gains, as part of the class stratification of castes.

Ravi Kumar (2008b) notes that in India "[T]he discourse on caste as located within the realm of capitalism is almost negligible" and that "[O]ne of the much frequently visited debates in the Indian context has been that of non-significance of 'class' and significance of 'caste' as the most significant category of social division or form of social relation." Kumar (2008b, developed in depth in Kumar 2008c) suggests that

> The emergence of elite among all castes (which could very well be identified with parallel class positions), especially among the so-called Backward Castes and Dalits (literally meaning "oppressed"), has shown how capital uses the existing identities to sustain and expand itself. *The direction in which Dalit politics has moved recently has been that of co-optation into the larger system of capitalism. In terms of "inclusion" of hitherto unrepresented social categories into the dominant forms of capital accumulation it can be said that there has been a democratization of opportunities to access the realm of competition* (italics in the original).

As Brosio (2008) notes, such co-option weakens the anti-capitalist struggle. To repeat, there is no denying the material reality, the daily living conditions, the deaths, arising from caste discrimination in India, or, indeed, from the 2008 ethnic strife/cleansing in Kenya, or the ethnocratic Zionist oppression and landgrabbing of Israeli Arab and Palestinian Arab land. Non-class ideologies can and do assume material reality, sometimes with lethal force. However, below, I advance a Marxist analysis of these ethnic, caste, and other forms of oppression.

Part 4: Marxist Analysis of Class, "Race," Caste, and Gender: Neoliberalism and Neoconservatism

Neoliberal capitalist policies of marketization, commodification, and privatization of public services, together with fiscal and other policy changes, comprise an intensification of "class war from above" (Harvey, 2005) by the capitalist class against the working class. It is worth noting that "class war from above" is a permanent feature of the labour-capital relation, more observable during crises of capital accumulation/major threats to the rate of profit, less observable during periods of class compromise, of "truce," but permanent, nevertheless.

These neoliberal policy changes *in the education sector* result, *inter alia*, in (1) widening social class educational inequalities, for example in wealth, income and educational attainment; (2) attacks on the key working class organizations, such as trade unions; and (3) worsening pay and conditions of education workers. These can be seen as three "fronts" in the current class war from above.[24]

The introduction and extension of neoliberal social policies in Britain, the USA after the New Right reactionary movements of the 1980s, and more globally (notably in Chile under Pinochet, elsewhere in Latin America under an assortment of generals and "big business" control) offer fertile ground for Marxist analysis since economic inequality and class division has sharpened markedly, within countries and internationally.[25]

Social Class and Marxist Critique of Identitarian Politics

Young (2006) notes that "in terms of race, an Althusserian account is presented in Stuart Hall's, 1980 article, "Race, Articulation, and Societies Structured in Dominance":

> By the 1990s, Hall shifts to a semiotic notion of race, and sees race as a "floating signifier." In many ways, Hall's intellectual trajectory on race mirrors the larger shift from the "material" to the "semiotic" in social theory. (from Young, 2006)

In a similar critique of Hall's "New Times" analysis, I also trace the Stuart Hall's (and other post-Marxist and postmodernist) progression from materialist analyses to semiotic/culturalist analyses) (Hill, 2001, 2005a). So does Jenny Bourne, in her discussion of the rise of cultural studies, the "Hokum of New Times," and her critique of Hall over his post-Marxist position on "race," "identity," and difference. She writes:

> The politics of identity and difference were now being clearly used to justify the break with class politics and, indeed, with the concept of Left politics

> altogether. (idem)
> The "personal is the political" also helped to shift the centre of gravity of struggle from the community and society to the individual. "What has to be done?" was replaced by "who am I?" as the blacks, feminists and gays, previously part of the pressure groups in Left parties or in social movements campaigning for rights, turned to Identity Politics. Articulating one's identity changed from being a path to political action to being the political action itself. (2002:200)

Bourne, continues,

> Sivanandan critiques postmodernism not so much in terms of the inward-looking self-referencing type of debate, beloved of academics, as in terms of the danger it spells to anti-racist practice. First, he takes issue with those intellectuals who, at a time when racism against the black working class is getting worse, "have retreated into culturalism and ethnicity or, worse, fled into discourse and deconstruction and representation—as though to interpret the world is more important than to change it, as though changing the interpretation is all we could do to change the world."

And in an acerbic aside Sivanandan adds: "Marxists interpret the world in order to change it, postmodernists change the interpretation" (cited in Bourne, 2002, p. 203).

Class is absolutely central to Marxist ontology and epistemology. Ultimately, it is economically induced and it conditions and permeates all social reality in capitalist systems. Marxists therefore critique postmodern and post-structural arguments that class is, or ever can be, "constructed extra-economically," or equally that it can be "deconstructed politically"—an epistemic position which has underwritten in the previous two decades numerous so-called "death of class" theories, arguably the most significant of which are Laclau and Mouffe (1985) and Laclau (1996).

I am not arguing against the complexities of subjective identities. People have different subjectivities. Some individual coalminers in Britain were gay, black, Betty Page or Madonna fetishists, heavily influenced by Biggles or Punk, their male gym teacher or their female History teacher, by Robert Tressell or by Daily Porn masturbation, by Radical Socialists or by Fascist ideology. But the coal mining industry has virtually ceased to exist in Britain, and the police occupation of mining villages such as Orgreave during the Great Coalminers' Strike (in Britain) of 1984-85 and the privatization of British Coal and virtual wiping out of the coal mining industry was motivated by class warfare of the ruling capitalist fraction. It was class warfare from above. Whatever individuals in mining families like to do in bed, their dreams, and in their transmutation of television images, they suffered because of their particular class fraction position—

they were miners—and historically the political shock troops of the British manual working class.

Postmodernism's rejection of metanarratives can be seen as symptomatic of the theoretical inability to construct a mass solidaristic oppositional transformatory political project, and that it is based on the refusal to recognize the validity or existence of solidaristic social class. More importantly, this general theoretical shortcoming is politically disabling because the effect of eschewing mass solidaristic policy is, in effect, supporting a reactionary status quo. Both as an analysis and as a vision, post-modernism has its dangers—but more so as a vision. It fragments and denies economic, social, political, and cultural relations. In particular, it rejects the solidaristic metanarratives of neo-Marxism and socialism. It thereby serves to disempower the oppressed and to uphold the hegemonic Radical Right in their privileging of individualism and in their stress on patterns and relations of consumption as opposed to relations of production. Postmodernism analysis, in effect if not in intention, justifies ideologically the current Radical Right economic, political, and educational project.

Marxism and Class

At this point it might be useful to discuss, briefly, Marxist analysis of social class. There are significant issues concerning intra-class differentiation and about class consciousness. It is important to recognize that class, for Marx, is neither simply monolithic nor static. Marx conceived of classes as internally differentiated entities. Under capitalist economic laws of motion, the working class in particular is constantly decomposed and reconstituted due to changes in the forces of production—forces of which members of the working class are themselves a part (6). Furthermore, Marx had taken great pains to stress that social class as distinct from economic class necessarily includes a political dimension, which is in the broadest sense of the term "culturally" rather than "economically" determined.

And, class consciousness does not follow automatically or inevitably from the fact of class position. *The Poverty of Philosophy* [1847] distinguishes between a "class-in-itself" (class position) and a "class-for-itself" (class consciousness); *The Communist Manifesto* [1848] explicitly identifies the "formation of the proletariat into a class" as the key political task facing the communists. In *The Eighteenth Brumaire of Louis Napoleon* [1852] Marx observes:

> In so far as millions of families live under economic conditions of existence that divide their mode of life, their interests and their cultural formation from those of the other classes and bring them into conflict with those classes, they form a class. In so far as these small peasant proprietors are merely connected on a local basis, and the identity of their interests fails to produce a feeling of community, national links, or a political organization, they do not form a class. (Marx, 1999 [1852])

Thus social class exists in a contingent rather than a necessary relation to economic class. The process (and conceptual category) that links economic and social class is that of "class consciousness." This is arguably the most contentious and problematic term in the debate over class.

Marxism, Class, and Capitalist Education and Economy

Classical Marxian scholarship with respect to education theorizes the relationship between education and the inequality in society as an inevitable feature of capitalist society/economy. Glenn Rikowski focuses on the relationship between social class and the process of capitalization of education (e.g. Rikowski, 2005) in the USA and UK, where neoliberal drivers are working to condition the education sector more tightly to the needs of capital. A global study I carried out in 2005 for the International Labour Organization (Hill, 2005b; Hill et al., 2006) shows clearly the similarity of these drivers, the similarity of policy developments, and the similarity of impacts across many countries. Empirical evidence (e.g. Greaves, Hill, Maisuria, 2006; Hill, Greaves, and Maisuria, 2008) shows how capital accumulation is the principal objective of national and international government policy, and of global capitalist organizations, "capitalist clubs," such as the World Trade Organization.

To repeat from above the key ontological claim of Marxist education theorists is that education serves to complement, regiment, and replicate the dominant-subordinate nature of class relations upon which capitalism depends, the labour-capital relation. Education services the capitalist economy, though this servicing is not unproblematic or uncontested. Education (schools, universities) helps reproduce the necessary social, political, ideological and economic conditions for capitalism, and therefore, helps reflect and reproduce the organic inequalities of capitalism originating in the relations of production.

But education is also a site of cultural contestation and resistance, a key site of "the culture wars" between neoconservative and neoliberal, liberal, social democratic, and socialist visions of and articulations of culture, correctness and common sense. Education reflects, supports and reproduces the social inequalities of capitalist culture. The "education industry" is a significant state apparatus (Althusser, 1971) in the reproduction and replication of the capitalist social form necessary for the continuation of "surplus value" extraction and economic inequality. Hence, Marxists argue that there are material linkages between educational inequality, exploitation, and capitalist inequalities in general.

In contrast to both Critical Race Theorists and revisionist socialists/left liberals/equivalence theorists, and those who see caste as the primary form of oppression, Marxists would agree that objectively—whatever our "race" or gender or sexuality or current level of academic attainment or religious identity, whatever the individual and group history and fear of oppression and attack—the fundamental objective and material form of oppression in capitalism is class oppression.

Black and Women capitalists, or Jewish and Arab capitalists, or Dalit capitalists in India, exploit the labour power of their multi-ethnic men and women workers, essentially (in terms of the exploitation of labour power and the appropriation of surplus value) in just the same way as do white male capitalists, or upper caste capitalists. But the subjective consciousness of identity, this subjective affirmation of one particular identity, while seared into the souls of its victims, should not mask the objective nature of contemporary oppression under capitalism—class oppression that, of course, hits some "raced" and gendered and caste and occupational sections of the working class harder than others.

Martha Gimenez (2001:24) succinctly explains that "class is not simply another ideology legitimating oppression." Rather, class denotes "exploitative relations between people mediated by their relations to the means of production." Apple's "parallellist," or equivalence model of exploitation (equivalence of exploitation based on "race," class and gender, his "tryptarchic" model of inequality) produces valuable data and insights into aspects of and the extent and manifestations of gender oppression and "race" oppression in capitalist USA. However, such analyses serve to occlude the class-capital relation, the class struggle, to obscure an essential and defining nature of capitalism, class conflict.

Objectively, whatever our "race" or gender or caste or sexual orientation or scholastic attainment, whatever the individual and group history and fear of oppression and attack, the fundamental form of oppression in capitalism is class oppression. While the capitalist class is predominantly white and male, capital in theory and in practice can be blind to colour and gender and caste—even if that does not happen very often. African Marxist-Leninists such as Ngugiwa Thiong'o (e.g. Ngugiwa

Thiong'o and Ngugiwa Mirii, 1985) know very well that when the white colonialist oppressors were ejected from direct rule over African states in the 1950s and 60s, the white bourgeoisie in some African states such as Kenya was replaced by a black bourgeoisie, acting in concert with transnational capital and/or capital(ists) of the former colonial power. Similarly in India, capitalism is no longer exclusively white. It is Indian, not white British alone.

As Bellamy observes, the diminution of class analysis "denies immanent critique of any critical bite," effectively disarming a meaningful opposition to the capitalist thesis (Bellamy, 1997:25). And as Harvey notes,

> neoliberal rhetoric, with its foundational emphasis upon individual freedoms, has the power to split off libertarianism, identity politics, multiculturalism, and eventually narcissistic consumerism from the social forces ranged in pursuit of justice through the conquest of state power. (Harvey, 2005:41)

To return to the broader relationship between "race," gender, and social class, and to turn to the USA, are there many who would deny that Condoleeza Rice and Colin Powell have more in common with the Bushes and the rest of the United States capitalist class, be it white, black or Latina/o, than they do with the workers whose individual ownership of wealth and power is an infinitesimal fraction of those individual members of the ruling and capitalist class?

The various oppressions, of caste, gender, "race," religion, for example, are functional in dividing the working class and securing the reproduction of capital; constructing social conflict between men and women, or black and white, or different castes, or tribes, or religious groups, or skilled and unskilled, thereby tending to dissolve the conflict between capital and labour, thus occluding the class-capital relation, the class struggle, and to obscure the essential and defining nature of capitalism, the labour-capital relation and its attendant class conflict.

Class is clearly not the only form of oppression in contemporary society. People get demeaned, discriminated against, labelled, attacked, raped, murdered and massacred because of a variety of presenting characteristics and identities, such as gender, "race," caste, sexuality, religion. As Marx (1852/1969) notes,

> Men [*sic*] make their own history, but they do not make it just as they please; they do not make it under circumstances chosen by themselves, but under circumstances directly encountered, given and transmitted from the past. The tradition of all dead generations weighs like a nightmare on the brains of the living.

Non-reductionist Class Analysis

I now refer to a non-reductionist analysis of the role of ideology, knowledge workers, and the material practices of racism and Dalit discrimination. As Motala and Vally (writing about South Africa, but with global analytical relevance) analyse,

> Simply rejecting these deeply embedded social norms, practices and histories, often developed over many centuries preceding the advent of capitalist accumulation, as "hypocrisy" is disarming and does not provide a basis for understanding them. In other words, the idea that "race" (or other such conceptions and practices) is a social construct does not automatically imply that it has no explanatory value (especially about how power is constituted through racist categories and/or gender to reinforce the structural attributes and impediments of working class lives). The explanatory value of "race" and gender lies in the power to reveal the relationship between these social constructs and class without suggesting that they provide a better explanation of exploitation. (2009, n.p.; italics added)

They recognize that

> [u]nderstanding the role of ideology fully and its construction of forms of subjectivity that reinforces class domination [is] essential. Ideology allows capitalist relations to be concealed, blocked from being grasped conceptually, by the empirico-experiential actuality of racist practices. (idem)

This comment, I might interject, is also relevant to the empirico-experientialist actuality of caste oppression in India and the Indian diaspora.

Motala and Vally continue,

> And because the empirio-experiential trumps the theoretical, the root cause of inequity is accepted as and ascribed to the empirical—to "race," in this case—rather than to capitalist relations. Ideology is rooted in and impacts on the material and cannot be reduced to falsehood.

Thus this analysis in this paper does not ignore the material reality of "race" oppression, caste oppression, or gender oppression. The analysis I am putting forward is a Marxist argument located within Marxist reproduction theory, the theory that education systems, together with other ideological and repressive state apparatuses, work to reproduce existing patterns of economic, social and political life. While not subscribing to an Althusserian relative autonomy analysis (one developed, inter alia, by Michael W. Apple), this analysis is not an "iron chain of command"—

from capital to government to state apparatuses to effective impact. The analysis offered here, while it will no doubt be criticized as "vulgar Marxism" and as deterministic, reductionist, and essentialist (for such critiques, see Apple, 2005, 2006), does recognize developments within neo-Marxist theory, especially state theory, that this cultural, economic, and ideological reproduction is mediated and resisted. (See Hill, 2001, 2005a.) However, such an analysis is more deterministic, reductionist, and essentialist than those of relative autonomy "culturalist (neo-)Marxists" and, most certainly, postmodernists. But not in terms of the "vulgar Marxism" attributed by its critics.

Such an analysis sees class as central to the social relations of production and essential for producing and reproducing the cultural and economic activities of humans under a capitalist mode of production. Whereas the abolition of racism and sexism or caste does not guarantee the abolition of capitalist social relations of production, the abolition of class inequalities, or the abolition of class itself, by definition, denotes the abolition of capitalism.

As Motala and Vally (2009, n.p.) argue:

> the absence of class analysis leads to a debilitating failure to appreciate the deeper characteristics of society; de-links poverty and inequality from the political, economic and social system—capitalism—which underpins them; obscures the class nature of the post-apartheid state; renders ineffective social and educational reforms and denies the importance of class struggle and the agency of working communities in the struggle for social transformation.

Part 5: Social Democracy, Reforms and the Transition to Socialism

Social democratic reforms, and social democratic or "revisionist left" analyses and theorists and the policies related to those theories and class/political mobilizations/struggle, are immensely valuable. Clean water, free schooling, social welfare benefits, the creating of Welfare States, are, of course, life enhancing/life changing/life lengthening for billions, in rich countries like Britain and the USA as well as in developing countries such as India, and are therefore intrinsically valuable. Thus, in India, for example, or in Britain or the USA, a common school system (known in Britain as a comprehensive school system)—with no private purchase of educational privilege via the existence of private, or semi-private school systems—would, if properly funded, be an immensely valuable, "welfarist" social reform.[26]

And in India, the caste-based system of quotas for entry into universities and into government jobs (termed "reservation") has indeed been invaluable in millions of individual cases of advancing repressed and poor sections of the people.

Ravi Kumar points out that,

> There is a great deal of debate on the issue of reservation in India. The Left has been in forefront of supporting it. My argument regarding it is as following: If one looks at the reservation policy it has, on paper, democratized access of the lower class/caste population to education/jobs.

So that is the value of a social democratic reform. But Kumar goes on to look at the class impact of such a policy:

> However, it has also, as an analysis of the past decades demonstrates led to the emergence of an elite. Reservation demand for the backward castes, for instance, since 1990 has clearly indicated this, as the majority of the BC population remains landless workers, or poor peasantry. The reservations democratize the access but only for those who have reached such a position to access it. For example, when the majority of children are not able to cross Class V in schools. Would reservation in Higher Education mean democracy in access for majority? Rather, it will only increase access for those who could afford to go beyond schools. In other words, those who can afford to purchase education.

Thus, within a social democratic welfarist framework, involving, in various countries, quota/reservation systems, assistance for poor students, and other measures of positive discrimination, education continues to play a key role in the perpetuation of the labour-capital relation, of capitalism itself. Referring to social democratic, left-liberal and "revisionist left" theorists, Kelsh and Hill (2006) explain,

> By "revisionist left," we mean, following Rosa Luxemburg (1899/1970), those theorists who consider themselves to be "left" but who believe there is no alternative to capitalism, and thus do "not expect to see the contradictions of capitalism mature." Their theories consequently aim "to lessen, to attenuate, the capitalist contradictions"—in short, to "adjust" "the antagonism between capital and labour." As Luxemburg explained, the core aim of the revisionist left is the "bettering of the situation of the workers and ... the conservation of the middle classes."

In contrast, egalitarian, socialist, reforms, affecting the lives, life chances material conditions of, for example, South Asian and other school students and communities in Britain, as elsewhere, require an end not only to neoliberal/neoconservative globalizing capitalism, but to capitalism itself, and through a localising and globalising of resistance, a transition to a socialist society, economy, and polity.

As Marx and Engels, 1977a [1847], p. 62) put it:

> The Communists fight for the attainment of the immediate aims, for the enforcement of the momentary interests of the working class; but in the movement of the present, they also represent and take care of the future of the movement.

In this, socialist and Marxist teachers and other cultural workers, community and political activists have a dual role: to act as critical transformative socialist public intellectuals, and to act with others in wider arenas of the anti-capitalist struggle.

Political Strategies

The analyses and statistics used or misused by knowledge workers can impact on the foci of political action—street action, propaganda, and programmes of progressive and egalitarian political parties and groups. Theories of oppression and of exploitation, with their statistical underpinnings and justifications, also impact on progressive political action. This was exampled in the 2009 European Parliament election campaign and current political action and developments in Britain, such as the Spring 2010 general election campaign.

The question for progressives, egalitarians, socialists, and Marxists is the balance between focusing on anti-racist campaigns and class-based campaigns. The necessity for and viability of such strategies does of course vary historically and geographically. In Britain, currently, the two major anti-racist organisations are "Hope not Hate" and Unite Against Fascism (UAF). During the June 2009 European election campaign, they both called on voters to "vote anyone but the BNP." On the other hand, some socialist/Marxist/Communist campaigns such as the NO2EU-Yesto Democracy and the SLP campaigns prioritised class-based campaigns of anti-racism and anti-sexism, but also of working class unity, as does the current (2010) TUSC (Trade Unionist and Socialist Coalition) and the programme/analysis of the Socialist Party. In strategic terms this is the difference between a Popular Front and a United Front.[27] Thus, two alternative political strategies were evident in the 2009 European election campaign in Britain, and will be again in the 2010 Parliamentary election campaign. The first strategy in 2009 (that of Unite Against Fascism – UAF – and the "Hope Not Hate" campaign, and the tactical voting urged by some sections of RESPECT, such as Salma Yaqub and the North-West region of RESPECT) was that the most important issue of all in the European election campaign was the anti-racist issue, to "Stop the BNP." Hence the call by the above mentioned sections of RESPECT to "Vote Green' to `stop the BNP."

This particular view would seem to theoretically align with the view of Critical Race Theorists that "race" and racism are *the key* forms of structural discrimination and oppression in Britain and in the USA. David Gillborn's insistence, like the Racism Awareness Training theorists of the 1970s, and like the various incarnations of black separatists and nationalists in various countries, seeks to blame all whites, and serves to divide the working class, black from white. At the political level this was paralleled by the various groups within the socialist and Marxist Left who sought to prioritize anti-racism and who were furious with NO2EU for "splitting the anti-racist vote" during the 2009 European election campaign.

A class-based Marxist analysis is that it was the collapse of New Labour's vote— due to its abandonment of working class interests in the interests of neoliberalism—that depressed the voting turnout, enabling the BNP to get elected. This was despite the BNP gaining fewer votes than in the previous European elections. But they got elected because of the collapse in the Labour vote. This is paralleled in various countries in Western Europe, where the decline of former social democratic parties (in Austria, France, and Italy, for example) has been stark, with fascist, racist, and anti-immigrant groups becoming beneficiaries of social democratic parties' embrace of neoliberalism.

Critical Race Theorists' prioritizing of the "race" issue is in contrast to the view of Marxists who took a class perspective—who prioritized the class issue. Such a class perspective was advanced within, for example, the NO2EU-Yesto Democracy campaign (supported principally by the RMT trade union, the Socialist Party and the Communist Party of Britain with its *Morning Star* daily newspaper, and—ultimately— the view of Socialist Resistance, to which I belong).

During that campaign, as a lead regional candidate for NO2EU-Yesto Democracy[28] at various venues, from doorstep campaigning, to addressing the Trades Union Congress national conference of Trades Councils (local TUCs), to conversations with Greens at the Regional Election count, I was one of those who advanced the view that anti-racism was and is a key policy/focus, but that there are others, such as resisting/opposing/stopping privatization of public services; opposing the European Union's privatizing policies, such as the Health Services Directive and the Postal Services Directive (which demand of member states the marketization of Health and Postal Services); renationalizing formerly public services such as the Railways; and stopping/reversing the Posted Workers' Directive, which, along the principles of the Bolkestein Directive, allows groups of workers to be imported by employers into member states and paid at the wages of the originating member state, thereby undercutting trade union national agreements.

The final aim of much of the NO2EU campaign was to set up a new "Workers' Party," backed by trade unions, as a socialist party, defending working class interests (of workers of all colours and creeds) occupying the space to the left of Labour. Indeed, the TUSC is a possible embryo for such a development, supported as it is not only by some trade union national leaders and by regional organizations of the RMT union, but also the major socialist and Marxist groups in Britain such as the Socialist Workers' Party, the Socialist Party, Socialist Resistance, the Indian Workers Association, and Respect.

The political focus made by socialists and Marxists in Britain during the period of the May-June 2009 European parliamentary election campaign was thus between two positions.

The first was prioritizing the "Don't Vote BNP" campaigns. The Socialist Workers' Party, the largest of the Marxist parties in Britain, with around 5,000 members, took the perspective highlighting race.

The second position, held by other parties (such as NO2EU and its constituent/supporting organisations, and the Socialist Labour Party) took the class perspective. This class perspective (at least that held by the Socialist Party constituent part of NO2EU) was about developing/setting up a new Workers Partyone that would unite various socialist political parties, groups, individuals, with trade unions. That is, to prioritize working class issues on behalf of/with the "raced" and gendered working class. This view, which I am advancing here, is to fight the class struggle for all workers, black, white, brown, or, to echo the anti-fascist slogan of the 1970s, "black and white unite and fight, smash the National Front." To echo an international slogan of working class revolutionaries and Marxists across different countries, "*o povounidojamaos sera vencido*," "the workers united will never be defeated".

This is not to deny the existence of "white privilege." Yes, Whites do have white privilege because of the colour of their/our skins. But the poor white English, Portuguese, African Caribbean, Black African, Indian, Pakistani, Bangladeshi, or Chinese have more *in common* in terms of the material conditions of their daily existence than they do with sons and daughters of the white English, Indian, Pakistani, African Caribbean or Chinese millionaire. As Bob Crow, leader of NO2EU-yestoDemocracy, and of the RMT says, "I have got more in common with a Chinese labourer than I have with Sir Fred Goodwin" (the multimillionaire ex-"boss" of the Royal Bank of Scotland) (Hattenstone, 2008).

Notes

1. I follow the convention of placing the word "race" in quotation marks to indicate that it is a social category, a social construct, rather than a biological category.
2. For an explanation of this classification, see Hessari and Hill, 1989. The relevant chapter, Chapter 2, is online at http://www.ieps.org.uk/PDFs/Multicultural.doc
3. The parties and leaders leading this transition from revolutionary rhetoric to social democratic rhetoric were the Italian Communist Party, the *PartitoComunistaltaliano* under the leadership of Enrico Berlinguer, and the Spanish Communist Party, the *PartidoComunistaEspañol*, led by Santiago Carrillo, when they adopted a Eurocommunist analysis and programme. Possibly the most important Eurocommunist theoretical publication was Santiago Carrillo's, *Eurocommunism and the State*, 1977. Trotskyites such as Mandel (1978) claimed that communist parties had abandoned revolutionary politics and the concept of proletarian revolution since 1924, when the Soviet Union abandoned the concept of world revolution and internationalism, replacing it with the concept of "socialism in one country," i.e. paramount support by communist parties throughout the world for the Soviet Union.
4. In the UK this debate is urgent with the likelihood of a Parliamentary (general) election in May or June 2010. Some socialists/Marxist support voting Green, which in the UK is broadly a social democratic party, others say vote Labour, while others are trying to set up an anti-capitalist socialist party, currently based around the Trade Unionist and Socialist Coalition (TUSC). I am, in fact, one of their Parliamentary candidates, in the Brighton Kemptown constituency.
5. For Marxist arguments against postmodernism, seeEagleton, 1996; Cole, Hill and Rikowski, 1997; Callinicos, 1989; Cole et al., 2001; Hill et al., 2002; and Cole, 2008a. Elsewhere in this paper I refer to Bourne, 2002.
6. This is not an argument against separate ethnic or religious language/culture/religion schooling for indigenous, migrant groups in schooling/education that is supplementary to, or complementary to, a common (or comprehensive) publicly funded, secular state school system with a common core curriculum.
7. See Miles, 1987, 19898, 1993; Abbass, 2007; and Cole, 2008. I am using the Marxist concept of racialization here. There are others, such as in Murji and Solomos, 2005.
8. Cole, 2004b, 2008a, b, 2009
9. In Britain 1.8 per cent of the population are Indian heritage (more than one million), 1.3% of Pakistani heritage (three quarters of a million, with over half of Pakistanis living in the West Midlands, Yorkshire and the North West), and 0.5 per cent of Bangladeshi heritage (280,000). London has the highest proportion of minority ethnic communities. Almost 50% of Londoners

describe themselves other than white British (National Statistics, 2001). (See also Commission for Racial Equality, 2007).

10. In the UK, in official data such as census data and school achievement data, "Asian" refers to South Asian. In the UK this is mainly Indian, Pakistani, and Bangladeshi. In the UK "Chinese" is a category distinct from "Asian." This is in contrast to usage/categorization in the USA, where "Asian" refers to East Asian (primarily Chinese, Japanese, Vietnamese, Cambodian, Laotian, and Korean).
11. For ethnographic, empirical and theoretical/analytical work on South Asian minority ethnic groups' identity and educational achievement, see, for example, Runneymede Trust, 2000; Sivanandan, 2001; and Abbas, 2004a, b.
12. See Mills, 1987, 1989, 1993, 1997, 2003; Bell, 1992, 2004; Delgado, 1995; Delgado and Stefanic, 2000, 2001; Gillborn, 2005, 20061, b, 2008; Preston, 2007a, b; and Chakrabarty and Preston, 2007.
13. See, for example, Apple, 2001, 2005, and 2006.
14. For critiques of the effects of caste in India, see Iliah, 2005; Kumar and Kumar, 2005; Murali Krishna, 2007 and Quadri and Kumar, 2003. For critiques of caste in Britain, see Borbas et al., 2006.
15. See Sivanandan, 2001; Cole, 2007a, 2007b, 2008a, b, 2009 forthcoming; Cole and Maisuria, 2007, 2009; and with respect to "race" salience theories—theories analysing "race" as the primary form of structural oppression—see Miles 1987, 1989, 1993; and Young, 2001.
16. I ask two questions, and make these two associated criticisms, concerning the representation of these statistics: Firstly, with respect to "race" and educational attainment, I question the validity of ignoring the presence of the (high achieving) Indian/Indian heritage group of pupils—one of the two largest minority groups in England and Wales. I make the point that this group has been ignored, indeed, left completely out of statistical representations —charts—showing educational achievement levels of different ethnic groups. Secondly with respect to social class and educational attainment, I question the validity of Gillborn's selection of two contiguous social class/strata in order to show social class differences in educational attainment. This is in sharp contrast to his earlier practice, for example in Gillborn and Mirza, 2000, of comparing social "classes" (strata) that are not contiguous.I have seen David Gillborn present his arguments at two separate conferences—the April 2009 AERA (American Educational Research Association Annual Conference in San Diego, California) (Gillborn, 2009c) and at the Race(ing) Forward: Transitions in Theorizing "Race" at the Education conference organized by The Higher Education Academy, in 2008, at the University of Northampton (Gillborn, 2008b).
17. An anti-Muslim group calling itself the "English Defence League" has been demonstrating outside mosques in London and Birmingham, chanting *"Muslim bombers off our streets"* and rampaging through ethnically mixed

areas such as Stoke. In January 2010 at Stoke, there were 1500 demonstrators, including known fascists and racists (BBC, 2010; Smith, 2010). Similar racist demonstrations have been held in Wales and in Scotland by the Welsh Defence League and the Scottish Defence League. This is serious; it is the first time since the defeat of the National Front in the late 1970s (by a combination of street-level anti-fascist mobilizations and Margaret Thatcher's 1979 election appeal to nationalist and racist voters) that fascists and racists are attempting to control the streets in some areas and intimidate minorities.

18. I have been actively involved in the anti-Fascist and anti-racist movement since the 1970s. From the Grunwicks mass picket in 1977, to being a local officer of the Anti-Nazi League in the 1970s, and being smoke bombed by NF supporters, to engaging in street confrontations against the fascist National Front, and twice being physically attacked by Fascists. I was also involved in ARTEN, the Anti-Racist Teacher Education network in Britain in the late 1980s, and joined the march to close down the NF headquarters in Welling in 1993. More recently I took part in and was a platform speaker at the 2009 anti-British National Party rally at the national conference of the Trades Union Congress Trades Councils.
19. See, for example, Apple, 2005:392; 2006:116.
20. See the section below on Identity and Identitarian Politics.
21. For critiques of Apple's analysis see, in addition to Kelsh and Hill, 2006, Farahmandpur, 2004, Rikowski, 2006, and Hill 2007a. This, my, critique is not an *ad hominem* critique. Apple, in a whole series of books, articles, and doctoral supervisions over three decades, has been a powerful figure in critiquing and analysing capitalist education from a left perspective—a reformist left perspective.
22. The writings in India of, for example, Murali Krishna (2007) and Kancha Ilaiah (2005) regarding Hindu Dalits and of Quadri and Kumar (2003) on oppression of Muslim Dalits are very powerful testimonies to the oppression of Dalits in India.
23. Dalits are not a separate caste, but it is considered a politically correct term to be used for the Scheduled Castes, as it literally means "repressed." The Scheduled Castes comprise 16.2% of India's total population, and the Scheduled Tribes comprise 8.2% of the population as per the 2001 census.
24. Hill et al., 2005a, 2007a, c, d.
25. See Dumenil and Levy, 2002; Harvey, 2005; Hill and Kumar, 2009.
26. For some suggestions concerning the development of an eco-socialist education policy, see Hill and Boxley, 2007. See Glenn Rikowski's, "Marx and the Education of the Future," 2004, where Rikowski, with close reference to Karl Marx's writings on education, outlines the education of the future as anti-capitalist education. In starting out from a conception of communism as the "real movement which abolishes the present state of things" (Marx), Rikowski argues that the anti-capitalist education of the future consists of three moments: critique, addressing human needs, and realms of freedom.

He also argues that all three moments are essential for an anti-capitalist education of the future, but the emphasis on particular moments *changes* (a movement from moment one to three) as capitalist society and education are left behind through social transformation. In the light of this framework, Rikowski critically examines Marx's views on the relation between labour and education, and his views on education run by the state. He concludes with a consideration of two trends that are gaining strength in contemporary education in England: the social production of labour-power and the business takeover of education. These trends, and this analysis, clearly have global resonance.

27. A Popular Front is a broad-based, multi-class alliance, involving for example liberals and even conservatives in an anti-war movement, or an anti-fascist or anti-racist movement. While valuable in mobilizing (sometimes very) large numbers and forces, its politics are usually the politics of the lowest common denominator. Extremely important though that might be, the Popular Front is different from a United Front in that a United Front is a coming together of socialist forces. It is class based, with a (working) class perspective. For a discussion of the differences between these two forms of organization/political tactics, see, for example, Goldfield, 1999; Bensaid, 2007; Choonara, 2007. Choonara also points out the difference between the United Front and the revolutionary, Marxist, party. The United Front 'is not a substitute for a revolutionary party. The United Front tactic can never, under any circumstances, mean the subordination of revolutionary politics and organization to reformist politics and organization.
28. I was the lead candidate for the NO2EU-Yesto Democracy campaign in the May-June 2009 European Parliament election campaign, for the Southeast region of England. See <http://www.no2eusoutheast. blogspot.com/> for some aspects of the campaign. The election leaflets in the Southeast region highlighted anti-racism as one of the four key points of the campaign. See also the interview I did (Hill, 2009b) with *Weekly Worker*, online at the Respect blogspot, *Interview with Dave Hill who tops the No2EU list in the South East* at <http://respectuk.blogspot.com/2009/05/interview-with-dave-hill-tops-no2eu.html>. The main organizations supporting NO2EU-Yesto Democracy were the RMT trade union, Socialist Party of England and Wales, the Communist Party of Britain, the Alliance for Green Socialism, and the Indian Workers Association. Groups such as Socialist Resistance also gave their general support.

References

Abbas, T. (2004a). *The Rise and Fall of Multiculturalism: Philosophical Considerations*. Centre for Research on Nationalism, Ethnicity and Multiculturalism. University of Surrey. Centre for Research on Nationalism, Ethnicity and Multiculturalism. Online at<http://www.surrey.ac.uk/Arts/ CRONEM/seminar-04-03-15-Abbas.htm>.

Abbass, T. (2004b). *The Education of British South Asians: Ethnicity, Capital and Class Structure*. London: Palgrave MacMillan.

Abbass, T. (2007). "British South Asians and pathways into selective schooling: Social class, culture and ethnicity." *British Education Research Journal*, 33 (1), pp. 75-90.

Althusser, L. (1971). "Ideology and Ideological State Apparatuses: Notes Towards an Investigation." In L. Althusser, *Lenin and Philosophy and Other Essays*. New York and London: Monthly Review Press. Online at <http://www.marx2mao.com/Other/LPOE70ii.html - s5>.Also available at <http://www.marx2mao.com/Other/LPOE70ii.html - s5>.

Apple, M.W. (1988). "Facing the Complexity of Power; For a Parallelist Position in Critical Educational Studies." In M. Cole (ed.) *Bowles and Gintis Revisited*. Lewes, UK: Falmer Press.

Apple, M.W. (1993). *Official knowledge: Democratic education in a conservative age*. New York: Routledge & Kegan Paul.

Apple, M.W. (1996). *Education and cultural politics*. New York: Teachers College Press.

Apple, M.W. (1999). *Power, meaning, and identity: Essays in critical educational studies*. New York: Peter Lang.

Apple, M. W. (2001). *Educating the "right" way: Markets, standards, God, and inequality*. New York and London: Routledge/Falmer.

Apple, M.W. (2005). "Audit cultures, commodification, and class and race strategies in education." *Policy Futures in Education*, 3 (4), pp. 379-399. Online athttp://www.wwwords.co.uk/pdf/viewpdf.asp?j=pfie&vol=3&issue=4&year=2005&article= 6_Apple_PFIE_3_4_web&id=81.158.104.85>.

Apple, M. W. (2006). "Review Essay: Rhetoric and reality in critical educational studies in the United States." *British Journal of Sociology of Education*, 27 (5) (November), pp. 679-687.

Apple, M. W. and Weiss, L. (1983).*Ideology and Practice in Schooling*. Philadelphia, PA: Temple University Press.

Asante, M. (1987).*The Afrocentric Idea*. Philadelphia: Temple University Press, 1987.

Banfield, G. (2009a). Comments on this essay.Unpublished.

Banfield, G. (2009b). Marxism, Critical Realism and Class: Implications for a Socialist Pedagogy pp. 128-152 in D. Kelsh, D. Hill and S. Macrine, (eds.) *Teaching Class: Knowledge, Pedagogy, Subjectivity*. London: Routledge.

Bell, D. (1992). *Faces at the Bottom of the Well: The permanence of racism*. New York: Basic Books.

Bell, D. (2004). *Silent Covenants: Brown V. Board of Education and the Unfulfilled Hopes for Racial Reform*. New York: Oxford University Press.

Bellamy, R. (1997). "The Intellectual as Social Critic: Antonio Gramsci and Michael Walzer." In A. Kemp-Welsh and J. Jennings (eds.) *Intellectuals in Politics: From the Dreyfus Affair to Salmon Rushdie*. London: Routledge.

Bensaid, D. (2010). Trouble at Stoke-on-Trent English Defence League Rally.

BBC News, 24 January. Online at http://news.bbc.co.uk/1/hi/england/staffordshire/8476873.stm>.

Bensaid, D. (2009). "Notes on recent developments in the European radical Left." *International Viewpoint Online Magazine*, IV419, December. Online at <http://www. internationalviewpoint.org/spip.php?article1785>.

Bhatti, G. (1999). *Asian Children at Home and School: An Ethnographic Study*. London: Routledge Falmer.

Borges, S., Garcia, S. and Vivas, V. (2008). "The Bolivarian Revolution at the crossroads between imperialism, constitutional reform and the socialist discourse." *International Viewpoint Online Magazine*, IV397, February. Online at <http://www.internationalviewpoint.org/spip.php?article1428>.

Borbas, G., Haslam, D. and Sampla, B. (2006). *No Escape: Caste Discrimination in the UK: Dalit Solidarity Network UK Report*. London: Institute for Race Relations. Online at http://www.irr.org.uk/pdf/No_escape.doc>.

Bourne, J. (2002). "Racism, Postmodernism and the Flight from Class." In D. Hill, P. McLaren, M. Cole and G. Rikowski (eds.), *Marxism Against Postmodernism in Educational Theory*. Lanham, MD: Lexington Books.

Brosio, R. (1994). *A Radical Democratic Critique of Capitalist Education*. New York: Peter Lang.

Brosio, R. (2008). Comments on this chapter. Unpublished.

Callinicos, A. (1989). *Against Postmodernism: a Marxist Critique*. Cambridge, UK: Polity.

Carillo, S. (1977). *Eurocommunism and the State*. London: Lawrence and Wishart.

Chakrabarty, N. and Preston, P. (2007)."Putnam's pink umbrella?Transgressing melancholic social capital." In H. Helve and J. Bynner (eds.). *Capitals, Cultures and Identities*. London: Tufnell Press.

Cole, M. (2004a). "'Brutal and Stinking' and 'difficult to handle': The historical and contemporary manifestations of racialisation, institutional racism, and schooling in Britain." *Race, Ethnicity and Education*, Vol. 7, No. 1, pp. 35-56.

Cole, M. (2004b). "'F*** you' – human sewage: Contemporary global capitalism and the xeno-racialization of asylum seekers." *Contemporary Politics*, Vol. 10, No. 2, pp. 159-165.

Cole, M. (2006). "Marxism and Educational Theory: An E-Interview with Mike Cole." Interviewed by Glenn Rikowski.*Information for Social Change*, 23.Online at <http://libr.org/isc/issues/ISC23/C4 Mike Cole and GlennRikowski.pdfhttp>.

Cole, M. (2007). "'Racism' is about more than colour." *Times Higher Education Supplement*, 23 November. Online at <http://www.timeshigher-education.co.uk/story.asp?storyCode= 310855§ioncode=26>.

Cole, M. (2008a). *Marxism and Educational Theory: Origins and Issues*. London: Routledge.

Cole, M.(2008b). "Critical race theory comes to the UK: A Marxist response." *Ethnicities*.

Cole, M. (2009). *Critical Race Theory and Education: A Marxist Response*. New York: Palgrave Macmillan.

Cole, M. and Maisuria, A. (2007). "'Shut the f*** up,' 'you have no rights here': Critical Race Theory and Racialization in post-7/7 racist Britain." *Journal for Critical Education Policy Studies*, 5(1). Online at <http://www.jceps.com/index.php?pageID=article&articleID=85>.

Cole, M., Hill, D., McLaren, P. and Rikowski, G. (2001). *Red Chalk: On Schooling, Capitalism and Politics*. Brighton: Institute for Education Policy Studies. Online at http://www.ieps.org.uk.cwc.net/redchalk.html>.

Commission for Racial Equality (2007).*Diversity and Integration*. London: CRE. Online at <http://www.cre.gov.uk/diversity/diversity.html>.

Cox, O. Cromwell [1948] (1959). *Caste, Class, and Race*. New York: Monthly Review Press.

Cox, O. Cromwell [1948] (2000). *Race: A Study in Social Dynamics*. (Fiftieth anniversary edition of *Caste, Class and Race*.) New York: Monthly Review Press.

Dehal, I. (2006). *Still Aiming High*. London: Department for Education and Skills. Online at <http://www.blss.portsmouth.sch.uk/training/ppt/DFES_ID_KD.ppt - 13htt>. Delgado, R. (1995). *The Rodrigo Chronicles: Conversations about America and Race*. New York: New York University Press.

Delgado, R. and Stefancic, J. (eds.) (2000). *Critical race theory: The cutting edge*. Philadelphia, PA: Temple University Press. (2nd Edition).

Delgado, R. and Stefancic, J. (2001). *Critical Race Theory: An Introduction*. New York: New York University Press

Demie, F., Lewis, K. and McLean, C. (2007). *Raising the Achievement of Somali Pupils: Challenges and School Responses*. London: Lambeth Research and Statistics Unit.

Demie, F. and Tong, R. (2007). *Education Statistics*. London: Lambeth Research and Statistics Unit.

DfES (2007). National Curriculum assessments, *GCSE and equivalent attainment and post-16 attainment by pupil characteristics in England 2005/06* (Revised). SFR04/2007. London: DfES.

Dumenil, G. and Levy, D. (2004). *Capital Resurgent: Roots of the Neoliberal Revolution*. London: Harvard University Press.

Eagleton, T. (1996). *The Illusions of Postmodernism*. Malden, MASS: Blackwell.

Esteban, F. (2008). "The Bolivarian revolution at the Crossroads."*International Viewpoint Online Magazine*, IV403, August. Online at<http://www.internationalviewpoint.org/spip.php?article1504>.

Farahmandpur, R. (2004). "Essay Review: A Marxist critique of Michael Apple's neo-Marxist approach to education reform." *Journal of Critical Education Policy Studies*, 2 (1). Online at <http://www.jceps.com/index.php?pageID=article&articleID=24>.

Fekete, L. (2001). "The Emergence of Xeno-racism."*Institute of Race Relations*. Online at http://www.irr.org.uk/2001/september/ak000001.html>.

Gillborn, D. (2005). "Education policy as an act of white supremacy; whiteness, critical race theory and education reform."*Journal of Education Policy*, 20 4, pp. 485-505.

Gillborn, D. (2006a). "Critical Race Theory and Education: Racism and Antiracism in Educational Theory and Praxis." *Discourse: Studies in the Cultural Politics of Education*, 27 (1), pp. 11-32.

Gillborn, D. (2006b). "Rethinking white supremacy: Who counts in 'WhiteWorld.'" *Ethnicities*, 6 (3), pp. 318-340.

Gillborn, D. (2008a). *Racism and Education: Coincidence or Conspiracy?* London: Routledge.

Gillborn, D. (2008b). "Critical Race Theory Race(ing) Forward: Transitions in theorising "race" in education Conference. University of Northampton, Friday, 1 February.

Gillborn, D. (2009a). "Education: The Numbers Game and the Construction of White Racial Victimhood," in Kjartan Pall Sveinsson (ed.) *Who Cares About the White Working Class?*, Runneymede Trust. Online at <http://www.scie-socialcareonline.org.uk/profile.asp?guid=016038da-dc8a-47c9-afea-b9da67bae8fe>.

Gillborn, D. (2009b). "Whatever happened to institutional racism? How the 'White working class' were made into the new race victims." National Arts Learning Network, Annual Conference 2009. Online at <http://www.naln.ac.uk/en/conference/keynote-presentations/professor-david-gillborn.cfm>.

Gillborn, D. (2009c). "Reform, Racism, and the Recentering of Whiteness." Paper presented at the Annual meeting of the American Education Research Association Annual Meeting, San Diego, Thursday, 16 April.

Gillborn, D. and Mirza, H. (2000). *Educational Inequality; Mapping race, class and gender – a synthesis of research evidence*. London: Ofsted.

Gilroy, P. (2000). *Against Race*. Cambridge, MASS: Harvard University Press.

Gimenez, M. (2001). "Marxism and Class, Gender and Race: Rethinking the Trilogy." *Race, Gender and Class*, 8, 2, pp. 23-33.

Greaves, N.M., Hill, D. and Maisuria, A. (2006). "Embourgeoisment, Immiseration, Commodification – Marxism Revisited: A Critique of Education in Capitalist Systems." *Journal for Critical Education Policy Studies* 5 (1). Online at <http://www.jceps.com/?pageID=article&article ID=83>.

Hall, S. (1980/1996). "Race, Articulation, and Societies Structured in Dominance." In H. A. Baker Jr, M. Diawara and Lindeberg (eds.), *Black British Cultural Studies Reader*. Chicago: University of Chicago Press, 1996).

Harvey, D. (2005). *A Brief History of Neoliberalism*. Oxford, England: Oxford University Press.

Hessari, R. and Hill, D. (1989). *Practical Ideas for Multi-cultural Learning and Teaching in the Primary Classroom.* London: Routledge.

Hill, D. (2001). "State theory and the Neo-Liberal reconstruction of schooling and teacher education: a structuralist Neo-Marxist critique of Postmodernist,

Quasi-Postmodernist, and Culturalist Neo-Marxist theory." *The British Journal of Sociology of Education*, 22, (1) pp. 137-157.

Hill, D. (2005a). "State Theory and the Neoliberal Reconstruction of Schooling and Teacher Education."In G. Fischman, P. McLaren, H. Sünker and C. Lankshear (eds.), *Critical Theories, Radical Pedagogies and Global Conflicts*. Boulder, CO: Rowman and Littlefield.

Hill, D. (2005b). "Globalisation and its educational discontents: Neoliberalisation and its impacts on education workers' rights, pay, and conditions." *International Studies in the Sociology of Education* 15 (3) pp. 257-288.

Hill, D. (2007a). "Education, Class and Capital in the Epoch of Neoliberal Globalization."In A. Green and G. Rikowski (eds), *Marxism and Education: Renewing dialogues. Vol. 1, Opening the Dialogue*. London: Palgrave Macmillan.

Hill, D. (2007b). "Critical Teacher Education, New Labour in Britain, and the Global Project of Neoliberal Capital." *Policy Futures*, 5 (2). Online at<http://www.wwwords.co.uk/pfie/content/pdfs/5/issue5_2.asp>.

Hill, D. (2007c). "Socialist Educators and Capitalist Education." *Socialist Outlook*, 13. Online at <http://www.isg-fi.org.uk/spip.php?article576>.

Hill, D. (2007d). "Education: Their Agenda and Ours." *Socialist Resistance*, 49, p. 9. November. Online at <http://www.socialistresistance.net/49resistance.pdf>.

Hill, D. (2009). "Race and Class in Britain: A Critique of the statistical basis for Critical Race Theory in Britain: and some political implications." *Journal for Critical Education Policy Studies*, 7(2).Online at <http://www.jceps.com/index.php?pageID=article&articleID=159>.

Hill, D. with Anijar, K., Brown, C., Carroll, E., Davidson-Harden, A., Gabbard, D.,Gindin, J., Kuehn, et al. (2006). "Education Services Liberalization."In E. Rosskam (ed.), *Winners or Losers? Liberalizing public services*. Geneva: International Labour Organization.

Hill, D., McLaren, P., Cole, M., and Rikowski, G. (eds.) (2002). *Marxism Against Postmodernism in Educational Theory*. Lanham, MD: Lexington Books.

Hill, D., Greaves, N., and Maisuria, A. (2009). "Education, Inequality and Neoliberal Capitalism: A Classical Marxist Analysis." In Hill, D. and Kumar, R. (eds.), *Global Neoliberalism and Education and its Consequences*. New York: Routledge.

Hill, D. and Kumar, R. (eds.) (2009). *Global Neoliberalism and Education and its Consequences*. New York: Routledge.

Iliaiah, K. (2005). *Why I am not a Hindu: A Sudra Critique of Hindutva Philosophy, Culture and Political Economy*. Calcutta, India: Samya.

Independent Working Class Association 2005. Cheering News to Celebrate? Online at <http://www.iwca.info/news/news0070.htm>.

Kelsh, D. (2001). "(D)evolutionary socialism and the containment of class: For a red theory of class." *The Red Critique: Marxist Theory and Critique of the Contemporary* 1(1), 9-13. Online at <http://redcritique.org/spring2001/devolutionarysocialism.htm>.

Kelsh, D. and Hill, D. (2006). "The Culturalization of Class and the Occluding of Class Consciousness: The Knowledge Industry in/of Education." *Journal for Critical Education Policy Studies*, 4 (1). Online at <http://www.jceps.com/index.php?pageID=article&article ID=59>.

Kelsh, D., Hill, D. and Macrine, S. (eds.) (2009). *Teaching Class: Knowledge, Pedagogy, Subjectivity*. London: Routledge.

Kumar, Ashwani (2008). Personal comments on a draft of this paper following the Canadian Society for the Study of Education Annual Conference, University of British Columbia, Vancouver, Canada. May 31- June 3.

Kumar, Arun and Kumar, Sanjay (eds.) (2005). *Dalit Studies in Higher Education*. Delhi: Deshkal Publications.

Kumar, Ravi (2008a). Unpublished comments on a draft of this chapter.

Kumar, Ravi (2008b). "State, Class and Critical Framework of Praxis: The Missing Link of Indian Educational Debates." In Kelsh, D., Hill, D. and Macrine, S. (eds.), *Teaching Class: Knowledge, Pedagogy, Subjectivity*. Routledge: New York.

Kumar, Ravi (2008c). "Dynamics of Identity Formation: Political Economy of Backward Castes in Bihar." Ph.D. Thesis, Jawaharlal Nehru University, Delhi, India. Unpublished.

Kumar, Ravi (2008d). "Against Neoliberal Assault on Education in India: A Counternarrative of Resistance." *Journal for Critical Education PolicyStudies*, 6 (1). Online at <http://www.jceps.com/index.php?pageID=article&articleID=112>.

Kumar, Ravi (2010). "India: General Elections 2009 and the Neoliberal Consensus." *New Politics*, Vol. XII, No. 4, Whole Number 48, Winter, pp. 206-210.

Laclau, E. (1996). "Deconstruction, Pragmatism, Hegemony." In Mouffe, C. (ed.), *Deconstruction and Pragmatism*. London: Routledge, pp. 47-67.

Laclau, E. and Mouffe, C. (1985). *Hegemony and Socialist Strategy*. London: NLB.

Leonardo, Z. (2004). "The Unhappy Marriage between Marxism and Race Critique: Political economy and the production of racialized knowledge." *Policy Futures in Education*, 2, 3-4. Online at <http://www.wwwords.co.uk/pdf/viewpdf.asp?j=pfie&vol=2&issue=3&year=2004&article=4_leonardo_pfie_2_3- 4_web&id=142.179.108.96>.

Luxemburg, R. (1899/1900/1970). *"Reform or Revolution": Rosa Luxemburg Speaks*. NY: Pathfinder. Online at <http://www.marxists.org/archive/luxemburg/1900/reform-revolution/index.htm>.

Mandel, E. (1978). *From Stalinism to Eurocommunism:The Bitter Fruits of "Socialism in One Country."* London: New Left Books.

Marx, K. [1852] (1969)."The Eighteenth Brumaire of Louis Bonaparte." In Karl Marx and Frederick Engels, *Selected Works*, Moscow: Progress Publishers. Online at http://www.marxists.org/archive/marx/works/1852/18thbrumaire/index.htm>.

Marx, K. [1867] (1996). *Capital, Vol.1*. In *Collected Works 5*. New York: International Publishers. Online at <http://www.marxists.org/archive/marx/works/1867-c1/index.htm>.

Marx, K. (1977). *Selected Writings* (ed. D. McLellan). Oxford, England: Oxford University Press.

Marx, K. and Engels, F. (1848/1985). *The Communist Manifesto*. New York: Penguin Books. Online at http://www.marxists.org/archive/marx/works/1848/communist-manifesto/>.

McLaren, P. and Farahmandpur, R. (2005). *Teaching against Global Capitalism and the New Imperialism*. Lanham, MD: Rowman and Littlefield.

McLaren, P. and Jaramillo, N. (2007). *Pedagogy and Praxis in the Age of Empire*. Rotterdam: Sense Publishers.

McLaren, P. and Rikowski, G. (2006). "Critical Pedagogy Reloaded: An Interview with Peter McLaren (interviewed by Glenn Rikowski)." *Information for Social Change*, 23. Online at http://libr.org/isc/issues/ISC23/C3 PeterMcLaren.pdfhtt>.

Miles, R. (1987). *Capitalism and Unfree Labour: Anomaly or Necessity?* London: Tavistock.

Miles, R. (1989). *Racism*. London: Routledge.

Miles, R. (1993). *Racism after "Race Relations."* London: Routledge.

Mills, C. (1997). *The Racial Contract*. New York: Cornell University Press.

Mills, C. (2003). *From Class To Race: Essays in White Marxism and Black Radicalism*. Lanham, MD: Rowman and Littlefield.

Motala, E. and Vally, S. (2009). Class, "Race" and State in Post-Apartheid Education. In Kelsh, D., Hill, D. and Macrine, S. (eds.) (2009), *Teaching Class: Knowledge, Pedagogy, Subjectivity*. London: Routledge.

Murali Krishna, M. (2007). "Marginalization of Dalits: Role of Oppressive Pedagogic Practices in Indian Schools: A Dalit Perspective," Paper presented to the Deshkal Society International Conference: School Education, Pluralism and Marginality: Comparative Perspectives, December 14-16, 2007, New Delhi.

Murji, K. and Solomos, J. (2005). *Racialization: Studies in Theory and Practice*. Oxford, UK: Oxford University Press.

National Statistics (2001). "Census 2001 – Ethnicity and identity." Online at <http://www.statistics.gov.uk/cci/nugget.asp?id=455>.

Ngugiwa Thiong'o and Ngugiwa Mirii (1985). *I Will Marry When I Want*. London: Heinemann.

Preston, J. (2007). *Whiteness and class in education*. Dordrecht: Springer.

Preston, J. (2007). "All shades of a wide white world." *Times Higher Education*, 27 October. Online at <http://www.timeshighereducation.co.uk/story.asp?storyCode=310855& sectioncode=26>.

Quadri, S.I. and Kumar, S. (eds.) (2003). *Marginalization of Dalit Muslims in Indian Democracy.* Delhi: Deshkal Publications.

Reed, A. (Jnr.) (2001). "Race and Class in the Work of Oliver Cromwell Cox." Monthly Review, Feb. Online at <http://www.monthlyreview.org/201reed.htm>.

Rikowski, G. (2004). "Marx and the Education of the Future."*Policy Futures in Education*, 2 (3 and 4), pp. 565-577. Online at <http://www.wwwords.co.uk/pdf/viewpdf.asp?j=pfie&vol=2&issue=3& year=2004&article=10_Rikowski_PFEO_2_3-4_web&id=86.167.13.74>.

Rikowski, G. (2005). "The Education White Paper and the Marketization and Capitalization of the Secondary Schools System in England, 24 October. Part I." *The Volumizer*. Online at <http://journals.aol.co.uk/rikowskigr/Volumizer/entries/571>.

Rikowski, G. (2006). "In Retro Glide."*Journal for Critical Education Policy Studies*, 5 (1). Online at fhttp://www.jceps.com/index.php?pageID=article&articleID=81>.

Runneymede Trust (2000). *The Future of Multi-Ethnic Britain: The Parekh Report*. London: The Runnymede Trust.

Simpson, L., Purdam, K., Tajar, A., Feildhouse, E., Gavalas, V., Tramer, M., Pritchard, J., and Dorling, D. (2002). "Ethnic minority populations and the labour market: An analysis of the 1991 and 2001 Census." London: Department for Work and Pensions. Online at <http://asp.ccsr.ac.uk/dwp/info/ SUMM333.pdf>.

Sivanandan, A. (2001). "Poverty is the New Black." *Race and Class*, 43 (2), pp. 2-5. Edited version online at <http://www.guardian.co.uk/globalisation/story/0,7369,538225,00.html>.

Smith, V. (2010). "EDL Stoke rampage must never happen again." *Socialist Worker*, Issue 2186, 30 January Online at <http://www.socialistworker.co.uk/art.php?id=20080>.

Strand, S. (2007). *Minority Ethnic Pupils in the Longitudinal Study of Young People in England*. DfES Research Report RR-002. London: Department for Children Families and Schools (DCFS). Online at <http://www.dfes.gov.uk/research/data/uploadfiles/DCSF-RR002.pdf>.

Strand, S. (2008a). *Minority Ethnic Pupils in the Longitudinal Study of Young People in England*. Warwick: Warwick Institute of education. Online at: <http://www2.warwick.ac.uk/fac/soc/wie/research/policy/recent_projects/minority/>.

Strand, S. (2008b). *Minority Ethnic Pupils in the Longitudinal Study of Young People in England Extension Report on Performance in Public Examinations at Age 16*. Research Report DCSF-RR029. London: Department for Children Families and Schools (DCFS). Online at <http://www.dfes.gov.uk/research/data/uploadfiles/DCSF-RR029.pdf>.

Tudor, H. and Tudor, J.M. (eds.) (1988). *Marxism and Social Democracy: The Revisionist Debate, 1896-1898*. Cambridge: Cambridge University Press.

Young, R. (2006). "Putting materialism back into Race Theory: Towards

Transformative Theory of Race." *The Red Critique*, 11. Online at <http://www.redcritique.org/WinterSpring2006/puttingmaterialismbackintoracetheory.htm>.

Zavarzadeh, M. (2002). "On 'Class' and Related Concepts in Classical Marxism, and Why is the Post-Al Left Saying Such Terrible Things About Them?" Online at <http://www.etext.org/Politics/AlternativeOrange/3/v3n3_onrc.html>.

PART 2

Neoliberalism, Immiseration and Workers' Rights

4

Books, Banks and Bullets: Controlling Our Minds: The Global Project of Imperialistic and Militaristic Neoliberalism and its Effect on Education Policy

Dave Hill

Summary

This article focuses on global trends in education policy during the current epoch of imperializing, militaristic, neoliberal global capital. It is based on an analysis that global capital, in the form of dominant US multinational capital, together with its client governments, uses the repressive and ideological apparatuses of the state to advance its interests, and to marginalize, terrorize, weaken, or kill those who stand in its way. What we are seeing is class war from above–war by national and global capitalist classes against national and global working classes. The author identifies global and national characteristics of the ideological and repressive state apparatuses that impose (broadly neoliberal) educational and wider social, cultural, economic, and fiscal policy as part of the hegemonic activity of US-led global neoliberal capital. In particular, he examines the repression of critical thought and oppositional activity within the sites of teacher education, schooling, and university/higher education–the compression and repression of critical space in education today.

Introduction

Trends in Contemporary Capitalism

There are five major trends in contemporary global capitalism. These global-level trends are evident in different states to different degrees. They are as follows:

1. *Spread of capital(ism), both geographically* throughout the states of the world, and sectorally within those states. This embraces the

'businessification' of education —privatization, deregulation of controls on profits, the introduction of business forms of management, and the intensification of labour.

2. *Deepening of capitalist social relations* with the commodification of everyday life.This is carried out, in particular through the media and educational state apparatuses, to recompose human personality.

3. *Increasing use of repressive* economic, legal, military, and other *state and multi-state apparatuses globally* and within states.This is to ensure compliance and subordination to multinational capital and its state agents. The means used include repressive state apparatuses such as the police, incarceration/imprisonment, legal systems/laws, surveillance procedures, threat of and actual job dismissals, and stalled or non-promotion. At the international level they include the enhanced US 'neocon' project of militaristic imperialism, with its self-proclaimed right/carte blanche to attack any nation, such as Iraq, or group at any time and in any place.

4. *Increasing use of ideological state apparatuses in the media and education systems.* On the one hand, they are used in particular to both 'naturalize' and promote capitalist social and economic relations. On the other, they are used to marginalize, demonize, and justify punishing resistant/anti-(capitalist), hegemonic, oppositional ideologies, actions, and activists.

5. *Increasing concentration of wealth and power* (power to retain and increase that wealth) in the hands of the capitalist class. This embraces fiscal policy (cutting back), social and public welfare programmes and policies, and opening to the market divisive, marketized, stratified programmes in pensions, healthcare, schooling, and higher education. Such programmes increase hierarchies of provision, resulting in increasing racialized and gendered social class inequalities.[1]

In this article I wish to comment on the first four of these developments in order to show how some of these developments impact on education policy in advanced capitalist states, such as the United Kingdom, the USA, and European states. I focus on three sectors of education policy*: schooling, teacher education, and university/higher education.*

Part 1. The Spread of Capital(ism) Geographically and Sectorally

Numerous writers detail the current expansion and intensification of the rule of capital geographically and sectorally.[2] Marx and Engels describe the development of capitalism in *The Communist Manifesto:*

> The markets kept ever growing, the demand ever rising... The place of manufacture was taken by the giant, Modern Industry, the place of the industrial middle class, by industrial millionaires... Modern industry has established the world-market... The need of a constantly expanding market for its products chases the bourgeoisie over the whole surface of the globe. It must nestle everywhere, settle everywhere, establish connexion severy where ...In one word, it creates a world after its own image. (Marx and Engels, [1847]1987, pp. 23-25)

Glenn Rikowski (2002)argues that 'globalization' is essentially capitalist globalization: the globalization of capital, which is at the core of all the economic, social, political, and cultural trends that have been associated with conventional (and more superficial) notions of 'globalization'. Rikowski points out that capital's social universe is an expanding one.

This expansion takes three main forms:

- First, *spatially*, as capital fills all known socio-physical space. The *physical* space comprises not only spreading throughout the globe, but also into space—with spy satellites, space probes, and the sci-fi type of quest for space colonies and raw materials. The *social* space comprises, for example, the incorporation of simple commodity production and non-capitalist enterprise (such as the production of tribal remedies) into the circuit of global capital. These are aspects of capital's *extension*.
- Secondly, capital expands as *the differentiated form of the commodity* through the invention of new types of commodity. It expands through variegated and differentiated examples of itself. This is *capital's differentiation.* For example, there are different types of schools placed in the market of 'choice'.
- Thirdly, capital expands through *intensification*–it deepens and develops with in its own domain. That is to say that capital deepens and develops in the ways in which it is increasingly penetrating educational institutions. This embraces the new ways in which profit-making and profit-taking enter the *'public sector'*.

The World Trade Organization and the General Agreement on Trade in Services

Rikowski (2002) points out that globalization and education relate in quite specific ways. The World Trade Organization (WTO) facilitates globalization through opening up all spheres of social life—including public services—to international capital.The WTO's 'education agenda', therefore, is to facilitate the penetration of education services by corporate capital. The key WTO agreement for this purpose is the General Agreement on Trade in Services(GATS).This Agreement incorporates the aim of unleashing the progressive liberalization of trade in services, including public services such as education. In the long term, no area of social life is exempt from these developments (see also Rikowski, 2003b, c; Leher, 2004).

Kaplan emphasizes that the GATS will open the door to the commercialization of education services:

> The fact is that nowadays big international corporations want their share of the world 'market' in education, which in 1999 was estimated to be worth US$2.2 trillion. Their aim is to transform education into just another commodity, into some kind of industry selling its products (courses) to 'customers' (pupils and students) in a market ruled by the law of supply and demand ... It is clear that the big corporations and financiers are listened to carefully by governments of different political colours, all of which are tending more and more towards dismantling the public education service in each of their countries. Those corporations and financiers have undertaken a huge project which aims to replace 'formal education' (school) with what they call 'non-formal education' (the workplace) and 'informal education' (everyday life). This logic would lead to the replacement of qualified teachers with volunteers, social workers or street vendors. (Kaplan, 2002)

Rikowski (2002) further notes that at the national level it is the nation states that have to deal with and plan for the business takeover of public services. Governments, or collective state organizations such as the European Union (EU), also have to manage the politics of the corporate takeover of public services. He points out that national governments draw up and re-form the national faces of the GATS for each public service.

National governments have to open up all aspects of social life to corporate capital while simultaneously 'reassuring' their populations that this does not entail the privatization of public services. The progressive privatization of state enterprises, functions, and services over the last 15 years has made this task an onerous one. Indeed, in recent years there have been mass mobilizations and protests in a number of European states against the privatization of (or other attack on) pension rights and publicly run services such as railways, with millions pouring onto French and Italian streets, for example.

Spread of Capital(ism) within the Education System

Contemporary governments and society serve to perpetuate the interests of capital at the expense of workers, and to reproduce the existing economic system and power relations. At different historical periods it does this in more, or less, hidden ways, with greater or lesser use of the repressive and controlling functions of the state.

In the current and recent periods, education has been increasingly—and increasingly nakedly—subordinated, not just to the general requirements of capital, but also to the specific demands made of governments by the capitalist class. The relative autonomy of education from the requirements of capital, from the government, and within education at various levels, has been blow torched—the rhetorical and policy accretions of 'professionalism' and of relative autonomy have been burned away, leaving the skeletal structure of command in its unadorned nakedness (Cole et al., 2001; Hill, 2001a, 2003, 2004, 2005).

This increasing subordination of education to the nakedly expressed requirements of national and international capital runs through school education and teacher education to university education. Education and humanity itself have become increasingly commodified, with education being restructured internationally under pressure from international capitalist organizations and compliant governments. Thus, in Britain, education at all levels is seen as serving 'UK plc' in the global competitive labour market and economy.

This restructuring has two major aspects:

1. The capitalist agenda for education—what capital wants education to provide, i.e. how capital wants to make indirect profits from education.

2. The capitalist agenda in education (Hatcher and Hirtt, 1999; Hatcher, 2001, 2002; Hill, 2003a)—how capital wants to make direct profits from education.

The Capitalist Agenda for Education

This agenda centres on socially producing labour-power (people's capacity to labour) for capitalist enterprises. Within universities and vocational further education in particular, the language of education has been very widely replaced by the language of the market, where lecturers 'deliver the product', 'operationalize delivery', and 'facilitate clients' learning' within a regime of 'quality management and enhancement'; where students have become 'customers' selecting 'modules' on a pick'n'mix basis; and where 'skill development' at universities has surged in importance to the derogation of the development of critical thought.

The capitalist agenda for education has resulted in controlling the curriculum, teachers, and education institutions through common mechanisms. Pauline Lipman (2000) notes:

> George W. Bush's 'blueprint' to 'reform' education, released in February 2001 (No Child Left Behind) (Bush, 2001), crystallizes key neoliberal, neo-conservative, and business-oriented education policies. The main components of Bush's plan are mandatory, high-stakes testing and vouchers and other supports for privatizing schools.

Lipman continues that the major aspects of this agenda and policy are: "Standards, accountability, and regulation of schools, teachers and students and an explicit linkage of corporate interests with educational practices and goals". This is so of the USA she is analysing, as it is of England and Wales.

Hursh (2001) details the interconnections and collabouration in the USA between corporations, (federal) government and education, and a series of educational summits. In sentiments startlingly reminiscent of critics of the test-driven agenda in England and Wales, Hursh (2001) notes that in the USA states are developing subject area standards and then aligning the standards with state-wide standardized tests. Increasingly, standardized test scores are being used by school districts to determine whether students should be promoted to the next grade or from high school. Further, some states, such as Florida and New York, are using test scores to rank schools and districts with the purpose of 'rewarding' those teachers and schools with high scores and 'punishing' those with low scores.

This is very redolent of the punitive rhetoric and policy of the Thatcher (1979-91), Major (1991-97) and first New Labour governments (1997-2001), with its accompanying policies of 'closing down "failing schools"' (i.e. schools—all of them to date in very poor areas—failing to reach national minimum Standard Assessment Tasks [SATS] results or exam passes), dismissing teachers, and restaffing the schools as 'fresh start' schools. To date, notes Hursh (2001), all but one of the states in the USA have followed the route of developing standards and implementing standardized tests. In England and Wales, local education authorities (LEAs) and schools have no choice in the matter. 'Non-compliant' head teachers are dismissed and non-compliant schools pilloried in the press.

Hursh (2001) suggests that 'the effort to impose standards, assessments, and accountability has been devastating for teachers and students'. He cites McNeil who, in Contradictions of School Reform: Educational Costs of Standardized Testing, concludes that:

> Standardization reduces the quality and quantity of what is taught and learned in schools ... over the long term, standardization creates inequities, widening the gap between the quality of education for poor and minority youth and that of more privileged students. (2000, p. 3)

McNeil's research revealed the emergence of:

> Phony curricula, reluctantly presented by teachers in class to conform to the forms of knowledge their students would encounter on centralized tests. The practice of teaching under these reforms shifted away from intellectual activity towards dispensing packaged fragments of information sent from an upper level of bureaucracy. And the role of students as contributors to classroom discourse, as thinkers, as people who brought their personal stories and life experiences into the classroom, was silenced or severely circumscribed by the need for the class to 'cover' a generic curriculum at a pace established by the district and the state for all the schools. (McNeil, 2000, p. 4)

In England and Wales, numerous commentators (e.g. Robertson & Hill, 2001) are now noting the increased standardization of pedagogy, with teachers teaching to the test, increasingly using closed instead of open questions, and mimicking the modelled pedagogy provided in the government videos about how to teach the National Literacy Strategy.

The 'businessification' of higher education. Higher education is also becoming big business. The GATS views state education as being liberalized so that it generates internationally tradable commodities. Students are viewed as paying customers, and the formal curriculum in higher education and the informal curriculum in non-elite universities are viewed widely as skills training and worker training. Rikowski (McLaren and Rikowski, 2001) claims that the 'ivory tower' no longer exists, if it ever did.Harvie (2000) shows that studies of higher education indicate that it too is increasingly under the truncheon of capitalist social relations. He suggests that a 'research-bourgeois' revolution in UK higher education is seeing research use-values subordinated to RAE- value, i.e. the degree to which universities are rated and rewarded by the Research Assessment Exercise method of allocating research funding. Research workers are becoming alienated from their work. 'With the enclosure of "intellectual commons", some research workers are being forced to alienate their own research-labour-power as two new classes are emerging within academia, a "research proletariat" and a class of "research capitalists"' (Harvie, 2000).

The Capitalist Agenda in Education

After the capitalist agenda for education, the capitalist agenda in education wants to make profits from education (as indeed from public or privatized services such as water supply and healthcare).

The New Labour government has introduced a plethora of policy initiatives opening up state schooling and LEAs to private ownership, private management, or private co-management. These range from private education companies being given contracts to run 'failing' LEAs (school districts in the USA)—or parts of their services, running 'failing schools', to the Private Finance Initiative, whereby private capital (in effect, of course, major national or multinational companies) finances and makes a profit out of building, maintaining, and running schools, educational buildings and settings.

The Education Act for England and Wales of 2002 really does open up the school system to private sector involvement to an unprecedented degree, facilitating further business takeovers of schools and LEA services. The 2002 Act enables school governing bodies to constitute themselves as companies. Once they have set themselves up as companies, these schools can invest in other companies. School companies can enter into deals with private sector operators; school companies can be part of a 'federation' or chain of schools (private companies can lead these federations and their leaders do not need teaching qualifications); school companies can also set up educational services and sell them to other schools; and the Secretary of State for Education has the power to form companies for involvement in any area of school life or LEA service.

With respect to schools in England and Wales, the 2002 Education Act also gives the private sector the freedom to vary or change the curriculum and change teachers' pay and conditions. This derives from the new 'earned autonomy' status that top-performing schools can obtain.

Privatization is also a major part of the agenda of US capital. Lipman (2000, para 7) discusses the Bush proposal to use federal funds for vouchers that students in failing schools (again determined by test scores) could use to attend private schools or to receive educational services from private providers. Other Bush plans that would promote privatization are: funding for the start-up of charter schools, creating a fund to promote 'school choice', and raising the ceiling on tax-free education savings accounts which could be used for K-12 (Kindergarten to grade 12) private schools as well as college tuition.

Mathison and Ross detail the many recommended interventions, both direct (the capitalist agenda in education) and indirect (the capitalist agenda for education), by capital in the US environment of the corporate takeover of schools and universities:

> In K-12 schools some examples are school choice plans (voucher systems, charter schools), comprehensive school designs based on business principles (such as economies of scale, standardization, cost efficiency, production line

> strategies), back to basics curricula, teacher merit pay, and strong systems of accountability. In universities some examples are the demand for common general education and core curricula (often not developed or supported by faculty), demands for common tests of student core knowledge, standardized tests of knowledge and skill for professional areas, promotion of 'classic' education, and elimination of 'new' content areas such as women's studies, post-modernism, and multiculturalism. (2002, para. 1.1)

Proletarianization, Casualization and Intensification of Labour in the Education State Apparatuses

One way that teachers as workers are kept in line is through job in security. McLaren et al. (2005, p.228) comment that:

> The last decade witnessed a rising tide of part-time and 'perma-temp' faculty and instructors who teach full-time at institutions of higher education but are nevertheless denied healthcare and pension benefits offered to tenure-track faculty. Leslie Berger of the *New York Times* reports that 43% of professors and instructors who are teaching at higher education institutions are part-time employees ... downsizing, outsourcing and 'flexible' methods of labour practices on production lines in factories have now trickled down to encompass universities and colleges across the United States.

The same writers point out that: 'In California more than 47,000 uncertified teachers are teaching in its public schools ... in Baltimore ... over one-third of the school district's teachers do not hold full teaching credentials'.

In the United Kingdom, the government wishes to increase the number of teaching assistants dramatically. This, taken together with the introduction of new higher grades of teacher and various sets of proposals that would allow schools and universities to set their own pay levels, can be seen as a downgrading of education workers. In England and Wales, for example, where it was once the case in the 1980s that teachers were recruited from the top 20 per cent of the attainment range, that figure is now 'from the top 40 per cent of the attainment range'.

Action in 2003 and 2004 by the National Union of Teachers (NUT) (the largest teachers' trade union in England and Wales) was to oppose the (2003) 'Workload Agreement', whereby school teachers in England and Wales are giving up various non-teaching administrative duties to be carried out by a dramatically increased force of 'teacher assistants'. The NUT's objection is that these 'teaching assistants' will become 'teachers on the cheap', which is redolent of the 'Mums' Army' proposed by the John Major government (to have non-graduate women trained mainly 'on the job', for one year only, to become infant teachers—see later).

Commodification and Personality Recomposition of Humanity

In *The Communist Manifesto,* Marx and Engels analyse the impact of global capital on the worker:

> It has resolved personal worth into exchange value, and in place of the numberless indefeasible chartered freedoms, has set up that single unconscionable freedom—Free Trade. In one word, for exploitation, veiled by religious and political illusions, it has substituted naked, shameless, direct, brutal exploitation. ([1847] 1987, p. 25)

They point out that capitalism 'left remaining no other nexus between man and man than naked self-interest, than callous "cash payment" and "egotistical calculation". All would be reduced to "paid labourers"' (Marx and Engels, [1847] 1987, p. 24).

Similarly, Polyani (1944) noted that market societies, rather than embedding the economy within social relations, embed their social relations within the economy. Individual gain motivates productive activity rather than what productivity lends to the welfare of the group. Individuals derive status from how much they gain from market activity. Today, Henry Giroux writes prolifically about the commodification of education and the consumerization of society.[3]

In capitalist society, 'well-being' is now equated with 'well-having'—we are what we consume. In educational terms our worth is how many years and credits we have accumulated. Indeed, being a student is now a serious game—to build up credits to get a better job. In the USA and England and Wales today, as in other advanced capitalist states, economic goals of education have sidelined social, societal and community goals (the traditional social-democratic goals of education), and have also replaced education/learning for its own sake (the traditional liberal and liberal- progressive goals of education).

The Importance of Education State Apparatuses: The Recomposition and Commodification of Personality

As Tomlinson (2001) states, the project of constructing the post-welfare state entails giving an unprecedented salience to the role of education, and relies heavily on shaping people's values and social identities. Gabbard's work supports this view, emphasizing the centrality of compulsory schooling to the enforcement of a market society (Gabbard, 2003, p. 68), that school students are learning to need school, with educational credentials being regarded as 'testimonials to the degree to which a person's use-value has been developed' (p. 69) (see also Saltman and Gabbard, 2003).

Rikowski (2001) asks: 'How does education fit into the neoliberal agenda?' Glenn Rikowski's work, such as *The Battle in Seattle* (2001, also set out in Hill, 2001a), develops a Marxist analysis based on an analysis of 'labour-power'. With respect to education, he suggests that teachers are the most dangerous of workers because they have a special role in shaping, developing, and forcing the single commodity on which the whole capitalist system rests: labour-power. In the capitalist labour process, labour-power is transformed into value-creating labour, and, at a certain point, surplus value —value over and above that represented in the worker's wage—is created. Surplus value is the first form of the existence of capital. It is the lifeblood of capital. As Rikowski notes, without it, capital could not be transformed into money on sale of the commodities that incorporate value and hence the capitalist could not purchase the necessary raw materials, means of production, and labour-power to set the whole cycle in motion once more. But, the most important element for the capitalist is that part of the surplus value forms his or her profit—and it is this that drives the capitalist on a personal basis. It is this that defines the personal agency of the capitalist!

Teachers are dangerous because they are intimately connected with the social production of labour- power, equipping students with skills, competences, abilities, knowledge, and the attitudes and personal qualities that can be expressed and expended in the capitalist labour process. Teachers are guardians of the quality of labour-power. This potential, latent power of teachers explains why representatives of the state might have sleepless nights worrying about their role in ensuring that the labourers of the future of the highest possible quality are delivered to workplaces throughout the national capital.

Rikowski suggests that the state needs to control the process for two reasons. First, to try to ensure that this occurs.Secondly, to try to ensure that modes of pedagogy that are antithetical to labour-power production do not and cannot exist. In particular, it becomes clear by this analysis that the capitalist state will seek to destroy any forms of pedagogy that attempt to educate students regarding their real predicament—to create an awareness of themselves as future labour-powers and to underpin this awareness with critical insight that seeks to undermine the smooth running of the social production of labour-power. This fear entails strict control, for example, of the curriculum for teacher education and training, of schooling, and of educational research.

As Boxley (2003) points out, it also entails strict regulation and self-regulation by teachers of their own pedagogy, where 'teachers are aware that the very ways in which they themselves relate to their students are being constrained by the expectations of performative measurability'. Boxley asks the question: 'Are they becoming to their very hearts Standardized Assessment Task teachers?' He also quotes Fielding (1999): 'How many teachers of young children are now able to listen attentively in a non-instrumental way without feeling guilty about the absence of criteria or the insistence of a target tugging at their sleeve?' (p. 280).

The Recomposition of the Teacher Education Force in England and Wales

This strict regulation now applies very noticeably to teacher trainers and educators. In England and Wales, new teacher educators (i.e. those appointed since the late 1980s and early 1990s)—recruits into the training and education of teachers—are now 'covered in chalk dust', not 'tainted by theory'. Of course, many are superb and analytical and theorize their work and are critical intellectuals. Most are not. Teacher education has been replaced by 'teacher training' in official discourse and in the concrete, non-theorized, skills-based lecture theatre and seminar room of teacher training courses. Even where teacher trainers and educators wish to engage in theory, in contextualization of experience, and in critical analysis and action (as many do), there is very little space now in the heavily policed and assessed undergraduate and postgraduate teacher training and education programmes. I will develop this point later.

The Recomposition of the School Teaching Force

The advert that was shown on television in England and Wales in the middle of 2003 to attract recruits into teaching clearly aimed at people's sense of rational individualistic self-interest. 'Use your head' was the visual and verbal message, showing headless (non-teaching) people going about their work lives.

This appeal was in marked contrast to the previous teacher recruitment adverts, which focused on non-acquisitive, affective,'use your heart' appeals. The 'everybody remembers a teacher' adverts appealed to notions of social good, altruism, and job-satisfaction. They further appealed to then on-cognitive, non-testable, non-exam-results aspects of teaching, highlighting the altruistic contribution teachers can make to children's social, affective, and aesthetic development—their development as people rather than as certificated cogs in a labour machine.

Policy by both Conservative and New Labour governments on teacher recruitment has been twofold. Firstly, it has been/is an attempt to solve the problem of the teacher shortage that was experienced throughout the 1980s and 1990s, a problem which has varied in acuteness. Secondly, policy was/is clearly intended to attract into teaching two new types of teacher and to restock the teaching force with new teachers who were/are differently constituted, in ideological terms, from teachers with initial professional socialization mediated through the theory-rich, analytical and sometimes radical/critical undergraduate and postgraduate programmes that were killed off by Conservative government regulations in 1992 and 1993, and interred by New Labour in 1997 and 1998.

The first 'new' target group (for the Conservative government) was ex-businessmen (sic) and ex-armed forces personnel, i.e. mature men and women variously accustomed to commercial and competitive—exploitative human relationships, and/or disciplinary—authoritarian relationships, whose approach to education (content and pedagogy) was likely to be instrumental, managerial, technical, and vocational.

My own experience of interviewing students and talking with student teachers over a 30-year period indicates that former commercial and armed forces personnel wishing to embark on a three- or four-year undergraduate initial teacher education (ITE) degree course frequently claim to do so precisely to escape such competitive—exploitative and/or disciplinary—authoritarian relationships, and opt for a four-year undergraduate 'professional' degree. This suggests a commitment to a teaching career prior to commencing higher education (unlike students who opt for a one-year postgraduate School Centred Initial Teacher Training (SCITT) scheme, or a Postgraduate Certificate in Education (PGCE) course, following a decision taken after starting higher education).

The second major group targeted by this Conservative government recruitment tactic (for primary schools) was that of mothers. Not any mothers, such as those wishing to study for a four-year teaching qualification, but those 'mums' who were happy or prepared to 'speed-train' as teachers and to qualify at sub-degree level. One example was the June 1993 proposal by the (then) Minister of Education John Patten to recruit mothers with A level qualifications. These had generally left school at 18. The plan was for them to receive their training on a one-year crash course instead of taking the four-year undergraduate Bachelor of Education course required at the time. Such 'Mums' Army' courses would, in fact, have been of the same duration as the (academically) lower-level, one-year nursery nurse courses, but the proposal was dropped after widespread criticism from teachers, teacher educators, and the media in general.

However, with the Specialist Teacher Assistant (STA) scheme in operation in England and Wales (since 1995), which provides a one-year, mainly school-based, training for primary school assistants, many 'mums' who are not qualified teachers now work alongside teachers in primary school classrooms. This number of assistants working in classrooms has increased very dramatically indeed under New Labour. It is likely that there will be as many 'teaching assistants' within schools in England and Wales as there are teachers.

Both these groups targeted by Conservative and New Labour governments share a number of characteristics: they would (i) be 'trained' rather than 'educated'; (ii) be trained largely on the job in schools; (iii) learn mainly in an apprenticeship system; (iv) not experience any variety of school ethos and style; (v) have minimal opportunity to collabouratively critique and evaluate what they had seen or done; and (vi) be largely denied theoretical and analytical perspectives, other than those of their school mentor and class teacher.

They would be 'trained', but not 'educated'. They would be trained to deliver, but not educated to question and evaluate systematically (Hill, 1992a, 1994a, 1997a, b, 2001a). They would also, in some cases, (vii) be non-graduates. This would have clear implications for both their pay and their status in the staff room.

And, once in the classroom, teachers stumble across the incessant and public demands for 'improvement' within a discourse (and funding and staffing policy) of school effectiveness.

Boxley analyses the certification and standards agenda of New Labour's education policy. He examines how the broad aim of the New Labour government's education policy is to 'improve standards'. He states:

> Within every corner of the educational establishment, 'improvement' is under way. The quality of our teachers and schools is to be raised to such an extent that, by 2002, an enormous upswing in the key skills of our children will be visible, evidenced by SATS [Standard Assessment Tasks] and GCSE [General Certificate of Secondary Education] results. The targets and tables commanding the exact increases in skills and knowledge for each region and every school are well known to the workers in all the educational establishments of Britain ... what they mean for the teachers and children they 'represent'. For every one of the charts and graphs represents no more or less than the work of very many men, women and children. The government's targets and the measurable means of establishing them demand a reconceptualization of what it actually is to be such a teacher or learner encrypted within these tabulatures, within this society and system. (2003)

Jane Mulderrig also discusses the instrumental rationality underlying (New Labour's) education policy discourse, which is manifested in the pervasive rhetoric and values of the market in the representation of educational participants and practices. She theorizes this as an indicator of a general shift towards the commodification of education and the concomitant consumerization of social actors:

> Discourse plays an important role, not only in bringing about these reforms, butalsoin legitimising and enacting the ongoing project of globalization and concomitant changes in the relationship between the State and the economy. Central to this work, is creating a hegemonic consensus on the inevitability of it all; that our educational practices and relationships must necessarily be shaped to meet the'challenges' posed by this rapidly changing and competitiveworld...an important role for the government is to represent its policy reforms as being both necessary for Britain's economic survival, in the interests of everyone involved, and socially just. (2003)

Hursh (2003), in a study entitled 'Discourse, Power and Resistance in New York: The Rise of Testing and Accountability and the Decline of Teacher Professionalism and Local Control', similarly analyses the way in which the discourse of neoliberalism (which, after all, 'represent[s] a significant shift in the state's role in promoting social welfare' [2003]) is accompanied by the discourses of 'fairness' and of 'objectivity'.

Considerable research attention has been given over the last two decades to the deprofessionalization of teachers. Ironically, the removal of their professional autonomy is legitimized and partly enacted through a 'discourse of professionalism', which constructs them as committed to self-improvement and the upgrading of their skills, ambitious, collabourative, and strategically oriented to the effectiveness of their work. This discourse institutes a mentality of self- regulation by which the teachers themselves become the mechanism for legitimizing the surveillance, marketization, and codification of their work practices.[4]

Part 2. Repressive and Ideological State Apparatuses and the Repression of Critical Thought

Ideological State Apparatuses (ISAs) and Repressive State Apparatuses (RSAs)

Currently, the capitalist class is ratcheting up the use of ideological state apparatuses in the media and education systems in particular to both 'naturalize' and promote capitalist social and economic relations on the one hand, and, on the other, to marginalize and demonize resistant/anti-(capitalist), hegemonic, oppositional ideologies, actions, and activists. In the current period of capitalism there is increasing and naked use of repressive economic, legal, and military force globally to assert, and ensure compliance and subordination to, multinational capital and its state agents. This includes repressive state apparatuses such as the police, goal/jail, legal systems, and surveillance procedures.

The term 'state apparatus' does not refer solely to apparatuses such as ministries and various levels of government. It applies to those societal apparatuses, institutions, and agencies that operate on behalf of, and maintain the existing economic and social relations of, production. In other words, the apparatuses that sustain capital, capitalism and capitalists.

Capital and neoliberal force and ideology seek to neutralize and destroy potential pockets of resistance to global corporate expansion and to its interests. Education and the media are the dominant ideological state apparatuses. Each of these ideological state apparatuses contains disciplinary repressive moments and effects. The most powerful restraint on capital (and the political parties funded and influenced by capitalists in their bountiful donations) is that capital needs to persuade the people that neoliberalism—competition, privatization, poorer standards of public services, greater inequalities between rich and poor—is legitimate. If it cannot do this, there is a delegitimation crisis, and government and the existing system are seen through as grossly unfair and inhumane. They may also be seen as being in the pocket of the international and/or national ruling classes and their weaponry.

In order to minimize this delegitimation, to ensure that the majority of the population considers that the government and the economic system of private monopoly ownership are legitimate, the state uses the ideological state apparatuses such as schools, colleges and the media to 'naturalize' capitalism—to make the existing status quo seem 'only natural' (of course, if and when this does not work, the repressive state apparatuses kick in—sometimes literally, with steel-capped military boots or incarceration programmes consigning more and more of the poor in the USA to prison).

The freedom of the press and the media belongs to those who own that press and media. Rupert Murdoch is more powerful than me, although the ideas he represents ultimately may not be. The freedom of school choice, despite the 'naturalization' of 'choice' and 'competition' in the mass media and schools and universities as 'common sense', is pretty much confined to those with the economic and cultural capital to be able to choose. A car helps, too. Similar (racialized) social-class-based, hierarchical economic reproduction is also apparent in higher education, but is broadly 'hidden from current history', unexposed by an education system and mass media that are overwhelmingly non-critical of capital and its effects.

The Naturalization of Capital and the Denaturalization of Dissent

As Peter McLaren notes, one of its greatest achievements is that capital presents itself as natural, free, and democratic:

> As if it has now replaced the natural environment. It announces itself through its business, leaders and politicians as coterminous with freedom, and indispensable to democracy such that any attack on capitalism as exploitative or hypocritical becomes an attack on world freedom and democracy itself. (McLaren, 2000, p. 32)

Or, in Bourdieu's words: 'Everywhere we hear it said, all day long—and this is what gives the dominant discourse its strength—that there is nothing to put forward in opposition to the neoliberal view, that it has succeeded in presenting itself as self-evident, that there is no alternative' (1999, p. 29).

When capitalism is not accepted as 'natural', 'God-given', 'the way things are and the way things always will be', then the 'delegitimization of the delegitimizers' sets in, sometimes brutally. James Petras (2002) perhaps says it best when he argues that the USA is a veritable police state, on the cusp of a totalitarian regime. He writes:

> One of the hallmarks of a totalitarian regime is the creation of a state of mutual suspicion in which civil society is turned into a network of secret police informers. The Federal Bureau of Investigation (FBI) soon after September 11 exhorted every US citizen to report any suspicious behavior by friends, neighbors, relatives, acquaintances, and strangers. Between September and the end of November almost 700,000 denunciations were registered. Thousands of Middle Eastern neighbours, local shop owners, and employees were denounced, as were numerous other US citizens. None of these denunciations led to any arrests or even information related to September 11. Yet hundreds and thousands of innocent persons were investigated and harassed by the federal police.

McMurtry (2001) considers 'America's new war' as the latest expression of a much deeper and wider terrorist campaign of an emergent totalitarian pattern of instituting world corporate rule with no limit on occupation or accountability beyond itself. He forcefully claims that the United States has effectively created a new form of totalitarianism. The old totalitarianism culture of the 'Big Lie' is marked by 'a pervasive overriding of the distinction between fact and fiction by saturating mass media falsehoods'. This 'Big Lie' is an all-pervasive lie that 'is disseminated by round-the-clock, centrally controlled multi-media which are watched, read or heard by people across the globe day and night without break in the occupation of public consciousness instead of national territories'.

McMurtry writes that: 'In the old totalitarian culture of the Big Lie, the truth is hidden. In the new totalitarianism, there is no line between truth and falsehood. The truth is what people can be conditioned to believe'.

The Education Ideological State Apparatuses

Changes to ITE and education more widely have been effected through the repressive as well as ideological means available to the state. Althusser argues that the ideological dominance of the ruling class is, like its political dominance, secured in and through definite institutional forms and practices: the ideological apparatuses of the state. As Althusser suggests, every ideological state apparatus is also in part a repressive state apparatus, punishing those who dissent:

> There is no such thing as a purely ideological apparatus ... Schools and Churches use suitable methods of punishment, expulsion, selection, etc., to 'discipline' not only their shepherds, but also their flocks. (Althusser, 1971, p. 138)

Ideological state apparatuses have internal 'coercive' practices (for example, forms of punishment, non-promotion, displacement, being 'out of favour'). Similarly, repressive state apparatuses attempt to secure significant internal unity and wider social authority through ideology (for example, through their ideologies of patriotism and national integrity). Every repressive state apparatus therefore has an ideological moment, propagating a version of common sense and attempting to legitimate it under threat of sanction.

For example, in England and Wales, by means of the government regulatory organizations' (such as the Council for the Accreditation of Teacher Education [CATE] and the Teacher Training Agency [TTA]) circulars and Education Acts, higher education institutions (HEIs) and education departments and faculties can now have their resources reduced, their staff contracted, and their specializations (in 'race', social class, gender, disability, or sexuality) thereby altered. Oppositional teachers and teacher educators can lose heart and lose pay; schools and HEIs can lose pupils/students and therefore income and therefore teachers' and lecturers' jobs (see Hill, 1997c, d for a description and analysis of my own dismissal/'redundancy'). Their successors are likely to be appointed because they are 'covered in chalk dust' and mandated national curriculum expertise, rather than equal opportunities policies or the lust for justice.

Governments, and the ruling classes in whose interests they act, prefer to use the second form of state apparatuses—the ideological state apparatuses (ISAs). Changing the school and initial teacher education curriculum, abandoning 'general studies' and liberal studies in the United Kingdom for working class 'trade' and skilled-worker students/apprentices in 'further education' (vocational) colleges is less messy than sending the troops onto the streets or visored baton-wielding police into strike-bound mining villages. And it is deemed more legitimate by the population in general.

As Althusser (1971) and Bourdieu (1999) have also noted, schooling and the other sectors of education are generally regarded as politically neutral, and not as agencies of cultural, ideological, and economic reproduction. The school, like other institutions in society such as the legal system and the police, is always presented in official discourse as neutral, non-political, and non-ideological (of course, those who have direct negative experiences of any of these institutions, such as being half-strangled in a police assault, or living in a community whose children are frequently excluded from school, and those who have a critical political consciousness do not see it this way).

The Suppression and Compression of Critical Space in Education Today

As David Harvey points out, on the one hand capital requires educated and flexible labourers, but on the other hand it refuses the idea that labourers should think for themselves. While education of the labourer is important, it cannot be the kind of education that permits freethinking (Harvey, 2000, p. 3). So freethinking, and oppositional thinking, has been chopped, curtailed and circumscribed.

Critical space for critical education studies and research is being compressed through curriculum control, through the remaking of human personality, and through a gamut of ideological and repressive state apparatuses. This is especially so for fundamental critique: 'How the core processes and phenomena of capitalist society (value, capital, labour, labour-power, value- creation and capital accumulation, and so on) generate contradictions and tensions in everyday life—for individuals, groups, classes, societies and on an international scale' (Rikowski, 2003a).

Within schools and universities in the USA, England and Wales, and other states there has been:

- increasing concentration of/on pro-capitalist formal curricula (in England and Wales this includes rigorously monitored and assessed formal national curricula in schooling and in 'teacher training'; in the USA it includes what is, in effect, the national

curricula of 'high stakes testing' and the tyranny of the approved textbook) (Apple, 1993);
- increased marginalization of resistant/anti-(capitalist), hegemonic, alternative/oppositional curricula, texts, and programmes;
- increasing concentration of/on pro-capitalist hidden/informal curricula and pedagogy;
- increased marginalization of resistant/anti-(capitalist), hegemonic alternative/oppositional education and educators, i.e. the compression and suppression of critical space.

The marginalization of resistant anti-capitalist forces, individuals, and ideas takes place through the compression and suppression of critical space within the media and within education. Critical space consists of those social places and spaces where critique (especially fundamental critique) is possible. Effective critical space is those social places and spaces where such critique actually occurs. Critical space is about the potential and actuality for criticism of the existing society and the search for and promulgation of alternatives. Critical space is being compressed in education today. There are becoming fewer opportunities for engaging with critiques of society and education within formal education, within schools, within further vocational education, and within higher and teacher education.

And for those who do protest, who do stick their heads above the parapet ... sometimes it gets blown off—in dramatic or in undramatic but effective ways. In the period prior to and since the US-led invasion of Iraq, oppositional school students, college students, and faculty have suffered from something of a witch-hunt (McLaren et al., 2005, pp. 223-224). McLaren et al. detail what they term 'witch-hunting' by teachers against students who participated in anti-war protests such as organizing teach-ins in both K-12 schools and higher education institutions, and against students who expressed opinions critical of US policy. They give examples of disciplinary actions taken by school managements and by the police.

On a less dramatic but more pervasive level, Gabbard describes the drip, drip repression and sidelining of 'those who have challenged the viability of the market as a mode of social organization'.They receive no (positive) attention.

> 'Neither does the school afford the vast majority of children the opportunity to study the lives of people like themselves, much less the opportunity to study their own lives' (Gabbard, 2003, p. 71).

The Teacher Education Curriculum in England and Wales: Detheorized, Sanitized, Technicist Skills Training

Priorto the1997general election, the message from the Labour Party leader, Tony Blair and the Labour Party Shadow Minister for Education, David Blunkett was that:

> The Labour Party intends to launch a back to basics drive in the classroom ... More emphasis on basic skills, classroom discipline and whole class teaching will become part of a drastic overhaul of teacher training. The plan has been sparked by the party's dissatisfaction with the quality of newly qualified teachers. (Times Educational Supplement, 1996a)

The British government has, in effect, expelled most potentially critical aspects of education, such as the critical, sociological, and political examination of education and society, from the national curriculum for schooling in England and Wales and from what is now termed 'teacher training'. This was formerly called 'teacher education'. The change in nomenclature is important both symbolically and in terms of actual accurate analysis of the new, 'safe', sanitized, and detheorized education and training of new teachers.

The Conservative government's restructuring of initial teacher education (ITE) in England and Wales between 1979 and 1997 has been virtually unamended by the New Labour government in office since 1997. The Conservatives set up a market in ITE, attempted to recompose the teaching force and established a tightly controlled national curriculum through the CATE Circulars 9/92 and 14/93 (Department for Education [DfE], 1992, 1993). This emphasized then, and does still, the development of practical skills, and the abjuring of theory per se as well as of critical reflection with its attendant social justice underpinnings.

The Content of Teacher Education/Training Courses in England and Wales

Wilkin (1996), in her survey of teacher education policy from the 1960s to the 1990s, discusses Thatcherism and the government regulatory body CATE's criteria of 1984 in depth (Department of Education and Science [DES], 1984). These criteria were, she notes, 'moderate in terms of curricular demands but unprecedented in terms of control' (Wilkin, 1996, p. 148). This initial, pre-marketization phase of Thatcherite policy on ITE under Keith Joseph was aimed at controlling the content of the ITE curriculum.

It also saw 'the redistribution of power both overtly and covertly from the institutions to the schools' and the change to 'the practical nature of the criteria and the non-reflective (i.e. non-theorizing) mode' (Wilkin, 1996, p. 151). The 'tactics embodied in the criteria', Wilkin suggests, 'reduce considerably the power of the theorists, the tutors, and ... enhance that of the practitioners, the teachers' (pp. 151-152). Also, the CATE criteria established for the first time 'the right of the Secretary of State to have a say in the detailed content and structure of Initial Teacher Education in England' (Furlong et al., 2000, p. 22).

Under the CATE criteria of 1989 and 1992/1993, the content and objectives—or input—for the undergraduate B.Ed., BA (qualified teacher status [QTS]), and the postgraduate PGCE courses became more rigidly circumscribed than at any other time in living memory. The ITE curriculum was locked into the schools' national curriculum, ensuring that student teachers were to learn how to teach the relevant (school) national curriculum subject(s). In itself, this was not a contentious requirement, but the criteria also, as I shall go on to argue, excluded other forms of learning from the ITE curriculum, or considerably marginalized them.

Significant changes occurred in the content of B.Ed. and PGCE courses following CATE Circular 24/89 (DES, 1989). These continued in exaggerated form after the promulgation of CATE Circulars 9/92 and 14/93 (DfE, 1992, 1993). Emphasis on and time for education issues such as 'race', gender, sexuality, special needs and social class factors in schooling were reduced. So too were policy responses to counter stereotyping and educational underachievement, the ideological and political analysis of classroom and school pedagogy, and of national policy and legislation (such as the 1988 Education Reform Act, opting out, the national curriculum, and assessment). Progressively, the 'squeeze' on time for 'education' courses affected issues such as bullying, styles of classroom management, child abuse, and the study of cross-curricular issues. This resulted in courses described by the *Times Educational Supplement* (TES) editorial of 20 September 1996 as 'Basics Training' (TES, 1996b). This 'Basics Training' has become even more basic in working class schools, now dominated by the National Literacy Strategy and the National Numeracy Strategy.

At Brighton Polytechnic (now University) and at the West Sussex Institute of Higher Education (renamed Chichester Institute of Higher Education, then University College, Chichester), core course units validated under the 1984 CATE criteria (DES, 1984), which had focused on contextual and egalitarian issues in education, were replaced in the late 1980s (set out in Hill, 1989). Their content and concepts became, under the 1989 and then the 1992/1993 CATE criteria (DES 1989; DfE

1992, 1993), less visible in the successor BA (QTS) courses at both institutions.

I have detailed some of the changes in ITE for England and Wales. I will now summarize them. The current (2003-2004) ITE curriculum under New Labour comprises:

- a neo-conservative, utilitarian national curriculum with increased focus on 'the basics' in the school curriculum and preparing student teachers for teaching, particularly language and numeracy;
- a neo-conservative, utilitarian national curriculum in ITE that prepares student teachers to uncritically 'deliver' the existing school national curriculum;
- an emphasis within the ITE curriculum on classroom management skills and technical reflection as opposed to/and leaving little space and less demand for critical reflection;
- an emphasis within the ITE curriculum on managerialist solutions to problems in schooling as opposed to solutions targeted at schools' financial, pupil intake, and curriculum solutions and policies;
- an acceptance that student teachers may need only two school-based experiences, thereby limiting students' comparative critical appreciation of school ethoses and procedures;
- the 'naming and shaming' and closures of 'failing' teacher training courses;
- overall (if not universal) denigration of the education research community, and an insistence on its focusing on applied technicist research.

Anti-intellectual Thuggery

Teacher education has, in England and Wales and in other states, been largely detheorized, technicized, deintellectualized. So, by and large, has school teaching. This anti-intellectual thuggery is the ideological and repressive aspects of the education state apparatus in action. Designer dissent is managed. 'Deep dissent' is damned. As McLaren et al. (2005, p. 252) put it, what capital has enforced is intellectual thuggery that pervades teacher education programmes, particularly the kind of programme that 'rejects "theory"' (the knowledge of totality) (Zavarzadeh and Morton, 1994, p. 3).

In contrast to and in opposition to this education for quiescence, this education for capital, I join with McLaren et al. (2005, p. 252) in:

> Acknowledging that capitalist education acts as a drag on the development of 'critical' or 'class' consciousness by presenting a lifeless world empty of contradictions, we argue for a theory of the 'big picture', which enables people to translate their daily free-floating frustrations with the 'system' into a set of other ideas, beliefs and feelings that provide the basis not only for coherence but also for action.

So, currently the banks (finance capital, together with other capitals) control the books, and where the books don't work, or reach, then bullets and bombs are used. Books, banks and bullets combine in a permanent war to control our minds in support of the global project of imperialistic and militaristic neoliberalism. Education policy is subordinated to and is part of the project of contemporary capital.

Resistance

But there is resistance; there are spaces, disarticulations, and contradictions.[5] And there are always, sometimes minor, sometimes major, awakenings—that the material conditions of existence, for teacher educators, teachers, students, and workers and families more widely—simply do not match or recognize the validity of neoliberal (or other capitalist) discourse and policy. It is then and there that coherent understanding, and action, in pursuit of economic justice and social justice can potentially triumph. And in a general socialist redistributive and egalitarian reorganization of the economy and society, develop schools, vocational education, teacher education and universities to suit nobler purposes than being the ideological and repressive state apparatuses of capital.

Notes

1. I do not deconstruct or elabourate on the increasing concentration of wealth and power (to retain and increase that wealth) in the hands of the capitalist class, in particular through fiscal policy, employment, and (cutting back) social and public welfare programmes and policies. Nor do I detail here how these policies, including education policies, increase inequalities.

    This has been widely addressed in respect of schooling (for example, in Gewirtz et al., 1995; Anyon, 1997; Whitty et al., 1999; Lipman, 2000, 2002) and in respect of global society (for example, in Monbiot, 2000; Hill and Cole, 2001; Klein, 2001, 2002; Mojab, 2001; Hill et al., 2002; Pilger, 2002; Hill, 2001b, 2003a, 2004, 2005; Cole, 2005; Giroux, 2005).

    In the USA, the two reports Dying for Growth: global inequality and the health of the poor (Kim et al., 2000) and Poverty, Inequality and Health (Leon and Walt, 2000) analyse the relationship between the neoliberal policies of the World Bank and the International Monetary Fund, and the collapse of the global public health system. In the United Kingdom, New Labour has kept to a regime of low public expenditure. Despite funding increases in the second New Labour term (2001–), by 2005 public spending has risen to only 40.5% of the gross domestic product, which is a smaller share than in most other developed countries and considerably less than the 49.9% in 1976 (Toynbee and Walker, 2001). Larry Elliott notes that spending on the nation's infrastructure was lower in each of New Labour's first four years in office (1997-2001) than in the final 12 months of John Major's Conservative government—and only one-quarter of what it was at the end of Jim Callaghan's (Old) Labour government in 1979 (Elliott, 2001). Toynbee and Walker (2005, p. 154) note that the level of net tax and social security contributions as a percentage of GDP is projected to rise to only the same level in 2006 as it was under Mrs Thatcher in the mid-1980s. On page 155, they continue, Chancellor Gordon Brown's budget of 2002 (March) and Spending Review (July) planned for public spending to rise towards 42% of GDP, which would mean spending had risen by five percentage points since Labour took power (Toynbee and Walker, 2005). This is, of course, still far lower than in 1976.

2. I have depicted this elsewhere as the bell of economic determination that is now tolling (see Hill, 1989, 1990, 2001a, b, 2003a, 2004, 2005). In two of my works (Hill, 2001a, 2005) I have tried to develop Althusser's (1971) concepts of economic determination. The 'bell' of economic determination that (for Althusser) 'never tolls' is, at the current juncture of capitalism, now tolling.Althusser's theory of 'economic determination in the last instance' is therefore inadequate. It needs to be extended by the concept of economic determination in the last resort. This is a periodized concept, applying to particular stages in the development of capitalism (e.g. the early 19th century laissez-faire period in Britain, and the post-1970s). Within such periodization, it is a concept referring to the nakedness of the primacy of the capital accumulation process. It is important to note that this is not a millennial or pre-revolutionary statement or stage. It refers to the current stage of capitalism. There are three ways in which this nakedness is asserted: (i) in the intentionality of governmental discourse; (ii) in media support for that intentionality; and (iii) in creating general awareness of those intentions within the population at large by conflating the interests of capital with those of society, where capitalism is naturalized as the unquestioned backdrop to everyday global life. This is recognized, for example, in the increased visibility and use of the term 'capitalism' itself, both by its supporters (e.g. 'venture capitalists') and its opponents (e.g. the anti-capitalism demonstrators in Seattle and London in 1999 and 2000).
3. See, for example, Giroux, 1997, 1999, 2000a, b, 2002, 2003, 2005, and Giroux and Myrsiades, 2001.
4. Mulderrig (2003) also argues that discourse plays a significant role in

constructing and legitimizing post-welfare learning policy as a key aspect of the ongoing project of globalization.

5. I have suggested critical anti-capitalist programmes for teacher education, for teachers to become skilled critical transformative intellectuals in Hill, 1992b, 1994b, 2002, 2003b, 2004b, forthcoming 2005.

References

Althusser, L. (1971). Ideology and Ideological State Apparatuses, in L. Althusser. *Lenin and Philosophy and Other Essays*, pp. 122-173. London: New Left Books.

Anyon, J. (1997). *Ghetto Schooling: A political economy of urban educational reform*. New York: Teachers College Press.

Apple, M. (1993). *Official Knowledge: Democratic education in a conservative age*. London: Routledge.

Bourdieu, P. (1999). *Acts of Resistance: Against the Tyranny of the Market*. New York: The New Press.

Boxley, S. (2003). Performativity and Capital in Schools, *Journal for Critical Education Policy Studies*, 1(1). Available at: www.jceps.com.

Bush, G.W. (2001). *No Child Left Behind.* Washington, DC: US Department of Education. Available at: http://www.ed.gov/nclb/landing.jhtml.

Cole, M. (2005). New Labour, Globalization and Social Justice: The role of education, in G. Fischman, P. McLaren, H. Sünker and C. Lankshear (eds) *Critical Theories, Radical Pedagogies and Global Conflicts,* pp. 3-22. Lanham: Rowman & Littlefield.

Cole, M., Hill, D., McLaren, P. and Rikowski, G. (2001). *Red Chalk: On Schooling, Capitalism and Politics. Brighton*: Institute for Education Policy Studies.

Department of Education and Science (DES) (1984). *Initial Teacher Training—Approval of Courses: Circular 3/84*. London: HMSO.

Department of Education and Science (DES) (1989). *Initial Teacher Training—Approval of Courses: Circular 24/89*. London: DES.

Department for Education (DfE) (1992). *Circular 9/92: The Initial Training of Secondary School Teachers*. London: DfE.

Department for Education (DfE) (1993). *Circular 14/93: The Initial Training of Primary School Teachers*. London: DfE.

Elliott, L. (2001). It's About Time Blair Had a Big Idea, *Guardian*, 2 April.

Fielding, M. (1999). Target Setting, Policy Pathology and Student Perspectives: Learning to labour in new times, *Cambridge Journal of Education*, 29(2), pp. 277-287.

Furlong, J., Barton, L., Miles, S., Whiting, C. and Whitty, G. (2000). *Teacher Education in Transition: Re-forming Professionalism?* Buckingham: Open University Press.

Gabbard, D.A. (2003). Education IS Enforcement: The centrality of compulsory schooling in market societies, in K. Saltman and D.A. Gabbard (eds) *Education as Enforcement: The militarization and corporatization of schools,* pp. 61-80. London: Routledge Falmer. Gewirtz, S., Ball, S. and Bowe, R. (1995). *Markets, Choice and Equity in Education*. Buckingham: Open University Press.

Giroux, H. (1997). *Pedagogy and the Politics of Hope: Theory, Culture and Schooling*. Boulder: Westview Press.

Giroux, H. (1999). *The Mouse that Roared: Disney and the End of Innocence*. New York: Rowman & Littlefield. Giroux, H. (2000a) *Stealing Innocence: Corporate Culture's War on Children*. New York: Palgrave.

Giroux, H. (2000b). *Impure Acts: The Practical Politics of Cultural Studies*. New York: Routledge.

Giroux, H. (2002). The Corporate War against Higher Education, *Workplace*, 5(1). Available at: www.louisville.edu/journal/workplace/issue5p1/giroux.html

Giroux, H. (2003). Selling Out Higher Education, *Policy Futures in Education*, 1(1), pp. 179-200. Available at: www.wwwords.co.uk/pfie/index.html?

Giroux, H. (2005). *The Terror of Neoliberalism*. Boulder: Paradigm.

Giroux, H. and Myrsiades, K. (2001). *Beyond the Corporate University: Culture and Pedagogy in the New Millennium*. Lanham: Rowman & Littlefield.

Harvey, D. (2000). *Spaces of Hope*. Berkeley: University of California Press.

Harvie, D. (2000). Alienation, Class and Enclosure in UK Universities, *Capital and Class*, 71, pp. 103-132.

Hatcher, R. (2001). Getting Down to the Business: Schooling in the Globalised Economy, *Education and Social Justice*, 3(2), pp. 45-59.

Hatcher, R. (2002). *The Business of Education: How Business Agendas Drive Labour Policies for Schools*. London: Socialist Education Association.

Hatcher, R. and Hirtt, N. (1999). The Business Agenda Behind Labour's Education Policy, in M. Allen, C. Benn, C. Chitty, M. Cole, R. Hatcher, N. Hirtt and G. Rikowski. *Business, Business, Business: New Labour's Education Policy*, pp. 12-23. London: Tufnell Press.

Hill, D. (1989). *Charge of the Right Brigade: The Radical Right's Attack on Teacher Education.* Brighton: Institute for Education Policy Studies.

Hill, D. (1990). *Something Old, Something New, Something Borrowed, Something Blue: Teacher Education, Schooling and the Radical Right in Britain and the USA.* London: Tufnell Press.

Hill, D. (1992a). What the Radical Right is Doing to Teacher Education: A Radical Left Critique, *Multicultural Teaching,* 10(3), pp. 31-34.

Hill, D. (1992b). *What's Left in Teacher Education?* London: Tufnell Press.

Hill, D. (1994a). Cultural Diversity and Initial Teacher Education, in G. Verma and P. Pumfrey (eds) *Cultural Diversity and the Curriculum,* vol. 4: *Cross-curricular Contexts, Themes and Dimensions in Primary Schools.* London: Falmer Press.

Hill, D. (1994b). A Radical Left Policy for Teacher Education, *Socialist Teacher*, 56, pp. 23-24.

Hill, D. (1997a). Equality and Primary Schooling: The Policy Context Intentions and Effects of the Conservative 'Reforms', in M. Cole, D. Hill and S. Shan

Equality and the National Curriculum in Primary Schools, pp. 15-47. London: Cassell.

Hill, D. (1997b). Reflection in Initial Teacher Education, in K. Watson, S. Modgil and C. Modgil (eds) *Educational Dilemmas: Debate and Diversity, Vol. 1: Teacher Education and Training*, pp. 193-208. London: Cassell.

Hill, D. (1997c). Brief Autobiography of a Bolshie Dismissed, General Educator, 44, pp. 15-17. Hill, D. (1997d). *Critical Research and the Death of Dissent, Research Intelligence*, 59, pp. 25-26.

Hill, D. (2001a). State Theory and the Neoliberal Reconstruction of Schooling and Teacher Education: A structuralist neo-Marxist critique of postmodernist, quasi-postmodernist, and culturalist neo-Marxist theory, *British Journal of Sociology of Education*, 22(1), pp. 137-157.

Hill, D. (2001b). Global Capital, Neoliberalism, and Privatization: the growth of educational inequality, in D. Hill and M. Cole (eds) *Schooling and Equality: Fact, Concept and Policy*, pp. 35-54. London: Kogan Page.

Hill, D. (2002). The Radical Left and Education Policy: Education for Economic and Social Justice, *Education and Social Justice,* 4(3), pp. 41-51.

Hill, D. (2003a) Global Neoliberalism, the Deformation of Education and Resistance, *Journal for Critical Education Policy Studies*, 1(1). Available at: www.jceps.com

Hill, D. (2003b). Critical Education for Economic and Social Justice, in M. Pruyn and L. Huerta-Charles (eds) *Teaching Peter McLaren: Paths of dissent*, pp. 132-173. New York: Peter Lang.

Hill, D. (2004). Educational Perversion and Global Neoliberalism: A Marxist critique, *Cultural Logic:* An Electronic Journal of Marxist Theory and practice. Available at: http://eserver.org/clogic/2004/2004.html

Hill, D. (2005). The State and Education: Structuralist Neo-Marxism, Theory and Education Policy, in G. Fischman, P. McLaren, H. Sünker and C. Lankshear (eds) *Critical Theories, Radical Pedagogies and Global Conflicts*, pp. 23-51. Lanham: Rowman & Littlefield.

Hill, D. (2005). Globalization and its Educational Discontents: Neoliberalisation and its impacts on access, equality, democracy, critical thought, and education workers' rights, pay and conditions, *International Studies in the Sociology of Education.*

Hill, D. and Cole, M. (eds) (2001). Social Class, in D. Hill and M. Cole (eds) *Schooling and Equality: Fact, concept and policy*, pp. 137-159. London: Kogan Page.

Hill, D., Sanders, M. and Hankin, T. (2002). Marxism, Class Analysis and Postmodernism, in D. Hill, P. McLaren, M. Cole and G. Rikowski (eds) *Marxism against Postmodernism in Educational Theory*, pp. 15-194. Lanham: Lexington Books.

Hursh, D.W. (2001). Neoliberalism and the Control of Teachers, Students, and Learning: The rise of standards, standardization and accountability, Cultural Logic, Special Issue: *Marxism and Education,* 4(1). Available at: http://www.eserver.org/clogic/4-1/4-1.html

Hursh, D. (2003). Discourse, Power and Resistance in New York: The rise of testing and accountability and the decline of teacher professionalism and local control, in J. Satterthwaite, E. Atkinson and K. Gale (eds) *Discourse, Power and Resistance: Challenging the rhetoric of contemporary education*, pp. 43-56. Stoke-on-Trent: Trentham Books.

Kaplan, D. (2002). *Education is Not a Commodity Fighting the Privatization of Higher Education Worldwide.* Available at: www.ieps.org.uk.cwc.net/kaplan2003b.pdf

Kim, J. Yong, Irwin, A., Millen, J.V. and Gershman, J. (eds) (2000) *Dying for Growth: global inequality and the health of the poor*. Monroe: Common Courage Press.

Klein, N. (2001). *No Logo*. London: Flamingo.

Klein, N. (2002). *Fences and Windows: Dispatches from the front lines of the globalization debate.* London: Flamingo.

Leher, R. (2004). A New Lord of Education?World Bank Policy for Peripheral Capitalism, *Journal for Critical Education Policy Studies*, 2(1).Available at: www.jceps.com

Leon, D. and Walt, G. (eds) (2000). *Poverty, Inequality and Health: An international perspective*. Oxford: Oxford University Press.

Lipman, P. (2000). Bush's Education Plan, Globalization and the Politics of Race, *Cultural Logic,* 4(1). Available at: http://www.eserver.org/clogic/4-1/4-1.html

Lipman, P. (2002). Making the Global City, Making Inequality: The political economy and cultural politics of Chicago school policy, *American Educational Research Journal*, 39(2), pp. 379-419.

McLaren, P. (2000). *Che Guevara, Paolo Freire and the Pedagogy of Revolution.* Boulder: Rowman & Littlefield.

McLaren, P. and Rikowski, G. (2001). Pedagogy for Revolution against Education for Capital: An e-dialogue on education in capitalism today, *Cultural Logic,* 4(1). Available at: http://www.eserver.org/clogic/4-1/4-1.html

McLaren, P., Martin, G., Farahmandpur, R. and Jaramillo, N. (2005). *Teaching against Global Capitalism and the New Imperialism.* Lanham: Rowman & Littlefield.

McMurtry, J. (2001). '*Why Is There a War in Afghanistan?*' Speech made at Science for Peace Forum and Teach-In, How Should Canada Respond to Terrorism and War? 9 December. Available at: scienceforpeace.sa.utoronto.ca/Special_Activities/McMurtry_Page.html

McNeil, L. (2000). *Contradictions of School Reform: Educational costs of standardized testing*. New York: Routledge.

Marx, K. and Engels, F. (1987). *The Communist Manifesto*. New York: Pathfinder Press. (Original work published 1847.)

Mathison, S. and Ross, E.W. (2002). The Hegemony of Accountability in Schools and Universities, *Workplace,* 5(1).

Mojab, S. (2001). New Resources for Revolutionary Critical Education, *Convergence*, 34(1), pp. 118-125. Monbiot, G. (2000) *Captive State: The corporate takeover of Britain*. London: Pan.

Mulderrig, J. (2003). Consuming Education: A critical discourse analysis of social actors in New Labour's education policy, *Journal for Critical Education Policy Studies,* 1(1). Available at: www.jceps.com

Petras, J. (2002). Si*gns of a Police State are Everywhere,* Z, 15(1). Available at: http://zmag.org/zmag/articles/jan02petras.htm

Pilger, J. (2002). *The New Rulers of the World.* London: Verso.

Polyani, K. (1944). *The Great Transformation.* New York: Farrar & Rinehart.

Rikowski, G. (2001). *The Battle in Seattle: Its significance for education.* London: Tufnell Press.

Rikowski, G. (2002). *Globalization and Education, paper prepared for the House of Lords Select Committee on Economic Affairs Inquiry into the Global Economy*, 22 January. Available at: www.ieps.org.uk.cwc.net/rikowski2002d.pdf

Rikowski, G. (2003a). *Critical Space*, unpublished manuscript.

Rikowski, G. (2003b). The Profit Virus: The business takeover of education, *Mediactive: ideas, knowledge, culture*, 1, pp. 91-108.

Rikowski, G. (2003c). The Business Takeover of Schools, Mediactive: ideas, knowledge, culture, 1, pp. 91-108. Robertson, L.H. and Hill, R. (2001) Excluded Voices: Educational exclusion and inclusion, in D. Hill and M. Cole (eds) *Schooling and Equality: Fact, concept and policy*, pp. 73-93. London: Kogan Page.

Saltman, K.J. and Gabbard, D.A. (2003). *Education as Enforcement: The militarization and corporatization of schools.* London: Routledge Falmer.

Times Educational Supplement (1996a). *Article on New Labour and Teacher Education*, 31 May.

Times Educational Supplement (1996b). *Basics Training*, 20 September.

Tomlinson, S. (2001). *Education in a Post-welfare Society*. Buckingham: Open University Press.

Toynbee, P. and Walker, D. (2001). *Hard Work: Life in low-pay Britain*. London: Penguin.

Toynbee, P. and Walker, D. (2005). *Better or Worse? Has Labour Delivered*? London: Bloomsbury.

Whitty, G., Power, S. and Halpin, D. (1999). *Devolution and Choice in Education: The school, the state, and the market.* Buckingham: Open University Press.

Wilkin, M. (1996*). Initial Teacher Training: The dialogue of ideology and culture*. London: Falmer Press.

Zavarzadeh, M. and Morton, D. (1994). *Theory as Resistance: Politics and culture after (post) structuralism*. New York: Guilford Press.

5

Globalization and its Educational Discontents: Neoliberalization and its Impacts on Education Workers' Rights Pay and Conditions

Dave Hill

Summary

This article examines some impacts of neoliberal education policies during the current period of the intensification of neoliberal capital. Section 1 examines the relationship between education and capital, identifying three plans capital has in relation to education. It sets out some of the major aspects of neoliberal policy developments in schooling and further education.

Section 2 describes, analyses and evaluates the research methodology used in developing this article, locating the methodology within the debate between 'methodological purists' on the one hand, and 'committed research' on the other. The research for this article, within the 'research for social justice' paradigm, is rationalized. Section 3 examines the impacts of neoliberalization on education workers' securities— their pay/salaries, conditions of employment, stresses and pressures at work, and their work identity and status. It also examines the impacts on the rights and powers of education trade unions. The article ends, in Section 4, by briefly calling for resistance to the global neoliberal capitalist agenda in schooling and education.

Introduction

Constant revolutionizing of production, uninterrupted disturbance of all social conditions, everlasting uncertainty and agitation distinguish the bourgeois epoch from all earlier ones. All fixed, fast-frozen relations ...

are swept away, all new-formed ones become antiquated before they can ossify. (Marx and Engels (1977 [1847], p. 38)

This article analyses some of the impacts of the neoliberalisation of schooling and further education on teaching and learning in current changing times of the intensification of neoliberal capitalism and the current revolutionization of production.[1]

Section 1 examines the relationship between education and capital, identifying three plans capital has in relation to education, and sets out some of the major aspects of neoliberal policy in schooling and further education.

Section 2 describes, analyses and evaluates the research methodology used in developing this article, locating the methodology within the debate between 'methodological purists' on the one hand, and 'committed research' on the other. The research for this article, within the 'research for social justice' paradigm, is rationalized.

Section 3 examines the impacts of neoliberalization on education workers' securities—their pay/salaries, conditions of employment, stresses and pressures at work, and their work identity and status. It also examines the impacts on the rights and powers of education trade unions. There are other major impacts of neoliberal education policies globally. These include, first, the increasing inequalities within and between countries, second, the diminution and bypassing of democratic local and national control over education, and third, the reconceptualization of the very concept of democracy together with the commodification of humanity.[2] The article ends, in Section 4, by briefly calling for resistance to the global neoliberal capitalist agenda in schooling and education.

Part 1. Impacts of Neoliberalization of Schooling: Neoliberal Capital, Schooling and Further Education

The fundamental principle of capitalism is the sanctification of private (individual or corporate) profit, based on the extraction of surplus labour (unpaid labour-time) as surplus value from the labour-power of workers. It is a creed and practice of (racialized and gendered) class exploitation, exploitation by the capitalist class of those who provide the profits through their labour, the national and international working class.[3]

There have been a number of changes in capitalism in this current period of neoliberal globalisation. One development is the growth in service, communications and technological industries in the developed world. One 'service industry' is education. As the International Chamber of Commerce (ICC) observes, 'services are coming to dominate the economic activities of countries at virtually every stage of development' (ICC, 1999, p. 1). The ICC then draws the conclusion—a contested conclusion—that this makes 'services trade liberalization a necessity for the integration of the world economy' (1999, p. 1).

Another development is the declining profitability of capital—the crisis of capital accumulation. This crisis has resulted in intensification of competition between capitals, between national and between transnational capitals and corporations. There is general agreement among Marxists that

> the pressure on nations to liberalize services at the national level can be seen, therefore, as a response to the declining profitability of manufacture (Beckmann and Cooper, 2004).

Globalization is not a qualitatively new phenomenon but a tendency which has always been integral to capitalism's growth. Within the Marxist paradigm there is growing recognition of the relevance of Marx's account expressed in the *Communist Manifesto* that globalization is the predictable outcome of capitalism's expansionary tendencies, evident since its emergence as a viable form of society (Cole, 1998, 2005; Bromley, 1999).

This crisis of capital accumulation, as predicted by Marx and Engels (1977 [1847]), has led to the intensification of the extraction of surplus value, the progressing global immiseration of workers, and the intensification of control of populations by the ideological and repressive state apparatuses identified and analysed by Althusser (Althusser, 1971; see also Hill, 1989, 2001, 2005a).

National and Global Aspects of Neoliberalism in Education

The major aspects of neoliberal education policies include the following: deregulation and decentralization; the importation of 'new public managerialism' into the management of schools and colleges and education services; a fiscal regime of cuts in publicly funded schooling and further education services; commercialization of and within schools; the charging of fees; outsourcing of services to privately owned companies; and the privatisation and ownership of schools and colleges by private corporations.

National and international legal frameworks are developing to ensure international accessibility to the privatized market in educational services.

One salient policy is employment policy: attacks on and downwards pressures on workers' rights and conditions, and on trade union rights.

Proponents of liberalisation claim that 'private is better than public', that 'competition improves standards', that privatization and other liberalizing policies and processes nationally and globally (such as free trade) improve productivity and efficiency. To take one example of such claims, the World Bank, one of the main global 'levers' for privatization, has proclaimed:

> The virtues of the private sector, especially compared to the public system, include: (a) internal efficiency and management – almost no waste, lean organizational chart, better decision-making flow, less discontinuity of administration, agility in crisis solution, better students/teacher and students/staff ratio; (b) flexibility to hire/fire teachers, determine their salaries according to market values and cost levels; and (c) flexibility to adapt quicker to labour market needs and thus change curricula ... Private institutions are often accused of getting excess profits and paying inadequate attention to quality ... although, claims the World Bank, there has never been a systematic demonstration of their existence. (World Bank, 1991, p. 69)[4]

Three Education Plans of Capital: Capital has a number of plans with respect to education[5]

The capitalist plan for education. A first plan of capital is to produce and reproduce a work force and citizenry and set of consumers fit for capital.

This has two functions, an ideological function and a labour-training function. These comprise socially producing labour-power for capitalist enterprises. This is people's capacity to labour—their skills and attitudes, together with their ideological compliance and suitability for capital—as workers, citizens and consumers. This is the Capitalist Plan for Education.[6]

The capitalist plan in education. A second plan of capital is to smooth the way for direct profit-taking/profiteering from education. It is about how capital wants to make *direct profits* from education.

This centres on setting business 'free' in education for profit-making and profit-taking by capital, extracting profits from privately controlled/owned schools and colleges or aspects of their functioning.

Common mechanisms are, for example, from managing, advising, controlling and owning them. So, in some countries, 'core' teaching services are privatized—the school/college itself becomes privately owned. Or its 'peripheral services' are privatised both within institutions (services such as catering, security, reprographics) and nationally. Examples are student fees or loans for staying on at school in England, or for attending community colleges in the United States, being run by private corporations rather than by the local or national state.

Privatisation of schools, the growth of the private sector in schooling and further education, and the setting up of nationally-owned or foreign-owned or franchised chains of schools is happening in a number of countries.

The growth of this private sector is occurring in developed states. It is occurring on a larger scale in developing and less-developed states, forced on often unwilling governments by the 'restructuring' demands made by multinational banking and finance agencies, such as the World Bank and the International Finance Corporation.

Capital's global plan for education corporations. This is the third plan of capital, and is a series of national capitalist plans for domestically based national or multinational corporations globally. It is a plan for edubusinesses and corporations based in Britain, the United States, Australia and New Zealand, as well as those based locally (e.g. in particular states such as Brazil in Latin America) to profit from international privatising, franchising and marketing activities.[7] With a worldwide education industry valued at $2 trillion annually (UNESCO, 2000, p.16), 'it is not surprising that many investors and "edupreneurs" are anxious to seize the opportunities to access this untapped gold mine' (Shugarensky and Davidson-Harden, 2003, p. 323).

It is not just national edubusinesses that are involved—it is large multiactivity national and global capitalist companies (Mahoney et al., 2003; Rikowski, 2005).

With respect to the United Kingdom, Richard Hatcher comments that as the export value of manufacturing, farming and some service industries declines, the government's policy is that Britain should become a market leader in exporting a new international business: privatized services. Hatcher suggests that the British government's intention may be to foster and promote the private education industry until it is strong enough to compete internationally. He further suggests that the attempt to develop 'a world class education system' is not for the benefit of our children but to maintain businesses in the future (Hatcher, 2001).

Relationship Between These Three Plans of Capital

What are the primary aims of capital regarding education—to make direct profits, whether nationally or globally, or to secure an 'appropriate' workforce'? In Hatcher's view, 'the education business sector, even though it is growing, is a tiny part of the British, or any other, economy'. He suggests that currently 'the overriding interest of the vast majority of employers, including the big bourgeoisie, is in the production of human capital, not the profitability of the edubusiness sector. He comments:

> The crucial question is do they rely on the state to deliver that future workforce itself, directly, through the public school system (suitably advised and pressured by the business lobby, of course, and with a healthy dose of input by for-profit companies), or have they lost confidence in the state's ability to deliver, to the point where they want to see public education handed over to the private sector to run (with all the very risky political as well as technical problems that would raise)? In my view there is no evidence to support this latter view, whereas there is plenty to support the former. (Hatcher, 2005b; see also Hatcher, 2005a)

However, it would appear from an examination of existing trends globally that the relative importance of direct profit-taking by capital could well become of far more significance than currently. Current worldwide spending in education is' estimated at around 2,000 billion dollars ... more than global automotive sales' (Santos, 2004, p. 17). According to Santos, 'capital growth in education has been exponential, showing one of the highest earning rates of the market: £1000 invested in 1996 generated £3405 four years later' (Santos, 2004, pp. 17-18, cited in Delgado-Ramos and Saxe-Fernandez, 2005). Santos continues, 'that is an increased value of 240 per cent, while the London Stock Exchange valorization rate accounted on the same period for 65 per cent. Other 2004 data indicate that, current commercialized education, incomplete as it is, already generates around $365 billion in profits worldwide' (2004, pp. 17-18).

Neoliberalization of Education: Global Similarities, National Variations

Whichever aim, and policy, become salient, or increase in importance and impact, varies from country to country. There are global similarities in liberalising education policy. There are, however, local variations in the type and extent of the various policies. These relate to different historical conditions and balance of forces—the relative strengths of the trade union movement, workers' trade union and political organizations on the one hand (with their varying strengths of resistance to neoliberal policies), and those of local or transnational capital on the other. We are not in an era of the unimpeded march to neoliberal capitalism. A comparison of three North American states (Canada, the United States and Mexico), for example, shows some similarities and some differences in context and policy. Pardíñaz-Solís (1997) points out the impact of the different histories of the three states of North America—in particular the corporatist history of the state and education policy in Mexico, which, unlike the USA, has state mandated textbooks and a national curriculum (with some variation between the regions of Mexico). However, he also draws attention to the similarities between policies in the three states, and suggests that, despite very different histories and state ideologies in the past, neoliberal trends in policy are continuing apace in Mexico. Hursh (2005) similarly examines differences and similarities between the neoliberal education agenda in England and Wales and the United States.

Privatization. Privatization takes many forms, different forms sometimes in different countries. In Britain, the Centre for Public Services' booklet of 2003, *Mortgaging Our Children's Future* (Hall, 2003), analyses the various policies and initiatives under way in secondary schools in England and Wales (see also Rikowski, 2005; Hill, 2006c). Hall discusses making markets, city academies and specialist schools, school companies, the 'Excellence in Cities' programme, privatizing local education authorities, the Private Finance Initiative (PFI), outsourcing/restructuring of school meals and the Education Action Zones policy.

These are seen by Rikowski as means of 'softening up' the education service to business control and various forms of profit-making by capital. Rikowski goes further, and suggests that any degree of privatization and private involvement acts as a 'profit virus'—that once a public service such as education is infected ('virused') by private company involvement, then it will inevitably become liable to the regulations of the General Agreement for Trade in Services (GATS), and open up to free trade in services by national and by multinational and foreign capital (Rikowski, 2003, 2005; see also Hill, 2005b).

In Britain there is currently what may be seen as the 'hidden' preprivatisation of state schools in England by enabling schools to function as 'little businesses' through increased autonomies and business-like managements and corporate aspects, and the ability, within the 2002 Education Act and the October 2005 White Paper, *Higher Standards, Better Schools for All: More Choice for Parents and Pupils* (Her Majesty's Government, 2005) for schools to act as capitalist enterprises in terms of their ability to merge and engage in takeovers of other schools (Rikowski, 2005a,b). Schools can enter into deals with private-sector outfits. They can also sell educational services to other schools.

In a number of states, such as Pakistan, governments simply request private companies to fill the gap of non-provision publicly built and staffed/equipped schooling. Private schools have mushroomed at all levels, from pre-school to postgraduate studies. There are an estimated 56,000 private institutions currently operating in Pakistan, providing education to about 6 million students (Government of Pakistan, 2004). The government has resolved to increase private-school enrolment from 15% to 40% by 2010 under the Education Sector Reforms project, which is being funded by all major donors, including the World Bank (Government of Pakistan, 2002, p. 34). In other countries, such as Haiti, public provision is of such poor quality that the effect is the same—effective schooling is left to private companies—some not-for-profit (such as some religious schools), others very much 'for profit'. Increasingly, for example in Latin America, the profits from 'for-profit' schools flow not only to 'national' corporations, but also to United States chains and brands of schools.

Commercialism and Marketization. One aspect of profit-taking in education is *commercialization* of education—both in ideology/awareness/acceptance and in concrete terms. *Direct* commercial penetration is evident in the increasing use of commercially sponsored materials in the classroom and around the school. Whitty (2000) notes that the growing influence of commercial organizations as consultants in public provision can itself contribute to a change in the ethos of the sector. He comments:

> while they might strictly be regarded as elements of marketization, they could also be considered a prelude to privatization in the fuller sense of the privately funded and privately provided education Many critics of devices like devolved budgeting, internal markets, cost-centres and self-governing state schools competing in the marketplace, have been seen as examples of 'creeping privatization'. (Whitty, 2000)

Whitty suggests that some aspects of marketisation contribute to privatisation in an ideological if not a strictly economic sense, even where quasi-markets are confined to public-sector providers. Aspects of ideological privatization include fostering the belief that the private-sector approach is superior to that traditionally adopted in the public sector; requiring public-sector institutions to operate more like those in the private sector; and encouraging private (individual/family) decision-making in place of political and professional judgements. The increasing emphasis on competition and choice has also brought with it what Whitty calls a 'hidden curriculum' of marketisation.

Schoolhouse Commercialism in the United States. Possibly the most consistent and thorough analysis of 'schoolhouse commercialism' is that by Alex Molnarin the United States (e.g. Molnar, 2001; Molnar et al., 2004). For example, his latest (sixth) *No Student Left Unsold* (annual report on schoolhouse commercialism trends) examines eight types of schoolhouse commercialism, with most showing a year-on-year increase (Molnar et al., 2004).

These types of 'schoolhouse commercialism' (measured on an annual basis by Molnar et al.) are corporate sponsorship of school programmes and activities; exclusive agreements—agreements giving marketers exclusive rights to sell a product or a service on school or district grounds; incentive programmes—the use of commercial products or services as rewards for achieving an academic goal; appropriation of space—the selling of naming rights or advertising space on school premises or property; corporately sponsored educational materials; through to actual privatization—the private ownership of publicly funded schools, private management of publicly funded schools, public charter schools, and, finally, private, for-profit school involvement in voucher programmes.

Global Levers for Neoliberalization[8]

Globally, the GATS of the World Trade Organization (WTO) represents a broad and ambitious strategy of the 'free market' capitalist global economy to increase trade liberalization/neoliberalization in the 'services' industry. The two big 'service industries' not yet widely privatized throughout the globe are those of health and education.

Grieshaber-Otto and Sanger (2002) argue that the discourse of the GATS serves as a major potential force in essentially enshrining or entrenching neoliberal educational policies. It sets out supranational and binding legal mechanisms and serves to act as an enforcer for the 'corporate rights' of private education providers. As Shugurensky and Davidson-Harden (2003, p. 322) point out, 'these agreements represent an intensified stage of the neoliberal agenda for education, as it plays out in the global arena in forms of regional and local policy and practice'.

Rikowski (2001) and others demonstrate how the WTO [9] and other 'global clubs for the mega-capitalists' are setting up this agenda in education across the globe. Promoting the cause of 'free trade' are national and international business/capitalist organizations such as the International Chamber of Commerce, the Confederation of British Industry (CBI) and the Institute of Directors in Britain, multinational employers'/capitalist organizations such as the European Round Table (ERT) and mixed public/private/state/employer/multinational organisations such as the Partnership for Educational Revitalization in the Americas (PREAL), which, in its own words, 'is a partnership of public and private organizations' (PREAL, 2004).

It is not only the WTO and its GATS that are levers for liberalization of trade in services. The World Bank, international monetary credit rating agencies and the Organisation for Economic and Cultural Development (OECD) are also significant bodies. In addition, there are hemispheric/regional free-trade agreements such as the North American Free Trade

Agreement (NAFTA), the Free Trade Area of the Americas (FTAA), the Common Market of the South (MERCOSUR) and the European Union (EU). There are/have been, however, many similar regional and bilateral measures and mechanisms.

Sometimes, as noted by Shugurensky and Davidson-Harden (2003) and Davidson-Harden below, 'the going gets tough' for those promulgating free trade in services. There is opposition, from trade unions, social movements, political parties and other organizations and groups—including some governments. One plan was the so-called Bolkestein Directive, the EU's draft services directive seeking to open up trade in services. The draft directive sought to expose almost all services to market-based competition. Though public-education services were specifically excluded, the draft directive would have applied to 'peripheral' services supplied to schools and, like the GATS, it was unclear where the line between public and private services would be drawn.

Under the 'country of origin' principle, a company providing services would follow the rules and laws of the country in which it was based or 'established', rather than the country in which the service was provided. An education multinational from the United States could, for example, 'establish' itself in Latvia, simply by registering its presence there. It would then be able to trade in the rest of the EU, such as Britain, while conforming only to Latvian law on matters such as health and safety, employees' rights or environmental protection. Latvia, not the country where the service was provided, would be expected to send inspectors to ensure compliance with its laws.

Critics say the draft directive would encourage 'social dumping' since companies would have an incentive to opt for establishment in the least regulated EU member requiring the lowest standards. The directive 'would have been quite a blow to national level regulation, as it would tend to make services available in the least regulated way, rather than bringing all services operators up to best standards' (Malins, 2005). However, the current EU Internal Market Commissioner, Charlie McCreevy, says he is committed to re-introducing the directive in some form during his five-year term, which ends in 2009. With 70% of economic activity in Europe being in services, 'you don't have to have a degree in economics to know that if you can open up the services market you're going to have an impact on economic activity and we need increased economic activity in the EU' (McCreevy, cited in McLauchlin, 2005).

Part 2. Methodology: The Context: The ILO Report on Workers' Socio-economic Securities

This article develops from research that I conducted in 2004-2005 for the International Labour Organization (ILO), investigating the impacts of the neoliberalization of education on what the ILO terms 'workers' socio-economic securities'.[10] The focus of the ILO report on workers' socio economic securities was on 'What kinds of control are being imposed on workers in social services, and on the populations needing services?' My particular responsibility was the contributory report on schooling and further education. Other parallel contributory reports focus on: higher education; the prison service; pensions; public employment services; labour market training; health services (including mental health services and nursing home provision); criminal care services (particularly prisons); and care work services. Various contributory reports for the ILO report examined these impacts worldwide, each commissioning and drawing on a number of country case studies, as is common with ILO reports and reports of other international organizations such as the World Bank and the WTO.

The Research Methodology for This Article

And that is what I did. For the schooling and further education report as a whole, I sought and commissioned eleven country case studies (or, in one case, Latin America, a continental case study), whose authors included academics and also trade union-elected officials or appointed officials. (Trade union writers collabourated in the England and Wales, Canada and Spain case studies.)

The methodologies of the eleven case studies commissioned for the schooling report included literature searches and, in some cases, interviews with trade union researchers and officials. In addition, I also interviewed two national trade union officials from Spain and two from England and Wales, and leading officials from organizations that speak/act on behalf of trade unions and workers' rights – the ILO, Education International, and the Public Services International.

Some of the literature search data come from trade union sources, both national and international, some from official government reports, some from contemporary reports (such as newspaper reports and *Hansard*, the official report of the House of Commons debates in the United Kingdom), and some, also, from pro-neoliberal world organizations such as the World Bank and the WTO.

There are good reasons for using these sources in addition to the normal academic journal articles and books cited in academic journal articles.

The first reason is that the information is not available from books and academic journal articles. The ILO requested, and is working on, collecting and establishing a strictly up-to-date, state-of-the-art report on what is happening to workers' securities, a report that is more contemporary than what is commonly the one or two years' out-of-datedness associated with book and journal articles. The ILO is gathering state-of-the-art information about the impacts of neoliberal policy on workers' rights, pay and conditions. That is why it has commissioned the various sectoral case studies.

The second reason for using this data, in particular data derived from trade union and trade union-friendly sources, is a recognition that research is not neutral. I will elabourate upon this in more detail.

Research for Social Justice

This research is clearly *engaged* or *committed research,* described by Sikes (in Griffiths, 1998, p. x) as 'research for social justice'. This research is 'about taking sides and getting change in education through educational research' (Griffiths, 1998, p. 3). I am aware of the ideological impetus that led the ILO to conduct this research, and for me to participate in it. Hence I would hope to make this article, and the data collection and its interpretation, as 'fireproof', as 'objective' as possible.

As Connolly notes:

> There is little point in producing research reports that are clearly regarded as biased and/or partisan. If the effectiveness of ... research is in its ability to convince others of the significance of the issues raised, then there is a need to provide research evidence that is generally acceptable among academics, policy-makers and practitioners. (Connolly, 2001, p. 167)

I agree with Phillips that

> what is crucial for the objectivity of any inquiry—whether it is qualitative or quantitative—is the critical spirit in which it has been carried out ... Objectivity is the label—the 'stamp of approval'—that is used for inquiries that are at one end of the continuum; they are inquiries that are prized because of the great care and responsiveness to criticism with which they have been carried out. (Phillips, 1993, p. 71)

Hence, for this article I have welcomed some of the reviewers' comments, those guided by an impetus to secure greater objectivity.[11] I have therefore attempted to follow the *procedural objectivity*—that is, examining extant data—reports, books, journal and press articles—not only from organizations and writers that would commonly be described as 'pro-worker/pro-trade union rights', but also those from organisations and individuals for whom the primary foci are 'efficiency', 'neoliberalisation' and/or 'profit'. Hence I have attempted procedural objectivity. For Eisner (1993) this is distinguished by 'using a method that eliminates, or aspires to eliminate, the scope for personal judgement. One of the most common examples of such a method is the objectively scored achievement test' (Eisner, 1993, pp. 50-51).

Clearly such a test is not possible in this case or type of study, which is, primarily a review of available up-to-date data. But examining, and reporting data deriving from, and exhibiting, a variety of ideological perspectives would seem to be procedurally objective.

This procedure does not, however, assume the possibility of *ontological objectivity* through which to obtain 'an undistorted view of reality', a 'pristine unmediated grasp of the world as it is' (Eisner, 1993, pp. 50, 52). I am happy to settle, in this article, for as much procedural objectivity as possible, recognizing that, in the 'clash of ideas', with the 'culture wars' over past, current, and desired future social and educational systems and regimes of workers' rights and powers, oppositional socialist and Marxist analyses, such as my own, do not command much space within either the press or high status academic educational journals.

This research is not only 'committed' research; it has a particular commitment – to social justice, and, within the context of the ILO study and this article, to workers' rights. In 'the continuing and often raging debate about bias, objectivity, positivism and the production of useful knowledge' (Griffiths, 1998, p. 7), my 'pre-eminent commitment' is 'to the fundamental principles of social justice, equality and participatory democracy' (Troyna and Carrington, 1989, p. 208). It is within the tradition of emancipatory or critical research (see, for example, Hood et al., 1999; Connolly, 2001, p. 166; Rose and Grosvenor, 2001).

This research can be located within discussions about the desirability and possibility of 'neutral' research. On the one hand, there are the self-styled 'methodological purists'[12] who claim that facts can be value-free, and they question the objectivity of committed research.

Hammersley maintains that the politicization of social research is not only misguided, but inherently dangerous (cited in Connolly, 2001, pp. 164-165), erasing 'the distinction between political struggle and academic discussion ... it turns sociology into a political morality play' (Hammersley, 2000, p. 149).

Criticizing the 'methodological purists', Griffiths (1998, pp. 44-64) and Connolly (2001, pp. 166-167) summarize and comment on these debates.[13] In summary, their comments are threefold.

First, both Connolly and Griffiths note that all research is political—the very choice of research question or problem is a political choice, as is the selection of whose voices and interests are expressed or likely to be expressed.

Second, they both suggest that the likely political effects of research have to be considered, for example, the impact on groups that are discriminated against, oppressed and exploited. Will it, or is it likely to, entrench the existing relations of social/economic/political domination and subordination?

Third, Griffiths goes on to argue, against the methodological purists, that the value-laden nature of all facts and information is 'not helpfully described as "bias", since the term "bias" depends on the possibility of there being a neutral view ... [hence] "perspective" is a better description than "bias" since knowledge of human beings gets its meaning from the value system of the knowers' (Griffiths, 1998, p. 46).

Griffiths then (1998) proceeds to argue the merits of postmodernist and poststructuralist approaches to social research. However, my own research position is not poststructuralist or postmodernist. I adhere to and attempt to develop the structuralist neo-Marxist analysis and theory (for example in Hill, 1989, 2001, 2005a, c, 2006d). Griffith's first two points span the breadth of critical and social justice research perspectives, from poststructuralist to Marxist. However, in relation to her third point, my own research would insist on locating the 'value systems of the knowers' within their 'positions of domination and subordination that characterize social relations' (Connolly, 1992, p. 137).

This is my justification for using, *inter alia*, documents produced by trade unions and national and international organizations and individuals sympathetic to maintaining and extending labour rights, and interviews/discussions with national trade union officials and representatives from a number of countries and with global headquarters officials from various international organizations sympathetic to 'the cause(s) of labour'.

To repeat, I have interrogated their responses in the light of official publications from neoliberalizing governments and international organizations. But I do not suffer from the delusion of ontological objectivity.

Part 3. Impacts of Neoliberalization of Schooling on Workers' Pay, Conditions and Securities

In this section of the article it is suggested that neoliberalization of education has a major effect in many countries on the pay, rights and conditions of education and education support workers. The labour of academic and academic support staff is becoming both more proletarianized and more subservient to the interests of capital.

Workers' Rights and Conditions

Job security is defined by the International Labour Organization as: 'A niche designated as an occupation or "career", the opportunity to develop a sense of occupation' (ILO, 2002). Case studies of schooling and further education throughout the globe indicate some effects on the securities of education service workers.

Globally, where neoliberalism has triumphed in education, common results have been increased casualization of academic labour, increased proletarianization, increased pay and conditions differentials within education sectors, pay cuts, increased intensification of labour, with larger classes, and decreased autonomy for school and college teachers over curriculum and pedagogy, accompanying increases in levels of surveillance, monitoring and report-writing, and accompanying increased levels of stress. There is also the curtailment of trade union rights and the suppression of critical thinking (Hill, 2001, 2004b).[14]

Radical change, or restructuring, of an education institution commonly means either fewer and/or different teachers, professional staff, and support workers. This means lay-offs, forced early retirements, or major retraining and reassignment, as in the closure of institutions deemed ineffective or failing; and the radical alteration of the mission and production function of education institutions. This means radically altering who the teachers are, how they behave, the way they are organised, and the way they work and are compensated (Johnstone et al., 1998).

There is also the trend to individualisation of workers' pay, with performance-related pay (PRP) bonuses for some—for example, for teachers in England and Wales. Globally, the World Bank insists on PRP in some cases, as a condition for loans. In Brazil it insisted on the introduction of an additional remuneration for federal higher institution teaching personnel based on individual performance (Siqueira, 2005). As will be seen below, this has implications for trade union rights and powers.

The common neoliberal diagnosis of education identifies teachers and their traditional protections as the obstacle to market-based efficiencies. In its future scenario, education would become less dependent upon teachers' skills.

Casualisation, Temporary Contracts and the Trend to a Part-time Workforce

One way that teachers as workers are kept in line is through job insecurity. Staff on fixed-term contracts have the least job security in the sector, and often have inferior terms and conditions to their permanent colleagues. Fixed-term contracts: leave many staff feeling very exposed and undervalued; lead to staff having difficulty finding things such as loans, mortgages and other financial benefits; lead to significant recruitment and retention problems in the sector; are discriminatory (as their use disproportionately affects women, black and other minority groups of workers); destroy the possibility of career progression as individuals find themselves stuck on the lowest pay grades on a succession of short-term, poorly funded projects which offer no room for staff development; and mean staff coming to the end of contracts must inevitably spend time applying for funding or other posts (AUT, 2004).

Part-time staff members' employment arrangements usually do not allow them to spend time on research or the administration of the campus or the department. Finally, most part-time workers are hourly paid rather than on permanent fractional contracts and hence have no job security other than a commonly agreed contract for the year ahead. Private institutions are in the vanguard of the trends examined here. They tend to provide less employment security, particularly in low-ranking institutions and in countries where tenure is regulated through civil-service rules.

The increasing competition between public/not-for-profit and for-profit institutions risks enhancing this trend to the detriment of the labour conditions of the teaching and support staff. In addition, the status/rank of an institution seems to be related to its number of part-time faculty members.

According to a survey carried out by the United States Department of Education, the percentage of part-time work within all faculty at American community colleges rose from 22 per cent in 1970 to 60 per cent in 2001 (Longmate and Cosco, 2002, p. B14).

The increase in part-time teaching has been accompanied by a clear trend towards a 'feminization' of part-time work. In the United States, whereas the proportion of women among all full-time faculty members (in further/community education and in higher education) had reached 36 per cent in 1998, the proportion they made up of all part-time instructors was, at 47.9 per cent, significantly higher (see Wilson 2001, p. A14).

The increase in the proportion of part-time and, especially hourly paid, staff means that more and more of the administrative workload (such as course leadership, module leadership, membership of faculty and of university committees and the increasingly onerous writing up of annual reports, such as the increasingly monitored annual course reviews, and the myriad of other documents that course leaders need to respond to and write) is falling on fewer and fewer shoulders. This is a real intensification of the work of the full-time workers.

Unqualified Teachers

In a number of states, there is a growth in the numbers of uncertified teachers. McLaren et al. (2004, p. 1) comment that 'In California more than 47,000 uncertified teachers are teaching in its public schools ... in Baltimore… over one third of the school district's teachers do not hold full teaching credentials'. Substitutability is one of the defining characteristics of deprofessionalisation, or proletarianisation.

Not only is there a growth in uncertified teachers, there is also an acceptance that school head teachers/principals do not need teaching experience. In September 2002, in England and Wales, David Miliband (then Schools Minister) indicated that business leaders running school federations did not need teaching qualifications (Kelly, 2002).

Pay and Conditions

A key element of capital's plans for education is to cut its labour costs. For this, a deregulated labour market is essential—with schools and colleges able to set their own pay scales and sets of conditions—busting national trade union agreements and weakening union powers to protect their workforces.

In England and Wales, under the 2002 Education Act around 1000 schools are to be given the freedom to vary the curriculum and change teachers' pay and conditions. Furthermore, in the new and rapidly growing 'academies' sector of secondary schools in England and Wales (publicly funded independent schools with voluntary or private-sector sponsors and control), statutory pay and conditions arrangements do not apply. The government intends to have at least 200 academies established or in the pipeline by 2010 (Her Majesty's Government, 2005, Chapter 2, Summary).

These schools can set their own pay rates and conditions of service for teachers, a considerable breach of national pay and conditions. These ideas have been relaunched and extended in New Labour's Education

White Paper of October 2005 (Her Majesty's Government, 2005) (see Rikowski, 2005b, for an analysis). Para 2.16 of the White Paper states that the proposed 'Self-governing Trust schools' could have the power and 'freedoms over pay and conditions, where the Trust can demonstrate that these will raise standards'.

These policy developments could, potentially, destroy national pay bargaining in England. With respect to income security, the experience in England and Wales following the widespread contracting out of school meals, school cleaning and other services to schools and colleges in the 1980s led to severe deterioration of pay and conditions for thousands of low-paid, mainly women, workers. This can be seen in the stark differences within the 'two-tier workforce'. The pay (and rights and conditions) of those workers (such as cleaning and catering workers) who remain on public sector pay and conditions is, as the British trade union UNISON established, considerably superior to those of workers doing the same jobs who are on contracted-out, non-public sector pay and conditions.[15]

The Thatcher Government paved the way for contracting out in 1983 by denouncing ILO Convention No. 94 and repealing the Fair Wages Resolution, in place since 1891. It was thought that in labour-intensive public services, access to a cut-price workforce would be essential to attracting private bids. A downward spiral of pay and conditions followed for staff, mainly women, who were already the lowest paid in schools (Wing, 2003).

Compulsory competitive tendering forced local authorities to compete on the basis of cost. Contracts were often retained in house, but with worse pay and conditions. A survey for the Department of the Environment reported that 15% of authorities had withdrawn bonus schemes, 7% had cut wages, 18% had changed sick-pay arrangements and 12% had cut holiday entitlements. Workforce reduction and rearranged hours were the most common response to competition, with manual staff bearing the brunt of changes in working methods, pay and conditions (Walsh and Davis, 1993).

Research by the UNISON public-services trade union indicated that privatisation resulted in lower pay and that protection for staff transferring from the public sector contrasted with the inferior pay and conditions for recruits. Wing (2003, p. 4) suggests that gender had re-emerged as an issue, and that there had been no policy appraisal of the gender impact of the various policies that had led to the contracting out of thousands of jobs held by women.

UNISON established a Best Value Intelligence Unit and surveyed

190 private contracts in 2001. Comparisons were difficult as new staff in white collar jobs were often on personal contracts, but the findings suggest that basic pay in 62% of contracts had worsened, mainly affecting ancillary staff.

For school meals contracts, in Nottinghamshire, for example, pay for new staff was £4.60 an hour for 34 weeks as opposed to £4.80 an hour for 38 weeks paid to transferred staff. Conditions of service had also worsened for new starters: 73% had less leave, 58% had worse sick pay arrangements, 51% had inferior pensions, 44% had lost unsocial hours' payments and 44% reported less job security (UNISON, 2002, p. 6).

In the United States[16] a survey of 500 school districts found average teacher salary had declined by nearly 2% over the past ten years (Gewertz, 2004). Anijar and Gabbard also report on charter schools. These are state funded schools that have been handed over to private control, typically to an 'edubusiness' corporation, such as Edison Schools. Edison Schools describes charter schools as

> independently operated public schools that must meet the same academic requirements as traditional public schools but are free from most of the bureaucratic and regulatory constraints of their traditional counterparts. The charter establishing each such school is a performance contract detailing the school's mission, programme, goals, students served, and ways to measure success. A charter school is accountable to its sponsor –usually a university, state board, or local board. (Edison Schools, 2005)

Anijar and Gabbard (2004) report that they pay teachers less. According to the 1999-2000 Schools and Staffing Survey in the United States (SASS), 41% of charter-school teachers had total yearly earnings under $30,000 (compared with 20% in regular public schools). Research suggests that teachers choose charter schools for reasons such as working with like-minded colleagues in innovative educational settings, but it is difficult to create this environment when teacher turnover exceeds 35% (compared with about 15% in regular public schools; Nelson et al., 2003, p. 9).

In Pakistan [17], the workforce employed in private schools and colleges faces a 'corporate' rather than a 'social' employer. The profit-seeking private schools overwhelmingly ignore workers' rights, and private-sector employment in Pakistan lacks the international benchmarks of workers' socio-economic security. Private schools offer 35-80% less salary while job security and career prospectus are the missing elements in mostly short-term/temporary assignments. Pensions, medical and other facilities and group insurance, and so on are not taken care of by most of the schools in the private sector.

The primary-school teacher in public sector gets on average Rs. 4,000 per month while secondary-school teachers' average pay is Rs. 8,000 (Mukhtar, 2004, 2006). The private sector has worsened teaching standards by offering sub-standard salaries which are, on average, Rs. 2,500 for primary- and Rs. 5,000 for secondary-school teachers (Haq, 2004). About 16% of the private-school teachers are part-time workers.

Low-Income Countries

Education International, the international organization of education trade unions, notes and decries the fact that teacher salary levels in low-income countries are being determined by international aid agencies (Education International, 2003). The Fast Track Initiative (FTI), adopted in April 2002 by the World Bank and other agencies, included conditions attached to extra financial support. The World Bank (2005) states that 'the FTI is open to all low-income countries demonstrating serious intent toward achieving universal primary completion. As of June 2005 ... fifteen countries have had their education plans endorsed, and are receiving support'. The low-income countries [18] receive aid to help them achieve 'education for all', salient features of which are the achievement of universal primary schooling by 2015, and have moved towards gender parity. One condition is that teachers' pay will not be higher than 3.5 times the country's GNP per capita.

This condition undermines core labour standards, such as the right to collective bargaining. This rate might be considered quite high in industrialised countries: in Denmark for example, the GNP per capita is $27,950. This means that teachers' average salary would be $97,825! In reality, teachers' average salary in Denmark is struggling to reach 1.2 times GNP per capita. However, this is not the case in developing countries. In Niger, the GNP per capita reaches $170 and a teacher's average annual salary $1,630, representing 9.6 times the GNP per capita. In order to take advantage of the Fast Track financing initiative from the World Bank, Niger's government would have to reduce, in theory, teachers' salaries by 63 per cent. In the view of Education International, this is both unrealistic and unacceptable (Education International, 2003, p. 2).

Casualized Labour

With respect to further education colleges, prior to 1993, they were under the control of local government. Lecturers' pay and conditions were bargained nationally. Incorporation, laid down in the Further and Higher Education Act 1992, established colleges as publicly funded independent bodies. In England and Wales since 1993 there has been a growth in part-time staff, a reduction in teaching hours for students and an increased use of temporary and agency staff. In 1995-1996, the funding council estimated that 55 per cent of all college staff and 39 per cent of teaching staff worked part-time. This compares with a National Association of Teachers in Further and Higher Education (NATFHE) estimate of 15 per cent part-time working prior to incorporation.

As well as more part-time employment the post-incorporation college sector has made greater use of temporary staff. Using the census returns to the funding council 1994-95, NATFHE estimated that 42 per cent of staff employed for more than 15 hours per week had temporary contracts. This compared with a national average across all sectors of 9% (House of Commons, 1998, p. 287). It was suggested that the use of agency staff avoided contractual obligations. NATFHE cited an example where a number of colleges had dismissed their part-time lecturers and re-employed them through a third-party provider. Many were on lower pay, self-employed and responsible for their own professional indemnity (House of Commons, 1998, p. 293). Skill-reproduction security refers to the existence of opportunities to gain and retain skills, through innovative means as well as apprenticeships and employment training. This refers to the opportunity to go on training courses to develop new skills.

As commented above in connection with the decline in employment securities, workers on fixed-term temporary contracts and those on hourly paid contracts have their career progression damaged. Managements, whether public or private, are less willing to pay for in-service training for staff they may not re-employ. As Lewis (2004a) puts it, 'It's kind of obvious that casualization will lead to a training deficit. From the support staff point of view and looking at say, the school meals service, contracting out (or rather the competitive process) has led to demanning and deskilling'. She continues, 'most catering assistants work 10-15 hours a week and employers will not invest in them. They are just seen as units of labour'.

In England and Wales, Christine Lewis (2004b) points out that the increased use of casual staff in further education colleges impacts on the quality of the service as 'casual staff are disconnected from wider college matters, curriculum issues, student welfare and extra-curricular activities'.

Lewis cites the government body, the Further Education Development Agency (FEDA), which expressed concern that not all colleges took the opportunity to apply the full range of development opportunities to part-time staff (House of Commons, 1999, p. 291). FEDA continued,

> Clearly, this can threaten the quality of contribution that part-time staff can make. FEDA stated that 'the evidence [of part-time staff] shows that not all colleges are taking the opportunity to apply, for example, the full range of staff development opportunities, induction arrangements, briefing arrangements, that would be necessary to confirm that the quality of the input was as high as it could be. (House of Commons, 1999, p. 291)

Similar concerns are expressed in different countries. In Australia, for example, Federal Technical and Further Education (TAFE) President Pat Forward also comments on the fact that casual teachers 'have no capacity to plan their futures. They have reduced access to professional development, reduced capacity to form collegial relationships with their fellow teachers and little if no opportunity to participate in the community life of their workplace' (New South Wales Teachers Federation, 2004; see also Hester, 1998). Temporary and agency staff are likely to be even more disadvantaged.

In privatized schools, managements and owners tend to be less likely to bear the costs of in-service training (or, indeed, of other benefits) than in the publicly run schools. In Pakistan, for example, Mukhtar (2004, 2006) comments that 'there is no concept of on the job-training and retirement benefits in private schools' (Haq, 1994, cited in Mukhtar, 2004, 2006).

Mukhtar continues by asserting that 'private schools as employers do not pay attention to job security, on the job training, better working conditions and long term growth options etc. since they are not sure of the tenure of such their employees'.

Teachers' Work: Intensification, Surveillance and Stress

The common trend towards casualization of the labour conditions of higher education staff and the increased enrolment and class sizes has led to an intensification of work. This is justified through campaigns of vilification.

Siqueira (2005) reports that in Brazil, the Cardoso government of the mid- 1990s launched, using the media, a renewed and stronger campaign against civil servants, unions and retired public employees.

Some of the usual terms used by his government to refer to these groups were: sluggish, negligent, agitators, old-fashioned, unpatriotic, selfish and lazy. This is part of the global neoliberal critique of public-service workers for being expensive self-interested workers who have 'captured' the professions with their restrictive and expensive practices. In Britain, Stephen Ball (1990, p. 22) has called this denigration 'a discourse of derision'. In some right-wing newspapers, such as the *Daily Mail* in Britain, it is more like a 'discourse of hate'.

This 'new culture' of 'New Public Managerialism' entails a complementary and increasing governance of management bodies on the basis of mistrust targeted at both students and staff, resulting in an overkill of bureaucratic regimes of control and regulation. Formal assessment exercises require teachers to produce explicit 'learning aims and outcomes'. Students have become more subject to accountancy versions of educational values.

With regard to the conception of 'entrepreneurial management', Alexiadou argues this 'tougher' managerial discourse has direct implications for the work of educators: 'There is no attempt here to balance issues of professional autonomy with issues of control. "Trust" in teachers' professionalism is totally displaced by performativity' (Alexiadou, 2001, p. 429).

Soon after the abolition of the national negotiating machinery, the Education Reform Act of 1988 introduced local management of schools (LMS). Between 1994 and 2000, primary-school teachers' hours increased by 8 per cent and secondary teachers' hours by 5 per cent. Stress is now the main health and safety concern in schools; 82 per cent of school safety representatives cite it as a cause for concern in their school (TUC, 2000). Teachers are the most stressed occupational group, with over 40 per cent of teachers reporting high stress levels (Health and Safety Executive, 2000).

Education workers face increasing surveillance, while both their workload and its meaninglessness increase:

The consequences in terms of lowered morale of schoolteachers and university lecturers between 1992 and today are clearly measurable. In 1992 only 10 per cent of teachers and lecturers thought that they had to 'work at high speed all or most of the time', compared with 18 per cent for other occupations. By the end of the decade this position was reversed (33 per cent vs. 25 per cent), with teachers and lecturers experiencing a hefty rise in stress. Over the same period, the proportion of teachers who were 'dissatisfied with their job' more than doubled from 6 to 13 per cent. (Green, 2002, 16, cited in Beckman and Cooper, 2004)

There have been fewer resources for student-teacher contact, and thus greater pressure to standardise curricula and assessment criteria.[19] This is a form of loss of autonomy, one of the aspects of proletarianization of higher education work forces.

In sum, there has been increased managerialization of schooling and intensification of teachers' work, with 'teachers ...driven to burnout' (Whitty, 1997, p.305), and the proletarianization of teachers in schools and in further, higher and teacher education (Allen, 1999).

Trade Union Rights

Protection of the collective voice in the labour market, through independent trade unions and employer associations and other bodies able to represent the interests of workers and working communities, is one of the job securities identified by the ILO (2002).

This is under attack in some states through a number of means. Three of these are: the growth in individually negotiated/awarded performance related pay (PRP), the removal of trade union pay negotiating rights, and decentralization/deregulation.

PRP is being introduced in various states, undermining the collective bargaining function of trade unions. The current trend to introduce PRP in higher education, a trend that can be observed all over the world, is challenging the established structure of collective bargaining. This is a form of individual pay bargaining.

This is part of the deregulation agenda of neoliberal capital, to undermine nationally agreed pay and conditions, and to replace them with locally negotiated agreements. Furthermore, the decentralization of control and the autonomy of higher education institutions weaken the ability of unions to act.

Torres et al. (2004, pp. 3-4) note that decentralization erodes the bargaining power of teachers' unions. The transfer of negotiations from the national to the provincial or local level, such as, in England and Wales, school level or university level, can lead to different pay scales. Unions oppose this because 'it strikes at the heart of professional equity, under which teachers having similar qualifications can expect the same pay and conditions at any education institution of the same level across the country'. This weakens unions! Without strong unions, the pay and working conditions of average teachers/lecturers will further deteriorate, except for the few who receive PRP enhancements or other 'merit rewards', or work in a high paying 'independent state school', a self-governing Trust school promised in the 2005 White Paper on Education (Her Majesty's Government, 2005).

An example of the withdrawal of trade union pay negotiating rights can be found in England and Wales. Prior to 1988, Local Education Authorities (LEAs) in England and Wales had financial and managerial responsibility for schools and national collective bargaining machinery determined teachers' pay and conditions of employment. However, the Secretary of State for Education and Skills is, under the 1991 School Teachers' Pay and Conditions Act, now able to determine teachers' pay rates, the rules of the teachers' pay structure and provisions on conditions of service issues, such as working time. The Secretary of State's decisions are legally binding and set out in the statutory school teachers' pay and conditions document.

Part 4: Conclusion: Resistance and Restraints

Neoliberal developments in education policy are widely presented as inevitable, incontestable and irreversible. As Roberto Leher puts it:

> The structural adjustment that dismantles the precarious Social State is done in the name of globalization, a process presented as relentless and irresistible, against which nothing can be done, except fitting in, even though it may result in exponential unemployment, wild privatizations, exchange crisis, increasing taxes and destruction of labour rights. (Leher, 2004)

This article began by suggesting that the neoliberalization of education decreases in workers' pay, rights and conditions. It was argued that the reasons for education's massive expansion since the 1960s and 1970s are located in capital's ongoing drive for the extraction of more and more surplus value.

But there is resistance, there are spaces, disarticulations, and contradictions. And there are always awakenings, sometimes minor, sometimes major, that the material conditions of existence—for teacher educators, teachers, students, and workers and families more widely—simply do not match or recognize the validity of neoliberal (or other) capitalist discourse and policy.

Restraints on Neoliberal Policy

There are three restraining forces on the activities of neoliberal capitalism—infrastructural, consumer-related regulation, and legitimation. The first is the need for an educational, social, transport, welfare, housing, and so forth, infrastructure to enable workers to get to work, to be trained for different levels of the workforce and to be relatively fit and healthy. This restraint, though, is fairly minimal. It is a basic needs provision that says nothing, has no implications at all for equality in society or in education.

The second restraint is consumer dissatisfaction and consumer protection in the form of regulations. These, and inspectors of various sorts, are criticized as 'red tape' and as bureaucrats. Yet without regulation and enforcement in Britain, BSE ('mad cow disease' and foot-and-mouth disease have flourished and been exported to continental Europe. State regulation operates against the freedom of capitalism to do as it pleases. Hence Conservative Party policy in England and Wales in 2005 on schools is to deregulate them, to 'set them free', to allow them to charge what they want and run their own affairs. New Labour's policy in 2005 is similar though not, as yet, so extensive. Under current New Labour plans, not all schools are to be deregulated. (But see Rikowski, 2005.) This 'regulatory' model, of the state regulating standards (e.g. through Ofsted, Oftel, Ofgas, Ofwat, the Financial Services Commission, the Health and Safety Commission and the Rail Regulatory Body—regulatory bodies for various services and industries such as, respectively, education, water and sewage, electricity, finance, employment, railways), can be weak or strong. It can demand only basic standards (perhaps failing to inspect regularly) or it can demand strong controls, including controls over profits. (It is interesting that some of the most vigorously enforced standards are those in education—testimony perhaps to the crucial nature of the state apparatus of schooling.)

The third restraint is that capital (and the political parties they fund and influence) needs to persuade the people that neoliberalism—competition, privatisation, poorer standards of public services, greater inequalities between rich and poor—are legitimate. If not, there is a delegitimation crisis and government and the existing system are seen through as grossly unfair and inhumane. And people demonstrate. And/or elect alternatives. And/or revolt.

To stop this delegitimation happening, to ensure that the majority of the population consider that the government and the economic system of private monopoly ownership are legitimate, the state uses the ideological state apparatuses such as schools and colleges (see Althusser, 1971; Hill, 2001) to 'naturalize' capitalism—to make the existing status quo seem 'only natural'.

Increasingly, across Britain and more widely (currently most spectacularly in Venezuela [20]), neoliberal policy on education (and in other sectors) is being challenged—intellectually, electorally, organizationally—and in the streets.

Notes

1. This is explained and developed in the methodology section of this article.
2. These are beyond the remit of this article, but are addressed, *inter alia*, in Hill, 2004a, b, 2005, 2006a, b; Hill et al., 2005.
3. This is taken from Hill, 2004a, para 4. It is, of course, a common Marxist analysis.
4. There are very many apologia for neoliberalization, both by academics (such as Tooley, 1999, 2000, 2001) and by the organisations of international capital

themselves. See, for example, International Chamber of Commerce, 1999; International Finance Corporation, 2001; World Trade Organization, 2003a, b, c; World Bank Group, 2004.

5. For a fuller analysis, see Hatcher, 2003, 2005a; Hill, 2003, 2004a, b, 2006a.
6. These functions are well established in Marxist analysis. For example, see Althusser, 1971; Bowles and Gintis, 1976; Bourdieu and Passeron, 1977; Harris, 1982; Hill, 1989, 2001, 2005b, Rikowski, 2002a.
7. Hatcher first developed this analysis of this tripartite plan of capital. In 2001 he wrote of

   an agenda for that growing sector of the economy which sees the school system itself as a new market for profit. Business is driven to seek new potential markets, and the public sector, including education, is seen as one of the few major areas still left to colonise. So we can identify three related agendas—a business agenda for what the school system should produce, an agenda for how it should do it, and an agenda for what business itself should do within the school system. (Hatcher, 2001)

   See also Rikowski, 2001, 2002 b, c; Shugarensky and Davidson-Harden, 2003, for evidence of this third plan of capital.
8. I develop this further in Hill, 2005 and Hill et al, 2005.
9. See, for example, Coates, 2001; Delgado-Ramos and Saxe-Fernandez, 2005; Halimi, 2004; Hirtt, 2004; Pilger, 2002; Puiggros, 2002; Robertson et al, 2002; Robertson and Dale, 2003. For an explanation of the GATS and its powers and articles, see Devidal, 2004; Hill, 2005; Grieshaber-Otto, 2002; Rikowski, 2003; Shugurensky and Davidson- Harden, 2003.
10. This research is due to be published as Rosskam, 2005. More specifically, the project is exploring the following questions:
    1. What are the mechanisms leveraging the liberalization of social services? What roles are the international financial agencies playing? How do foreign firms enter the market for provision of services? What is the impact of GATS on these services?
    2. What is the impact on clients receiving services? Is equity improved orworsened as a result of liberalisation?
    3. What is the impact of liberalization on the quality of services?

       How are existing patterns and types of investment in health care, higher education, employment services, pension schemes, care work, and criminal care services influencing the seven forms of socio economic security for workers providing those services? (ILO, 2004)
11. As Kerlinger (1973) suggests:

    Objective methods of observation are those in which anyone following theprescribed rules will assign the same numerals to the objects and sets of objects as anyone else. An objective procedure is one in which agreement among observers is at a maximum. In variance terms, observer variance is at aminimum. This means that judgemental variance, the variance due to differences in judges' assignment of numerals to objects, is zero. (1973, p. 491, in Phillips, 1993, p. 70)

12. These include Foster, Gomm and Hammersley (e.g. Foster, 1990a, b, 1991; Hammersley, 1995, 1997, 1998, 2000; Foster et al., 1996; Foster & Hammersley, 1996; Hammersley's reply to his critics in Hammersley, 2001, and Patai, 2005). Critics of Hammersley's *Taking Sides in Social Research: Essays on partisanship and bias* (2000), with its demand for 'value-free' research, include Connolly, 2001; Delamont, 2001; Oliver, 2001.
13. See also Connolly, 1992; Troyna, 1994; Troyna and Carrington, 1989; Wright, 1990; Gillborn, 1995; Griffiths and Troyna, 1995; Mirza, 1995; Oliver, 2001.
14. These effects are regularly catalogued by Education International (http://www.ei-ie.org/)
(as well as by other organisations, such as the Public Service International, at www.psi.org, Public World, www.publicworld.org/., the Labour Research Department, at http://www.lrd.org.uk/default.php3?pagid=22, the Local Government Information Unit, at http://www.lgiu.gov.uk/
15. This was very much the stuff of trade union politics and campaigns in the 1980s in particular. I was engaged in these campaigns, first as the Leader of the Labour Group of Councillors on East Sussex County Council, which, like other Local Education Authorities, was privatizing school meals and school cleaning and catering services.
Second, I was involved as a regional (higher education) Chair of the lecturers' union, the National Association of Teachers in Further and Higher Education (NATFHE), which was active in anti-privatization campaigns. Third, I was Labour Parliamentary candidate (for Brighton Pavilion constituency) in the 1979 and 1987 general elections in Britain and active in local and national campaigns, for example, to protect and defend the pay and conditions of low paid public service workers. Anne Gray (2004) has examined casualisation and 'flexploitation' more recently in detail.
16. This derives from Anijar and Gabbard, 2004; Anijar-Appleton and Gabbard, 2006.
17. According to Mukhtar (2004, 2006).
18. As of June 2005, fifteen countries have had their education plans endorsed, and are receiving support from the FTI. They are: Burkina Faso, Ethiopia, Gambia, Ghana, Guinea, Guyana, Honduras, Madagascar, Mauritania, Moldova, Mozambique, Nicaragua, Niger, Vietnam and Yemen. The World Bank (2005) expects that '9 more countries will join FTI by the end of 2005, and an additional 36 countries by the end of 2007'. More information on the EFA-Fast Track Initiative is available online at www.worldbank.org/education/efafti. Rose (2003) also notes that in some countries, this stipulation should mean that teacher salaries will rise.
19. See, for example, Lipman, 2004; Hursh, 2005.
20. The striking success and popularity of President Hugo Chavez in Venezuela is widely reported in the liberal and left press internationally and regular coverage in Socialist and Marxist journals and magazines and weekly newspapers, worldwide (see also a more indepth analysis, Gott, 2005).

References

Alexiadou, N. (2001). Management Identities in Transition: A case study from further education, *Sociological Review*, 49(3), pp. 412-435.

Allen, M. (1999). Labour's Business Plan for Teachers, in M. Allen, C. Benn, C. Chitty, M. Cole, R. Hatcher, N. Hirrt and G. Rikowski, *New Labour's Education Policy*. London: Tufnell Press.

Althusser, L (1971). Ideology and State Apparatuses, in L. Althusser, *Lenin and Philosophy and Other Essays*. London: New Left Books.

Anijar, K. and Gabbard, D. (2004). USA Case Study written for D. Hill et al., Education Services Liberalization, in E. Rosskam (ed.) *Winners or Losers? Liberalizing public services*. Geneva: International Labour Organization. Unpublished.

Anijar-Appleton, K. and Gabbard, D. (2006) The USA, in D. Hill (ed.) *Globalisation/Neoliberalism/Education and Resistance*.Vol 4, *Rich Countries*. Brighton: Institute for Education Policy Studies.

Association of University Teachers (AUT) (2004). *Security Alert II – Ending the abuse of fixed-term contracts*. Available at: http://www.aut.org.uk/index.cfm?articleid=904.

Ball, S. (1990). *Politics and Policymaking in Education*. London: Routledge.

Beckmann, A. and Cooper, C. (2004). 'Globalization', the New Managerialism and Education: rethinking the purpose of education, *Journal for Critical Education Policy Studies*, 2(1). Online at: http://www.jceps.com/index.php?pageID =article&articleID=31.

Bourdieu, R. and Passeron, J. (1977). *Reproduction in Education, Society and Culture*. London: Sage.

Bowles, S. and Gintis, H. (1976). *Schooling in Capitalist America*. London: Routledge & Kegan Paul.

Bromley, S. (1999). Marxism and Globalization, in A. Gamble, D. Marsh and T. Tant (eds.) *Marxism and Social Science*. London: Macmillan.

Bruce Johnstone, D., Arora, A. and Experton, W. (1998). *The Financing and Management of Higher Education: A status report on worldwide reforms*.Washington, D.C.: World Bank, Departmental Working Paper. Available at: http://www-wds.worldbank.org.

Centre for Public Services (2003). *Mortgaging Our Children's Future*. Sheffield: Centre for Public Services. Available at: http://www.centre.public.org.uk/publications/briefings/mortgagingour-childrens-future-the-privatisat/.

Coates, B. (2001). GATS, in E. Bircham and J. Charlton (eds.) *Anti-Capitalism: A guide to the movement*. London: Bookmarks.

Cole, M. (1998). Globalization, Modernization and Competitiveness: A critique of the New Labour project in education, *International Studies in the Sociology of Education*, 8(3), pp. 315-332.

Cole, M. (2005). New Labour, Globalization and Social Justice: The role of education, in G. Fischman, P. McLaren, H. Sünker and C. Lankshear (eds.)

Global Conflicts, Critical Theories, and Radical Pedagogies. Lanham: Rowman & Littlefield.

Connolly, P. (1992). Playing it by the Rules; The politics of research in 'race' and education, *British Education Research Journal,* 18(2), pp.133-148.

Delamont, S. (2001). Review Symposium article on M. Hammersley (2000) 'Taking Sides in Social Research: Essays on partisanship and bias', *British Journal of Sociology of Education,* 22(1), pp. 157-160.

Delgado-Ramos, G. and Saxe-Fernandez, J. (2005). The World Bank and the Privatization of Public Education: A Mexican perspective, *Journal for Critical Education Policy Studies,* 3(1). Available at: http://www.jceps.com/index.php?pageID=article&articleID=44#sdfootnote10sym.

Devidal, P. (2004). Trading Away Human Rights? The GATS and the right to education, *Journal for Critical Education Policy Studies*, 2(2).

Education International (2003). Teacher Salary Levels Should not be Determined by International Aid Agencies, *Worlds of Education,* 2. Brussels: Education International.

Education International (2004). Decentralization in Norway, *Worlds of Education,* 7. Brussels: Education International.

Eisner, E. (1993). Objectivity in Educational Research, in M. Hammersley (ed.) *Educational Research: current issues*. London: Paul Chapman.

Foster, P. (1990a). *Policy and Practice in Multicultural and Anti-Racist Education*. London: Routledge.

Foster, P. (1990b). Cases not Proven: An evaluation of two studies of teacher racism, *British Education Research Journal,* 16(4), pp. 334-349.

Foster, P. (1991). Case Still not Proven: A reply to Cecile Wright, *British Education Research Journal,*19(2), pp.165-170.

Foster, P., Gomm, R. and Hammersley, M. (1996). *Constructing Educational Inequality.* London: Falmer Press.

Foster, P. and Hammersley, M. (1996). Researching Educational Inequality: A critique, *Research Intelligence,* 56, pp.18-20.

Gewertz, C. (2004). Schools Chiefs Lead the Way in Pay Trends, *Education Week*, 23 June.

Gillborn, D. (1995). *Racism and Antiracism in Real Schools.* Buckingham: Open University Press.

Gott, R. (2005). *The Bolivarian Revolution in Venezuela*. London: Verso Books.

Government of Pakistan (2002). *Education Sector Reforms Action Plan 2001-04.* Islamabad: Ministry of Education.

Government of Pakistan (2004). *Annual Report of the Federal Bureau of Statistics 2004.* Islamabad: Government of Pakistan.

Gray, A. (2004). *Unsocial Europe: Social protection or flexploitation?* London: Pluto.

Green, F. (2002). *Times Higher Education Supplement*, 12 April, p. 16.

Grieshaber-Otto, J. and Sanger, M. (2002). *Perilous Lessons: The impact of the WTO service agreement (GATS) on Canadian public education.* Ottowa: Canadian Centre for Policy Alternatives.

Griffiths, M. (1998). *Educational Research for Social Justice: Getting off the fence.* Buckingham: Open University Press.

Griffiths, M. and Troyna, B. (eds.) (1995). *Antiracism, Culture and Social Justice in Education* Stoke-on-Trent: Trentham.

Halimi, J. (2004). Road Map for Privatization: The great leap backwards, *Le Monde Diplomatique,* June. Online at: http://mondediplo.com/2004/06/08privatisationroadmap.

Hall, D. (2003). *Public Services Work! Information, insights and ideas for the future.* London: PSIRU, the public services international. Available at: http://www.worldpsi.org/Content/ContentGroups/English7/Publications1/En_Public_Services_Work.pdf. Also at: http://www.psiru.org/reports/2003-09-U-PSW.pdf.

Hammersley, M. (1995). *The Politics of Social Research.* London: Sage.

Hammersley, M. (1997). 'Educational Research and Teaching: A response to David Hargreaves' TTA lecture, *British Educational Research Journal,* 23(2), pp.141-161.

Hammersley, M. (2000). *Taking Sides in Social Research: Essays on partisanship and bias.* London: Routledge.

Hammersley, M. (2001). A Reply to Partisan Reviews, *British Journal of Sociology of Education,* 22(3), pp. 417-421.

Haq, R. (2004). Causal Link of Illiteracy with Poverty in Punjab, *Pakistan Development Review,* August.

Harris, K. (1982). *Teachers and Classes: A Marxist analysis.* London: Routledge & Kegan Paul.

Hatcher, R. (2001a). *The Business of Education: How business agendas drive Labour's policies for schools.* London: Socialist Educational Association.

Hatcher, R. (2001b). Getting Down to the Business: Schooling in the globalized economy, *Education and Social Justice,* 3(2), pp. 45-59.

Hatcher, R. (2003). Privatization and the US School System: Voucher programmes and Education Management Organisations. Paper presented at the ESRC Seminar 'Private Sector Participation in Public Sector Education', Institute of Education, London, 28 November 2003. Online at: http://www.socialistteacher.org/media/3B%20US%20privatisation%20%20paper%20FINAL.doc.

Hatcher, R. (2005a). Privatization and Sponsorship: The re-agenting of the school system in England, *Journal of Educational Policy.*

Hatcher, R. (2005b). E-mail discussion between Mike Cole, Richard Hatcher and Dave Hill. Unpublished.

Health and Safety Executive (2000). *The Scale of Occupational Stress: A further analysis of the impact of demographic factors and type of job.* Cardiff: Centre for Occupational and Health Psychology, School of Psychology, Cardiff University. Available at:http://www.hse.gov.uk/research/crr_pdf/2000/crr00311.pdf.

Her Majesty's Government (2005). *Higher Standards, Better Schools for All: More choice for parentsand pupils.* White Paper, Cm 6677, October. Norwich: Stationery Office.

Hester, N. (1998). *Precarious Employment and Working Time.*Australian Council of Trade Unions. Available at: http://www.actu.asn.au/public/news/1067407772_8147.html.

Hill, D. (1989). *Charge of the Right Brigade: The radical right's attack on teacher education.* Brighton, UK: Institute for Education Policy Studies. Onine at: http://www.ieps.org.uk.cwc.net/hill1989.pdf.

Hill, D. (2001). State Theory and the Neoliberal Reconstruction of Schooling and Teacher Education: a structuralist neo-Marxist critique of postmodernist, quasi-postmodernist, and culturalist neo-Marxist theory, *British Journal of Sociology of Education*, 22(1), pp. 137-157.

Hill, D. (2003). Global Neoliberalism, the Deformation of Education and Resistance, *Journal for Critical Education Policy Studies*, 1(1). Online at: http://www.jceps.com/index.php?pageID=articleandarticleID=7.

Hill, D. (2004a). Educational Perversion and Global Neoliberalism: A Marxist critique, *CulturalLogic: An electronic journal of Marxist theory and practice.* Available at: http://eserver.org/clogic/2004/2004.html.

Hill, D. (2004b). Books, Banks and Bullets: Controlling our minds—the global project of imperialistic and militaristic neoliberalism and its effect on education policy, *Policy Futures*, 2(3) (theme: Marxist futures in education). Online at: http://www.triangle.co.uk/pfie/.

Hill, D. (2005a). State Theory and the Neoliberal Reconstruction of Schooling and Teacher Education, in G. Fischman, P. McLaren, H. Sünker and C. Lankshear (eds.) *Critical Theories, Radical Pedagogies and Global Conflicts.* Boulder: Rowman & Littlefield.

Hill, D. (2005b). The WTO, the GATS and the Levers of Global (Neo-) Liberalization of Education, *Journal of Education Policy.*

Hill, D. (2005c). Six Theses on Class, Global Capital and Resistance by Education and Other Cultural Workers, in O.P. Moisio and J. Suoranta (eds.) *Education and the Spirit of Time.* Rotterdam: Sense Publishers.

Hill, D. (ed.) (2006a). *Globalization/Neoliberalism/Education and Resistance.* Vol. 4, *Rich Countries.* Brighton: Institute for Education Policy Studies.

Hill, D. (ed.) (2006b). *Globalization/Neoliberalism/Education and Resistance.* Vol. 3, *Low and Middle Income Countries.* Brighton: Institute for Education Policy Studies.

Hill, D. (2006c). *New Labour and Education: Ideology, (in)equality and capital.* London: Tufnell Press.

Hill, D. (2006d). Education, Class and Capital in the Epoch of Neoliberal Globalization, in A. Green and G. Rikowski (eds.) *Marxism and Education: Renewing dialogues.* Vol. 1, *Opening the Dialogue.* London: Palgrave Macmillan

Hill, D. with Anijar-Appleton, K., Davidson-Harden, A., Fawcett, B., Gabbard, D., Gindin, J., Kuehn, L., Lewis, C., Mukhtar, A., Pardinaz-Solis, R., Quiros,

B., Shugurensky, D., Smaller, H. and Templer, B. (2005). Education Services Liberalization, in E. Rosskam (ed.) *Winners or Losers? Liberalizing Public Services*. Geneva: International Labour Organization.

Hill, D., Fawcett, B. and Lewis, C. (2006). England and Wales in D. Hill (ed.) *Globalisation/Neoliberalism/Education and Resistance* Vol 4, *Rich Countries*. Brighton, UK: Institute for Education Policy Studies.

Hirtt, N. (2004). Three Axes of Merchandization, *European Educational Research Journal,* 3(2), pp. 442-453. Online at: http://www.wwwords.co.uk/eerj/

Hood, S., Mayall, B. and Oliver, S. (eds.). (1999). *Critical Issues in Social Research: Power and prejudice.* Buckingham: Open University Press.

House of Commons (1998). Select Committee on Education and Employment. Sixth Report. Session 1997-1998, in *Further Education,* Vol. 1 (London: HMSO). Online at: http://www.publications.parliament.uk/pa/cm199798/cmselect/cmeduemp/264/26413.htm.

Hursh, D. (2005). The Growth of High-stakes Testing in the USA: accountability, markets and the decline in educational equality, *British Education Research Journal,* 31(5), pp. 605-622.

International Chamber of Commerce (ICC) (1999). *The Benefits of Services Trade Liberalisation: Policy Statement.* Document 103/210. Paris: ICC. Online at http://www.iccwbo.org/home/case_for_the_globaleconomy/benefits_servicestrade_ liberalization.asp.

International Finance Corporation (IFC) (2001). *IFC and Education.* Online at: http://www.ifc.org/ar2001briefs/IFC_and_Education.pdf.

International Labour Organization (ILO) (2002). *Seven Forms of Security for Decent Work*. Geneva: ILO. Online at: http://www.ilo.org/public/english/protection/ses/index.htm.

International Labour Organization (ILO) (2004). *In Focus Programme on Socio-Economic Security.* Geneva: ILO. Available at: http://www.ilo.org/public/english/protection/ses/index.htm.

Kelly, J. (2002). Business People May Run State School Federations, *Financial Times*, 19 September, p. 4.

Kerlinger, F. (1973). *Foundations of Educational Research* (2nd edn). New York: Holt, Rinehart.

Ladd, H. (2002). *School Vouchers Don't Make The Grade*. Washington, D.C.: The Economic Policy Institute: Research and Ideas for Working People. Online at http://www.epinet.org/content.cfm/webfeatures_viewpoints_hl_testimony_200 30509.

Leher, R. (2004). A New Lord of Education? World Bank policy for peripheral capitalism, *Journal for Critical Education Policy Studies*, 2(1). Online at: http://www.jceps.com/index.php?pageID=articleandarticleID=20

Lewis, C. (2004a). Interview with Christine Lewis, National Officer for UNISON. Unpublished.

Lewis, C. (2004b). Some Impacts of the Liberalization of Further Education Colleges in England and Wales, in D. Hill, B. Fawcett and C. Lewis (2004).

England and Wales Case Study written for D. Hill et al., Education Services Liberalization, in E. Rosskam (ed.) *Winners or Losers? Liberalizing public services*. Geneva: International Labour Organization. Unpublished.

Lipman, P. (2004). *High Stakes Education: Inequality, globalization, and urban school reform*. New York: Routledge.

Longmate, J. and Cosco, F. (2002). Part-Time Instructors Deserve Equal Pay for Equal Work, *Chronicle of Higher Education* 48(34), p. B14.

Mahony, P., Menter, I. and Hextall, I. (2003). Edu-business: Are teachers working in a new world? Paper given at American Education Research Association Annual Conference, 2003, Chicago, April 21-25. Available at: http://www.roehampton.ac.uk/perc/iptatw/AERAEdubusiness.pdf.

Malins, C. (2005). Comment on 'Bolkestein legacy "too radical" for new Commission'. Online at: http://lists.aktivix.org/pipermail/ssf/2005-February/000880.html.

Marx, K. and Engels, F. [1847] (1977). The Communist Manifesto, in *Karl Marx and Frederick Engels, Selected Works*. London: Lawrence &Wishart.

McLaren, P, Martin, G., Farahmandpur, R. and Jaramillo, N. (2004). Teaching In and Against Empire: Critical pedagogy as revolutionary praxis, *Teacher Education Quarterly*, 31(3), pp. 131-153.

McLauchlin, A. (2005). The EU Services Directive, in *The Economist,* 11(4), 3 February. Online at: http://lists.aktivix.org/pipermail/ssf/2005-February/000880.html.

Mirza, M. (1995). Some Ethical Dilemmas in Field Work: Feminist and antiracist methodologies, in M.Griffiths and B. Troyna (eds.) *Antiracism, Culture and Social Justice in Education.* Stokeon-Trent: Trentham.

Molnar, A. (2001). *Giving Kids the Business: The Commercialization of America's schools* (2nd edn). Westview: HarperCollins.

Molnar, A., Wilson G. and Allen, D. (2004). *Profiles of For-Profit Education Management Companies: Sixth annual report, 2003-2004*. Arizona: Arizona State University Education Policy Studies Laboratory. Online at: http://www.asu.edu/educ/epsl/CERU/Documents/EPSL-0402-101-CERU.pdf and at: http://www.asu.edu/educ/epsl/EPRU/documents/EPSL-0402-101-CERU.pdf.

Mukhtar, A. (2004). Pakistan Case Study written for D. Hill et al., Education Services Liberalization, in E. Rosskam (ed.) *Winners or Losers? Liberalizing public services*. Geneva: International Labour Organization. Unpublished.

Mukhtar, A. (2006). Pakistan, in D. Hill (ed.) *Globalization/Neoliberalism/Education and Resistance*. Vol. 3, *Low and Middle Income Countries.* Brighton: Institute for Education Policy Studies.

Nelson, F.H., Muir, E. and Drown, R. (2003). *Paying for the Vision: Charter School revenue and expenditures.* Washington, D.C.: American Federation of Teachers. Online at: http://www.aft.org/topics/charters/.

New South Wales Teachers Federation (2004). The Casual Crisis in TAFE, *NSWTF Online,* 30 June. Online at: http://www.nswtf.org.au/edu_online/39/crisis.html.

Oliver, M. (2001). Review Symposium article on M. Hammersley (2000) Taking Sides in Social Research: essays on partisanship and bias', *British Journal of Sociology of Education,* 22(1), pp. 157-160.

Pardíñaz-Solís, R. (1997). *The Impact of the North American Free Trade Agreement on Mexican Teacher Education.* Ph.D. thesis, University of Birmingham, UK.

Partnership for Educational Revitalization in the Americas (PREAL) (2004) Homepage. Online at: http://www.preal.cl/.

Patai, D. (2005). You Say Social Justice, I Say Political Censorship, *Times Higher Educational Supplement*, 28 October, p. 12.

Phillips, D.C. (1993). Subjectivity and Objectivity: An objective inquiry, in M. Hammersley (ed.) *Educational Research: Current issues.* London: Paul Chapman.

Pilger, J. (2002). *The New Rulers of the World.* London: Verso.

Puiggrós A. (2002). World Bank Education Policy: Market liberalism meets ideological conservatism, in V. Navarro (ed.) *The Political Economy of Social Inequalities: consequences for health and quality of life.* Amityville, NY: Baywood.

Rikowski, G. (2001). *The Battle in Seattle: Its significance for education.* London: Tufnell Press.

Rikowski, G. (2002a). Fuel for the Living Fire: Labour-power!, in A. Dinerstein and M. Neary (eds.) *The Labour Debate: An investigation into the theory and reality of capitalist work.* Aldershot. Ashgate.

Rikowski, G. (2002b). Transfiguration: Globalization, the World Trade Organization and the national faces of the GATS, *Information for Social Change*, 14, pp. 8-17. Online at http://libr.org/ISC/.

Rikowski, G. (2003) Schools and the GATS Enigma, *Journal for Critical Education Policy Studies,* 1(1). Online at: http://www.jceps.com/index.php?pageID=article&articleID=8.

Rikowski, G. (2005a) *Silence on the Wolves: What is absent in New Labour's five year strategy for education.* Occasional paper published by the Education Research Centre, University of Brighton, UK.

Rikowski, G. (2005b). The Education White Paper and the Marketisation and Capitalisation of the Schools System in England, *The Volumizer*. Online at: http://journals.aol.co.uk/rikowskigr/volumizer.

Robertson, S., Bonal, X. and Dale, R. (2002). GATS and the Education Service Industry: The politics of scale and global territorialisation, *Comparative Education Review,* 46(3), pp. 472-496.

Robertson, S. and Dale, R. (2003). *The Implications of GATS for Education Systems in the North and the South.* Online Papers GENIE – Globalisation and Europeanisation Network in Education. Bristol: GENIE. Online at: http://www.genie-tn.net/paper001.htm.

Rose, P. (2003) *The Education Fast Track Initiative: Report prepared for Action Aid on behalf of the Global Campaign for Education.* London: Action Aid. Online at: http://www.actionaid.org.uk/775/our_research.html.

Rose, R. and Grosvenor, I. (2001). *Doing Research in Special Education.* London: David Fulton.

Rosskam, E. (ed.) (2005). *Winners or Losers? Liberalizing public services.* Geneva: ILO.

Santos, B. (2004). *A universidade no século XXI.* Sao Paolo, Brazil: Cortez.

Schugurensky, D. and Davidson-Harden, A. (2003). From Cordoba to Washington: WTO/GATS and Latin American education, *Globalization, Societies and Education,* 1(3).

Sinclair, S. and Grieshaber-Otto, J. (2002). *Facing the Facts: A guide to the GATS debate.* Ottawa: Canadian Centre for Policy Alternatives.

Siqueira, A. (2005). The Regulation of Education through the WTO/GATS: Path to the enhancement of human freedom? *Journal for Critical Education Policy Studies*, 3(1).

Tooley, J. (1999). *Introduction: Overview of global private education sector.* Presentation to International Finance Corporation Conference: Investment opportunities in private education in developing countries, June 2-3, Washington D.C. Tooley, J. (2000) *Reclaiming Education.* London: Continuum.

Tooley, J. (2001). *The Global Education Industry. Lessons from private education in developing countries* (2nd edn). London: Institute for Economic Affairs.

Torres, C.A., Cho, S., Kachur, J., Loyo, A., Mollis, M., Nagao, A. and Thompson, J. (2004). *Political Capital, Teachers' Unions and the State: Conflict and Collabouration in Educational Reform in the United States, Canada, Japan, Korea, Mexico, and Argentina.* Online at: http://www.isop.ucla.edu/lac/cat/montim.pdf.

Trades Union Congress (TUC) (2000). *TUC Safety Reps' Survey 2000.* London: Trades Union Congress.

Troyna, B. (1994). Blind Faith? Empowerment and educational research, *International Studies in the Sociology of Education,* 4(1), pp. 3-24.

Troyna, B. and Carrington, B. (1989). Whose Side Are We On? Ethical dilemmas in 'race' and education, in R. Burgess (ed.) *The Ethics of Educational Research.* London: Falmer Press.

UNESCO (2000). *World Education Report 2000.* Paris: UNESCO.

UNISON (2002). *Best Value and the Two-tier Workforce in Local Government.* London: UNISON. Available at: http://www.unison.org.uk/acrobat/B318.pdf.

Walsh, K. and Davis, H. (1993). *Competition and Service: The impact of the Local Government Act 1988.* London: HMSO.

Whitty, G. (1997). Marketization, the State, and the Re-formation of the Teaching Profession, in A.H. Halsey, H. Lauder, P. Brown and A. Stuart Wells (eds.) *Education, Culture and Economy.* Oxford: Oxford University Press.

Whitty, G. (2000). *Privatization and marketization in education policy.* Speech given to the National Union of Teachers (NUT) conference on 'Involving the Private Sector in Education: Value Added or High Risk?', London, 21 November 2000. Online at: http://k1.ioe.ac.uk/directorate/NUTPres%20web%20version%20(2%2001).doc.

Wilson, R. (2001). Proportion of Part-time Faculty Members Leveled Off from 1992 to 1998, Data Show, *Chronicle of Higher Education* 47(34), pp. A14.

Wing, M. (2003). *Ending the Two-tier Workforce: A comprehensive solution*? London: UNISON.

World Bank (1991). *Higher Education Reform in Brazil* (draft: confidential). Washington, D.C.: The World Bank, Population and Human Resources Division, Country Department I, Latin America and Caribbean Region.

World Bank Group (2004). *Making Services Work for Poor People: World development report 2004*. Washington, D.C.: the author. Online at: http://poverty.worldbank.org/files/14222_WDR04_Inst.pdf.

World Bank (2005). Education for All – Fast Track Initiative: Fact sheet: About the fast track initiative. Online at: http://www1.worldbank.org/education/efafti/documents/factsheet_basic.pdf.

World Trade Organization (WTO) (2003a). Introduction. Online at: http://www.wto.org/english/tratop_e/serv_e/gats_factfiction1_e.htm.

World Trade Organization (WTO) (2003b). Six Benefits of Services Liberalization Online at: http://www.wto.org/english/tratop_e/serv_e/gats_factfiction3_e.htm.

World Trade Organization (WTO) (2003c). GATS: Fact and fiction: misunderstandings and scare stories. Online at: http://www.wto.org/english/tratop_e/serv_e/gats_factfictionfalse_e.htm.

Wright, C. (1990). Comments in Reply to the Article by Peter Foster, *British Education Research Journal,* 16(4), pp. 351-355.

6

Embourgeoisment, Immiseration, Commodification—Marxism Revisited: A Critique of Education in Capitalist Systems

Nigel M. Greaves, Dave Hill, and Alpesh Maisuria

Summary

In this paper, we explore educational inequality through a theoretical and empirical analysis. We use classical Marxian scholarship and class-based analyses to theorize the relationship between education and the inequality in society that is an inevitable feature of capitalist society/ economy. The relationship between social class and the process of capitalization of education in the USA and UK is identified, where neoliberal drivers are working to condition the education sector more tightly to the needs of capital. The empirical evidence is utilized to show how capital accumulation is the principal objective of national and international government policy, and of global capitalist organizations such as the World Trade Organization. The key ontological claim of Marxist education theorists is that education serves to complement, regiment and replicate the dominant-subordinate nature of class relations upon which capitalism depends, the labour-capital relation. Through these arguments we show that education services the capitalist economy, helps reproduce the necessary social, political, ideological and economic conditions for capitalism, and therefore, reflects and reproduces the organic inequalities of capitalism originating in the relations of production. We also note that education is a site of cultural contestation and resistance. We conclude that, whether in terms of attainment, selection, or life chances, it is inevitable that education systems reflect and express the larger features of capitalist inequality.

Introduction

This paper examines the relationship between capitalism and educational inequality. From a Marxist perspective, inequality is a long-term and inevitable consequence of the capitalist system. Education does not stand alone and remote from the practices and thought processes of society in general. It both reflects and supports the social inequalities of capitalist culture. The "education industry" is a significant state apparatus in the reproduction and replication of the capitalist social form necessary for the continuation of "surplus value" extraction and economic inequality. Hence, Marxists argue that there are material linkages between educational inequality, exploitation and capitalist inequalities in general. This has been brought into much sharper relief during the current reactionary phase of neoliberal capitalism in such countries as Thatcherite/post-Thatcherite Britain and Reaganite/post-Reaganite USA.

The question as to whether the development of a capitalist society inevitably increases inequality in education will be explored in two ways. In Section One, the enquiry is addressed through the lens of Marxist theoretical analysis. Capitalism is a particular economic form driven by a relentless profit motive in which exploitation and inequality, for example of income, of life chances are in-built features. This section will explain why, therefore, we might expect to find evidence for a relationship between education and class inequality. In Section Two, the question of capitalism and inequality is investigated by drawing, *inter alia*,on recent empirical research and the near-universal agreement among a wide range of national, international, and comparative studies examining the impacts of neoliberal capitalist policies for education (such as pre-privatization, privatization, commercialization, commodification, and marketization of schools and universities).

The Conclusion attempts a synthesis of the empirical and theoretical concerns of the paper. As confirmation of the key substantive concern of Marxist education theorists, a distinct correlation between capitalist economic inequality and educational inequality is revealed. Our analysis is that this relationship is causal and reciprocal. Capitalism causes and increases economic and education inequalities, which then, in turn, become functional to capitalist production and culture. This effect is evident in the long term. Short term snapshots of certain instances and conjunctures (such as in the case of South Korea in this volume) do not tend to reveal the full historical picture. (For a discussion of 'termism', long and short-term policy and their impacts, see Hill, 2001, 2005a).

Part 1. Marxist Analysis of the Relationship Between Capital and Education: A Conceptual Approach Reconnaissance of Marxist Education Theory

Marxist educational theory, research and writing reached its last peak in the late-1970s and early-1980s (Rikowski, 2006), building on the work of Althusser (1971), Bowles and Gintis (1976), Sarup (1978) and Willis (1977), and the Marxist-inspired work of Bourdieu (1976). With a few historically significant exceptions (such as Callinicos, 1991, Morton and Zavarzadeh, 1991; Ahmad, 1992), the rest of the 1980s and the early-1990s witnessed a failure to develop this first wave of Marxist educational theory and research. Instead, Marxists and neo-Marxists interested in education typically found themselves shoring up and/or critiquing the many problems and weaknesses inherent in the first wave work or giving a culturalist post-Gramscian spin on the earlier "reproductionist" analysis of Althusser, Bowles and Gintis, and Bourdieu. (Henry Giroux is an example, e.g. 1983).

However, by the mid-1990s, Marxist educational theory and research re-emerged from a moribund period characterised by of internal degeneration and hyper-defensiveness in the face of external criticism (Rikowski, 1996, 1997, 2006). Works from Richard Brosio (1994) Kevin Harris (1994) Ebert (1996) and Michael Neary (1997) heralded a new period of development and experimentation in Marxist educational research and writing. In the last few years, Marxist educational theory and research and radical pedagogy have opened up a second wave of development following the mini-renaissance of the mid-1990s. Works by Paula Allman (1999, 2001), Richard Brosio (2000), Peter McLaren (2000, 2005a and 2005b); McLaren and Farahmandpur, (2005), Bertell Ollman (2001), Carmel Borg, John Buttigieg and Peter Mayo (2002), Dave Hill *et al* (2002) have gained international recognition Furthermore, many others are expanding Marxist analysis and encompassing an increasing range of education policy issues and theoretical concerns, such as lifelong learning, mentoring, the learning society, social justice, globalization, educational marketization, and many other areas. The second wave has generated renewed interest in theorizing and researching issues of class, gender and race in education from within Marxism (see Hill, 1999; Hill and Cole, 2001; and Kelsh and Hill, 2006) and the business takeover of education (see Glenn Rikowski, 2001, 2002, 2003, 2005; Kenneth Saltman and David Gabbard, 2003; and Saltman, 2005) and on public services related to education, such as libraries (Ruth Rikowski, 2005).

However, Marxists find themselves once more on the defensive and increasingly fighting today a rear-guard action for the maintenance of Marxism (historical materialism) against the epistemological instability caused by the intrusion of pluralist, non-essentialist (such as postmodernist) and Weberian-type schemata into the leftist debate (Rikowski, 2001; Kelsh and Hill, 2006).

Kelsh and Hill (2006), Paraskeva (2006) and Farahmandpur (2004) take as an example of "revisionist left" writers, the prominent writer Michael W. Apple. Apple writes prolifically and influentially among left educators against neoliberal and neo-conservative ideological and political hegemony in the USA. His analysis and political objective are that there is, and should be, an alliance of political interests in which the tryptych of social class, "race" and gender have equal importance as *both* explanatory and as organizing principles (e.g. Michael W. Apple, 2001). The introduction of extra-class determinants of social inequality follows a Weberian-derived notion of class as a tool of classification useful only to describe *strata* of people, as they appear at the level of culture and in terms of status derived from various possessions, economic, political, or cultural.

However, as a tool of *class* categorization, Weberian derived classifications of social strata cannot provide reliable knowledge to guide transformative praxis - that is, a guide to action that will result in the replacement of capitalism by socialism (a system whereby the means of production, distribution and exchange, are collectively, rather than privately, owned). In Weberian classifications, there is no capitalist class, and no working class; just myriad strata. Similar assumptions surface in anti-essentialist, post-modernist approaches (for a critique, see Hill, 2001, 2005a; Hill, Sanders and Hankin, 2002; Kelsh, 2006, McLaren and Scatamburlo D'Anibale, 2004). Such classification systems substituted for Marxist class theory fuel the ideological notion that "class is dead" (Pakulski and Waters, 1996).

It is interesting, and rarely remarked upon, that arguments about "the death of class" are not advanced regarding the capitalist class. Despite their horizontal and vertical cleavages (Dumenil and Levy, 2004), they appear to know very well who they are. Nobody is denying capitalist class consciousness. They are rich. They are powerful. And they are transnational as well as national. They exercise (contested) control over the lives of worker-labourers and worker-subjects.

Marxists agree that class is not the only form of oppression in contemporary society, yet it is also a fact that class is central to the social relations of production and essential for producing and reproducing the cultural and economic activities of humans under capitalist modes of production. Whereas the abolition of racism and sexism does not guarantee the abolition of capitalist social relations of production, the abolition of class inequalities, by definition, denotes the abolition of capitalism.

Hickey, for example, points to the functionality of various oppressions in dividing the working class and securing the reproduction of capital; constructing social conflict between men and women, or black and white, or skilled and unskilled, thereby tending to dissolve the conflict between capital and labour (Hickey, 2006:196). While Apple's "parallellist," or equivalence model of exploitation (equivalence of exploitation based on "race,". class and gender, his "tryptarch" (or tripartite) model of inequality produces valuable data and insights into aspects of gender oppression and "race" oppression in capitalist USA, such analyses serve, as Hickey (2006), Gimenez (2001) and Kelsh and Hill (2006) suggest, to occlude the class-capital relation, the class struggle, and to obscure the essential and defining nature of capitalism, the labour-capital relation and its attendant class conflict. With respect to one aspect of structural inequalities reproduced within the education system in England and Wales, that is, educational attainment, Gillborn and Mirza (2000), themselves using the "official" (British government census classification) Weberian derived categorizations of social strata, show very clearly that it is the difference between social strata that is the fundamental and stark feature of the education system, rather than "race" or gender.

In sum, there is a recognized need amongst Marxists, firstly, to restate the epistemic foundation of Marxism; and, in so doing, secondly, to reclaim the authentic voice of the left-wing critique of capitalist education practices and their ideological justification though a class-based ontology (Kelsh and Hill, 2006).

Restating Class

For Marxists, class is not an arbitrary or abstract concept. Rather, it is a verifiable feature of certain human life processes. According to *The German Ideology*, written by Marx and Engels in 1845-6, human society passed through different productive epochs and in each there were opposing groups of people defined according to the objectively different relationships they had to the means and products of material production. That is, in every epoch, economic practices structure human society into "classes" with diametrically opposed interests rooted in relations of ownership to the means of production.. These relations of ownership to the means of production constitute what Marx calls the "relations of production" and this is an arena of perpetual tension and struggle (1977, p. 179). When the relations of production are combined with the "forces of production" (factories, workplaces, plant, equipment and tools, and knowledge of their use) we arrive at a "mode of production" or "economic base" (Marx, 1977, p. 161; 168). This productive "infrastructure" forms the organizational rationale and dynamic for society in general and these are reflected in the social institutions (e.g., the state) that spring up and become established in accordance with the needs of productive relations.

However, the techniques and technologies of production under capitalism always dictate new working practices which exert pressure for change. The institutions which attempt to guard the existing relations of production from crises (principally the state) then begin, precisely and contradictorily by attempting to guard those relations from crises to obstruct the further development of the forces of production and eventually the pressure of contradictions rooted in the class contradiction becomes too great and the established institutions are transformed by revolution. At that point, new social and political institutions, appropriate to new relations of production, are developed, and these must accord with the further free development of the material forces of production. *The German Ideology* constitutes Marx's attempt to depart from the metaphysical abstraction of the Hegelian idealist method and locate the motor of historical change in living, human society and its sensuous processes.

For later thinkers, such as Lenin, the significance of Marx's transformation of dialectics is the identification of the concept of 'class struggle' as the essential historical dynamic. In any era, and most certainly in the capitalist, society is locked in conflict; since the needs of a certain group in the productive process are always subordinated to another. Marxists hold that this social conflict cannot be truly reconciled with the source of its economic causation, and this perpetual tension is the seedbed of revolution.

The capitalist era is both typical of human history and at the same time unique. It is typical in that its production techniques involve the exploitation of one human being by another, but it is unique in history in terms of its advancing this principle to unprecedented levels of efficiency and ruthlessness. For Marx, writing in the Preface to *A Critique of Political Economy* of 1859 (known simply as the "*Preface*"), the capitalist era marks the zenith of class struggle in history and human exploitation cannot be taken further (1977, p. 390). The only redeeming feature of capitalism is its assembling its own social antithesis in the "proletariat" or "working class" which is destined to rise up against the bourgeoisie (profiteering or "ruling class") and abolish class and exploitation and thus bring "the prehistory of human society to a close" (1977, p. 390).

What, though, do Marxists mean by capitalist "exploitation"? In the first volume of *Capital*, Marx argues that workers are the primary producers of wealth due to the expenditure of their labour in the production of commodities. However, the relationship between the owners of the means of production (the employers) and the workers is fundamentally exploitative since the full value of the workers' labour power is never reflected in the wages they receive. The difference between the value of the labour expenditure and the sum the worker receives for it is known as "surplus value," and this is pocketed by the employer as profit.

Marx saw surplus value as the distinguishing characteristic and ultimate source of class and class conflict within the capitalist system (Cuneo, 1982, p. 378). However, for Marx, surplus value is not merely an undesirable side-effect of the capitalist economy; it is its motive force and the entire system would readily collapse without it. Technically, while surplus value extraction is not wholly unique, historically, to capitalist systems, all capitalist systems are characterized by it. Marx is thus able to offer a "scientific" and objective definition of class in the capitalist epoch based on which side of the social equation of surplus value one stands and to show, moreover, that this economic arrangement is the fundamental source of all human inequality.

Class is therefore absolutely central to Marxist ontology. Ultimately, it is economically induced and it conditions and permeates all social reality in capitalist systems. Marxists are therefore largely hostile towards postmodern and post-structural arguments that class is, or ever can be, 'constructed extra-economically', or equally that it can be 'deconstructed politically'—an epistemic position which has underwritten in the previous two decades numerous so-called 'death of class' theories—arguably the most significant of which are Laclau and Mouffe (1985) and Laclau (1996).

Capital, Immiseration, Education and Ideology

Marx's views on education, rarely expressed, tend towards an articulation of its "commodifying" properties in relation to both teachers and pupils. In other words, education is assessed according to its practical or "use value" for capital. Marx writes:

> [i]f we may take an example from outside the sphere of production of material objects, a schoolmaster is a productive labourer, when, in addition to belabouring the heads of his scholars, he works like a horse to enrich the

> school proprietor. That the latter has laid out his capital in a teaching factory, instead of in a sausage factory, does not alter the relation. (Marx, 1867, p. 477)

As a "sausage factory" in itself, the school is unlikely to hold out much prospect that pupils could be geared for anything other than the interests of capital. Marx would certainly have scoffed at the humanist notion that education is geared to the interests of the child, although "resistance theorists" (such as Willis, Giroux, McLaren) and critical pedagogues such as Freire and McLaren assert the possibilities for teachers and students challenging the capitalist system within schools, and, in the case of Giroux, Freire and McLaren, engaging in liberatory and transformative education. However, as far as capital is concerned, education is merely instrumental in providing and setting a pupil's future "use value" in production. The importance of this is that there is no other standard in which to aspire, other than that defined by capital, for the purposes of capital.

More subtly perhaps, though no less crucially, education has a role in conditioning and institutionalizing children not only for exploitation at work but toward an acceptance of their future life conditions and expectations. This is as true of the supposedly broad liberal arts education of today in the USA, or the purportedly 'broad' national curriculum for schools in England, as of more obviously utilitarian vocational models such as Soviet technical and vocational schooling. In any case, Marxists seek the explanation of this phenomenon in the processes of what Marx in the *Preface* called the "superstructure" (1977, p. 389).

The dynamics of production permeate all other activities in society such that there arises alongside concrete state institutions a vast complementary superstructure on the level of human thought or "ideology." The superstructure—consisting of all those elements widely understood as "culture" and "politics"—becomes simultaneously a product and necessary agency of the economic base. It is the cauldron in which thoughts, opinions, biases and outlooks—rooted in class positions and interests—are formulated and exchanged and become, due to the power and control exerted by the ruling class, broadly supportive of existing economic practices. In other words, the superstructure tends to replicate in the ideological field class differentials by either presenting these as legitimate somehow or by covering up and disguising the original source of class inequality.

The superstructure has, therefore, a vital concrete function. In a negative sense, it protects the dominant economic group by deflecting and disguising the adverse sensations of production. During the period in which Marx and Engels produced their work, capitalist superstructures were in the process of development and certainly lacked the powers of conciliation we witness today.

Of course, during the period in which Marx and Engels wrote, Europe was rife with social criticism. For example, the literary works of Charles Dickens (1812-1870) in England and Victor Hugo (1802-1885) in France are replete with moral outrage. However, much of it tended to reflect disgust that the major privileges of liberal philosophy, such as 'individual empowerment', 'self-ownership' and so forth, were contradicted by the extant material conditions of the poorest members of society. In other words, such liberal social critics tended to assume that the liberal revolutions, those that had accompanied transitions to capitalist modes of production throughout Europe, were incomplete or that their highest ideals had been subsequently betrayed somehow.

In fact, many 19th century social critics exposed a fundamental internal paradox of liberal philosophy. On the one hand, freedom is sacrosanct and there should be minimal interference in individual choice and behaviour, on the one hand, the activation and preservation of freedom requires social intervention or 'big government'. We find this theme, for example, in the political theories of the Philosophic Radicals, Jeremy Bentham (1748-1832) and James Mill (1773-1836) who, along with their fellow critics in literature, assumed that what was required to meet dire social need was in effect more liberalism or indeed the 'right kind'.

Marx, however, raises the stakes of social criticism beyond liberalism; an ideology which he believed had largely run its course. For Marx, what was required was socialism but this was not so much an 'idea' as an entirely new social form in which capitalist economic practices and corresponding state support had been swept away by proletarian revolution.

Marx believed he had every reason to be confident. In *The Communist Manifesto* and elsewhere, and derived in part from his earlier humanist writings on alienation, Marx saw the increasing "immiseration" of the workers as a vital revolutionary factor. From a series of articles written in 1849 for the journal *Neue Rheinische Zeitung* and later in the first volumes of *Capital*, Marx's idea of immiseration is that as capitalism develops its cost in human terms would increase proportionately. Workers are singularly vulnerable since their only resource is their labour power, and they are dependent for their subsistence on selling this power to someone else, as we have seen, always for less (exchange value) than its true value. The workers have, therefore, limited material resources and ability to control the processes of capitalism and its long-term tendencies to drive workers' wages down.

In effect, the workers shoulder the cost of an inherently unstable system. For example, the uptake of labour by capital periodically falls short of labour availability. This leads to unemployment, the creation of a ("raced" and gendered) reserve army of labour, and competition for jobs. Sometimes the reserve army is over the border in *maquiladoras*, sometimes far away in colonies and neo-colonies, sometimes through the importation of formerly subject peoples into the colonial/imperial "motherland," sometimes through the simple "free movement" of labour, as in the newly enlarged European Union, sometimes through bringing more women-labourers into the paid economy. On the other hand, the downward pressure on wages relates directly to downward pressure on commodity prices—labour being a commodity itself.

Subject to stiff market competition, capitalists act on labour as an immediate and malleable factor in the pricing of the commodity. Capitalists are compelled to reduce their overhead costs and are ever-vigilant in their bid to gain an advantage over their competitors. Many variables are beyond the capacity of the capitalist to control, such as the price of raw commodities which, Marx assumed, will be roughly the same for all capitalists, but this is not necessarily the case for the variable labour. Here, the capitalist exerts some measure of control. Indeed, the demands of competition result in the general trend for downward pressure on labour costs.

Of course, this pressure clashes fundamentally with the interests of those whose sole means of subsistence is their labour power. The capitalist's ability to compete will therefore depend upon the self-organization and interest-recognition of a given labour force. For Marx, such recognition was inevitable. For it would prove difficult to disguise from the workers the source of their misery and alienation and the appeal of socialism would thus become unstoppable. However, the growth of superstructures in terms of democratic enfranchisement, "bourgeois democracy," trade unionism and welfare states resulted in what Marxists dub the "embourgeoisement" of the working class or what Marshall (1990, p. 31) calls the pressure for "upward mobility." Rose (1960) considered, for example, how the Conservative Party in Britain was able to command a broad appeal and concluded that an important factor was the increasing association of workers with the values of the middle class. Similarly, analysis can be made of other advanced capitalist countries such as the USA, France, Germany. Embourgeoisement results, subjectively, if not objectively, in a blurring of the distinction between classes and the de-radicalization of the workers. Patently, this effect is attributable to the superstructure rather than the economy *per se*.

Analysis of the role of the superstructure in the process of de-radicalization was initiated in large part by the Italian Marxist Antonio Gramsci (1891-1937). He argued from a fascist prison cell in the 1930s that the superstructure has a constructive (rather than exclusively negative) dimension—emphasizing an aspect of Marxist theory that had always been at its core but which, owing to the historical material conditions of the time Marx and Engels made their key arguments, remained de-emphasized in their works, as Engels was later to argue (Engels, Letter to Joseph Bloch (1890). Therefore, Marxists should take the initiative and become more positively engaged in the life of the superstructure. It is, he wrote, "the terrain on which men move, acquire consciousness of their position, struggle, etc" (Gramsci, 1971, p. 377). As a consequence, the idea of education in Gramsci's thinking is similar to his views on ideology. Education in the widest sense is a vital tool for the advancement of civilization to a necessary level to meet with productive need. For Gramsci, ideology becomes a force for the advancement of the interests of one class over another by its presenting its viewpoints as fair, moral, just and so forth—as just "plain common sense." Gramsci called this force "hegemony" and it represents a particular account of reality which promotes both its own advancement throughout society and the suppression of rival accounts. Of course, equally, Gramsci offers the prospect of turning the tables on the capitalist class by encouraging the proletariat to throw off its ideological subordination and to cultivate its own version of reality as the first stage in revolutionary preparation (Greaves, 2005). This is the classic task of Marxist and communist educators, to transform the working class from an objective "class in itself," into a "class for itself"—a class with class consciousness, aware of its political project to replace capitalism.

Gramsci (1971) perceived that in capitalist systems the task of permeating society with a particular version of reality is given over to the capitalist's "chiefs of staff," or dominant "intellectuals," that is, rather than capitalists themselves. School is, therefore, an obvious locus of intellectual recruitment and hegemonic exchange. As Gramsci puts it: "[s]chool is the instrument through which intellectuals of various levels are elabourated" (p. 10) "[and part of an] overall framework of a policy for forming modern intellectual cadres" (p. 26). Firstly, children learn at school the prevailing mores of society and adopt the conditions of "good citizenship." Secondly, children are selected for a future role in production either as producers themselves or as the intellectual legitimizing agents of productive logic in the superstructure.

Gramsci's ideas on the pedagogic and reproducing nature of the superstructure have been influential within the Marxist tradition. They are explored by Louis Althusser (1971) and Bowles and Gintis (1972; 1976; 1988). For Althusser, the needs of capital are reproduced ideologically by replicating capitalist practices and conditions at multiple social levels. Children are structuralized by education because the education system is part of a state apparatus that cannot do otherwise than work in the interests of capital. A state contrived in accordance with the dictates of a given economic form cannot be brought to perform in ways that are at odds with its structural character. One effect of this is that education systems of capitalist societies become inherently hierarchical and elitist.

This process prepares the student for passive acceptance of the inequalities in expectation and reward that will be faced in the world of capitalist production. Indeed, education is preparation for future market evaluation and the process of commodification through which capitalism assesses human value and worth. Bowles and Gintis (1988) track this analysis. They write:

> [t]he hierarchical order of the school system, admirably geared towards preparing students for their future positions in the hierarchy of production, limits the development of those personal capacities ... and reinforces social inequality by legitimating of students to inherently unequal "slots" in the social hierarchy (1988, p. 18).

Bowles and Gintis (1988) recognize that over and above the interest of the child and the free development of its faculties lies a "hidden curriculum." Education transmits a curriculum to students that is conditioned to the needs of both the forces of production (skills, techniques, know-how) and the relations of production (class, class differentials, inequality). In catering to the needs of the productive forces and the acquisition of skill, the curriculum is open in the sense that the purpose of education is fully apparent. However, Bowles and Gintis (1972) argue that a hidden message is smuggled into education alongside the dissemination of vocational know-how that serves to justify social relations.

The school is a bureaucratic order, with hierarchical authority, rule orientation, stratification by "ability" as well as by age, role differentiation by sex (physical education) ... etc., and a system of external incentives (marks, promises of promotion, and threat of failure) much like pay and status in the sphere of work. (p. 87)

Section One has offered a synopsis of the Marxist analysis of education and its*a priori* assumptions on education in capitalist systems. We now turn to provide supporting empirical data.

Part 2. Capital and Education—An Empirical Analysis: Turning the Screw—Neoliberalism and Fiscal Inequality

The introduction and extension of neoliberal social policies in Britain, the USA after the New Right reactionary movements of the 1980s, and more globally (notably in Chile under Pinochet, elsewhere in Latin America under an assortment of generals and "big business" control) offers fertile ground for Marxist analysis since economic inequality and class division has sharpened markedly (Dumenil and Levy, 2002; Harvey, 2005; Global Policy Forum, 2006). The immiseration of the worker that superstructures and state activities had done much to ameliorate since Marx's time might be making a comeback (Brennan, 2003; Glyn, 2006).

And so, with the economic gains of the thirty-year post–war "boom," from the 1940s to the 1970s, when (in advanced capitalist countries) real wages of the working classes and standards of living improved, (as did the "social wage" welfare and social benefits) the theory of immiseration went into decline. However, following the hidden economic depression of the 1970s ("hidden" because it was compensated for in the west by the large-scale drafting of women into the workforce), Marx's theory of immiseration has regained validity. Since 1970, especially in the case of the United States, real wages have fallen dramatically. However, real family income has remained relatively stable as women entered the workforce. Families have the same amount of money to spend as before, but a lot more hours are being worked. Recent research (Dumenil and Levy, 2002; Harvey, 2005; Hill, 2004, 2005b; Hill et al., 2006) testifies that the "class war from above" is in full swing, characterized by the increase in the rate of extraction of surplus value, in advanced capitalist and in developing countries—with the rich getting richer, the poor poorer, and workers and trade union rights and liberties under attack.

Currently there is a "race to the bottom" in which worldwide wages and conditions of labour are being held down by neoliberal national and global policies such as the structural readjustment programmes of the World Bank and the International Monetary Fund, and the "liberalization" of trade agenda of the World Bank's General Agreement of Trade in services (GATS) (2002, 2003; Hill, 2005b; Hill et al, 2006). Together with competition from the substantially lower-wage economies such as India and China, we see Marx's rising rate of exploitation re-emerging, a century and a half after he first predicted it (Glynn, 2006). In justifying the intensification of labour, the ideological state apparatuses such as education and the media, and of the repressive state apparatuses of the laws, army, police (Althusser, 1971, Hill, 2004)—play a full role in trying to "manage" citizens and workers into accepting the "common sense" of an individualistic, consumerist, and hierarchically stratified society.

Dumenil and Levy (2004) highlight the increasing inequality in the USA. Those in the highest tax bracket are paying tax at a tax rate around half that of the 1920s, whereas the current tax rate for those in the lowest tax bracket are more than double of what it was then. In a forerunner of George W. Bush's "trillion dollar tax giveaway to the rich," Reagan cut the top rate of personal tax from 70 to 28 per cent. The results can be seen most starkly in CEO remuneration packages whose income soared by 25 per cent in 2005 to $17.9 million, with six CEOs who accumulating between USD$100–$280 million that year (Strass and Hansen, 2006). This compares with the average worker in the USA gaining a meagre 3.1 per cent increase which is below inflation. Real-term wages are in decline and the wealth of the nation is being transferred to the few in the capitalist oligarchy class (Ibid.). In addition, both the US administration and British government have also dramatically cut taxes on businesses and multinational corporations inflating profits.

Similarly, in Britain, the working class is paying more tax. The richest groups are paying a smaller proportion of their income in taxes in comparison to 1949 and to the late 1970s. These dates were both in the closing stages, at the end of two periods, of what might be termed "Old Labour," or social democratic governments (in ideological contradistinction to the primarily neoliberal policies of "New Labour"). As a percentage of income, middle and high earners in Britain pay less tax in 2003 than at any time for 30 years. It is the poorest, the lowest paid (1/3 of the population are paid below the EU decency threshold of the minimum wage), who are paying more despite the economy having doubled since the 1950s (Toynbee, 2003). Compared with the late 1970s, the "fat cats" are now paying around half as much tax (income tax and insurance contribution rate). These people are paying less income tax and national insurance as a percentage of their earned income than in 1949. "As a percentage of income, middle and high earners pay less tax now than at any time in the past thirty years" (Johnson and Lynch, 2004), In contrast, the average tax rate for "the low paid" is roughly double that of the early 1970s—and nearly twice as much as in 1949 (Johnson and Lynch, 2004). The subtitle for Johnson and Lynch's article is, appropriately, "sponging off the poor."

The encroachment of capital into state/public education has intensified because of a decline in the rate of capital accumulation. New markets outside the traditional private sector domain were needed (Hursh and Martina, 2003), especially to take advantage of economies of scale. In order to accommodate the business imperative, the US and British governments opened up, and continue to liberalize, the public sector services including education.

In Britain, New Labour's neoliberalizing policies aimed at deregulating educational provisions are potentially paving the way for the private sector to take a stranglehold of state services (Hill, 2006). The private sector is involved in almost every element of the British education services with activities ranging from selling services to educational institutions, to managing and owning schools and other facilities. Education ancillary services such as cleaning, catering, security and reprographics have been outsourced to private sector companies. On a national scale, functions such as inspection, student fees and loans handling, and record keeping, are increasingly run by private corporations rather than by the Local Education Authority (LEA) or the national government. And the current pre-privatization of state schooling in England and Wales (Rikowski, 2005) could well see a system of publicly funded privately controlled schooling.

The "Sausage Factory" in Action: Standardization and Centralization of Education

It should not be thought that the struggle between classes, in part, played out in education can be eradicated by state provision and such measures as standardised national curricula. For Marxists, the state can never be neutral while serving a capitalist economy, even though it can be used as a site of struggle and can effect reforms. State involvement in education represents the attempt at regulation, harmonization, and rationalization. The standardizing and centralizing powers of the state allow for a practical and ideological correlation between national educational provision and national economic need. The state turns the interests of capital into national educational strategies. Of course, the rhetoric of government policies such as that of *No Child Left Behind* in the USA and the rhetoric of the Blair government in its 2006 Education Bill for England and Wales do not solely advance a vocational or human capital rationale. (But is it remarkable how demoted or absent, relative to the 1960s, are rationales based on liberal-progressivist child-centred ideology, or social democratic redistributionist ideology). There are other rationales, such as political competitive vote-winning, considerations. There is also the legitimacy question. Insocieties, such as Britain, the USA and other liberal democratic politics, where economic inequality is high and growing, upward mobility between social classes has to be seen to be attainable—the message is work hard and you'll be rewarded. If these messages permeate the masses who do not enjoy much of the spoils, then they are more likely to tolerate the riches that few enjoy within that society. However, if these meritocratic messages of attainable riches, and advancement through a meritocratic education system are not widely accepted, then this poses legitimacy—and political survival problems—for political and economic elites.

As part of a strategic state objective, education is driven by the need and desire of capital for capital accumulation. Currently, in advanced capitalist countries education has a particular, distinctive economic and business orientation: it seeks a specialist workforce, whether by a dual-track system such as in Germany, or through supposedly single track, more 'comprehensive' systems, as in the USA. Both types of system, and hybrid types are specialised in that they are both designed to train or educate for the purposes of capital.In both types students are differentially and hierarchically trained and/or educated (Hirtt, 2004) to maximize economic return in the development of a "knowledge economy." In the world-wide division of labour other education systems and the economies they serve, have different functions. In some historic-geographical spaces these include the production of raw materials and/or low-skilled factory assembly work, together with supervisory capacity. This has the effect of stratifying children into crude (gendered and "raced") class strata categories. One result is the failure to provide a holistic educational experience aiming to enrich pupils' personal developments and talents.

The state allows for, and encourages, therefore, the harmonizing and standardizing of education provision toward the needs of capital. As McNeill (2000) observes, state standardization and centralization nevertheless replicates capitalist social relations in that it: creates inequities, widening the gap between the quality of education for poor and minority youth and that of more privileged students. (p. 3)

The state is a key agency for the defence of extant relations of production. Hence, Marxists would point to the anti-radicalizing effect of education through the smothering of creativity, imagination, and critical thought . By this is meant, radical political creativity, imagination and political thought. Rikowski (2001) suggests that the State needs to control the social production of labour power for two reasons. First to try to ensure that *the social production of labour-power*, equipping students with skills, competences, occurs,.Secondly, to try to ensure that modes of pedagogy that are antithetical to labour-power production *do not and cannot exist*. In particular, it becomes clear, on this analysis, that the capitalist State will seek to destroy any forms of pedagogy *that attempt to educate students regarding their real predicament—to create an awareness of themselves as future labour-powers and to underpin this awareness with critical insight that seeks to undermine the smooth running of the social production of labour-power*. This fear entails strict control, for example, of the curriculum for teacher education and training, of schooling, and of educational research. Hill (2003, 2004, 2007) argues that neoliberal capital and governments stifle critical thought-by compressing and repressing critical space in education today, with Capital and neoliberal ideology and policy seeking to neutralize and destroy potential pockets of resistance to global corporate expansion and neoliberal Capital.

A historic example of this is the smothering and incorporation of independent working class educational provision (such as in 19th century Germany and Britain). National "homogenization" given over to "task-related knowledge" approaches of capitalized education systems (Kimbell and Perry, 2001; Maisuria 2005) is a destructive, as well as in some respects constructive process because it creates robotic people less able to *think* beyond the scope of their function in society. Creativity, imagination and critical thought are, of course valued within education systems, but primarily insofar as they are constrained within a capitalist framework, focussed on the development of relatively compliant human capital. A restrictive educational experience limits cognitive emancipation and empowerment by limiting human horizons to the requirements of capital.

Of course, there are some differences between capitalist countries. Social democratic countries have a low Gini coefficient—i.e. relatively lower levels of inequality resulting from decades of social democratic rule and reforms. This is exemplified by Sweden, a country with a large state, impressive welfarist policies, and nationalised public services.

2000, and the UK increased to 0.345 in 1999 from 0.270 in 1979 (Ibid.). Sweden's levels of inequality has barely increased (from a relatively low baseline) in the last 30 years. In addition, Sweden in the 21st century is significantly more equal than the UK was 30 years ago

(Ibid.). However, whether social democratic, redistributionist governments will continue to limit the intrusion of capitalist interests into state provision, against the backdrop of increasingly globalized neoliberalism, remains to be seen. Where in "the balance of class forces," the class struggle, is sufficiently strong- with millions poring onto the streets in defence of their pensions, public utilities and services, labour-rights, then neoliberal capital can be thwarted. And, with a rise in class consciousness nationally and globally, be replaced.

Choice and Inequality

In the UK, while in government from 1979 to 1997, the Conservatives established a *competitive market* for consumers (children and their parents) by setting up new types of schools in addition to the local (State, i.e. public) primary school or the local secondary comprehensive school.

Empirical evidence by Hoxby (2000, 2003a, 2003b) shows that the result of this "school choice" is that inequalities between schools increased because in many cases the "parental choice" of schools has become the "schools choice" of the most desirable parents and children—and rejection of others. In the UK, parental social class and income is the most important factor affecting educational attainment (Rueda and Vignoles, 2003).

Choice means that so-called "sink schools" have become more "sink-like" as more favoured schools have picked the children they think are likely to be successful. Where selection exists the sink schools just sink further and the privileged schools just become more privileged (this is particularly pertinent in England and Wales, in the wake of the 2006 Education Bill by the New Labour government, which proposes to permit increased selection "by aptitude" in schools). The Association of Teachers and Lecturers lambasts marketization in education: "The trouble with choice is that those least able to choose find that, if the market rules, it tends to prioritize those customers which do not take up too much of its resources" (Bousted, 2006, p. XX).

Teachers in these "ghetto schools for the underclass" (p. XX) are publicly pilloried, and, under New Labour the schools "named and shamed" as "Failing Schools," and, in some cases either re-opened with a new "Superhead" as a "Fresh Start School" (with dismissals of "failing" teachers), or shut down (see, for example, Hill, 1997; Whitty, Power and Halpin, 1998). Similar policies and effects are seen in the US as a result of the *No Child Left Behind* legislation of the American congress (Hursh, 2003).

Hierarchical differentiation is the consequence of experiments with choice. This is so of the tripartite system in the US—private, suburban, and urban schooling—and in Britain, with the tripartite system of private fee-paying schools, schools (such as Academies) opted out of local authority/school district control, and working class local council and authority schools. Further differentiation is spurred on by the publication of various test results such as SATS.

Differentiation is being formally replicated in higher education (Machin and Vignoles, 2006). This is easily understood in the US where elite universities charge student fees many times those of lower status universities. In the USA university fees are assessed on a need/income basis for each student, with many poor and needs-based students paying little or nothing for fees at institutions like Harvard and Yale. This has, however led to comments such as 'in order to attend an expensive university, one has to be "either very rich, or very poor." Overall, the correlation between size of fees and size of working class attendance at universities in the USA is marked. In the UK, the turn-of-the-millennium differentiation between Oxbridge and the elite "Russell Group" of universities, the other "old" universities; the "new" (i.e. ex-Polytechnic) universities and the institutes/colleges of higher education is formalized. It is widely expected that elitist universities will be permitted to charge higher fees. (Until 2006 all universities in Britain charged the same fees, indeed, until the late 1990s the government paid all fees for all citizens). Now there is the further development of a ("racialized") class-based hierarchicalization of universities entry, essentially pricing the poor out of the system, or at least into the lower divisions of higher education.

Research by the Centre for Economics of Education at the London School of Economics found that "poorer students are [in 2006] more likely to go to higher education than they were in the past, [however] the likelihood of them doing so relative to their richer peers is actually lower than it was the case in earlier decades" (Machin and Vignoles, 2006, p.14) .

Markets have exacerbated existing inequalities in education. There is considerable data, most notably Whitty, Power, and Halpin (1998) and Machin and Vignoles (2006), on how poor schools have become poorer (in terms of relative education results, retention of students, and in terms of total income) and how elitist rich schools (in the same terms) have got richer through marketization in the US, Sweden, England and Wales, Australia, and New Zealand.

In order to foresee the future, there is some worth in looking at diktats and structural readjustment programmes of the World Bank, the International Monetary Fund, and other agencies of international capital, 'often push highly controversial economic policy reforms on poor countries, like trade liberalization and privatisation of essential services' (Eurodad, 2006. See also Shugurensky and Davidson-Harden, 2004; Hill, 2005b; Hill et al., 2006; Rosskam, 2006; Tomasevski, 2006a, 2006b). The 2006 Eurodad report continues,

Our research found that 18 out of the 20 poor countries we assessed had privatization related conditions attached to their development finance from the World Bank or IMF. And the number of 'aggregate' privatization-related conditions that the World Bank and IMF impose on developing countries has risen between 2002 and 2006. For many countries privatization-related conditions make up a substantial part of their overall conditions from the World Bank and IMF (p.3).

Increasing the role of the private sector (including *for*-profit) organizations at primary, secondary and tertiary levels create unequal access to schooling based on social class, despite compensatory measures, such as subsidies, intended to limit the stratifying effects of capitalization. Private schools cherry-pick, or "cream off" the children of wealthier families who are more equipped to succeed at school, leaving the public school system to admit more challenging students with greater needs. Furthermore, state schools generally have fewer resources than private schools, and therefore need the "investments" from pupils from wealthier backgrounds to replenish books, furniture, and materials.

Ironically, but not unexpectedly, the World Bank's corporate lending arm, the International Finance Corporation (IFC) (2001), has claimed that fee-paying educational institutions can "improve" equity:

> [p]rivate education can indirectly benefit the lowest socio-economic groups by attracting families who can afford some level of fee away from the public system, thereby increasing capacity and per student spending for the students who remain in the public system. Similarly, the emergence of private tertiary institutions allows governments to reduce funding in such institutions and instead to invest in lower levels of education, thus improving distributive efficiency. (p. 5)

The idea that the siphoning off "education investments" from wealthier pupils away from the public system actually increases equity is based on a highly contestable argument. Reimers (2000) notes that:

> [t]he poor have less access to pre-school, secondary, and tertiary education; they also attend schools of lower quality where they are socially segregated. Poor parents have fewer resources to support the education of their children, and they have less financial, cultural, and social capital to transmit. Only policies that explicitly address inequality, with a major redistributive purpose,

> therefore, could make education an equalizing force in social opportunity. (p. 55).

Indeed, principles of universal access, for example, as enshrined in international covenants such as the United Nations convention on economic, social and cultural rights, reflect a quite different notion of educational equity than that based on "choice" promoted by the World Bank and the IFC (Schugurensky and Davidson-Harden, 2003) and subscribed to by successive governments in the US and Britain. The arguments about inequality in this section is succinctly articulated by a Council's Director of Education in North-East England:

> Everything is to be done to keep middle England happy, to give them their choice of school—so they don't have to pay for private schools—to guarantee them the places that other children ought to have and, worst of all, to give their schools the powers to keep out those other children they don't want their own children to mix with (Mitchell, 2006).

Conclusion: How Capitalism (Exaggerated by Neoliberalism) Inevitably Increases Educational Inequality

In Section One, it was suggested that class should remain central to the leftist critique of capitalist education systems and that Karl Marx and subsequent Marxist thinkers possess the epistemic and explanatory upper hand over pluralist, Weberian, and deconstructionist (such as postmodernist) accounts of society.

Section Two reinforced the theoretical claim that education is functional to capitalism in two essential ways. Firstly, education imposes division amongst children in preparation for the stratification of labour within the labour process. Suitably selected for tasks in production, the child is then educated and skilled to the level deemed suitable by capital for work. The child's individual needs are, despite the best will and effort of many teachers, deemed secondary to the needs of production by capital and the governments funded and supported by capital. Secondly, education conditions the child for a career of exploitation, inequality and differentials, conformity and passivity. For the majority, education, despite the best will and efforts of many teachers, lowers expectation, and confines and fragments outlooks into myriad specialist skills that block the attainment of the bigger life picture. In short, education prepares and cultivates future workers to become both useful and productive and obedient and docile.

Section Two located empirically the actual linkage between the capitalist economy and educational outcome by examining neoliberal policy, the role of the state and the effect of the commodification of education by its increasing exposure to market ethics and practices. The evidence tended to support the Marxist claim that in capitalism a sector such as education is tightly controlled in the interests of capital, despite the resistant and counter-hegemonic efforts of students, teachers and communities. Education is embedded in class relations and reflects, reinforces and replicates the tendency of capital to produce and reproduce inequality.

Capital leads to capitalization of education, and the principal capitalist objective then is to accumulate value and surplus-value in order to make profits. Capitalism is ambivalent to the obvious inequalities, disadvantage, and discrimination they perpetuate, for them the end (profit making) justifies the means. The upshot is clear then: in the long-term and in macro-political terms, capitalism does indeed lead to increasing education inequality.

In many countries, capitalism has been fairly successfully regulated, the Gini co-efficient depicting levels of inequality in the distribution of education in the labour force, diminished. But, when the crunch comes of declining capital accumulation, then capitalists do not abolish themselves. They turn to Nazism or Fascism, or to a permanent "war on terror," taking away rights of protest and dissent. Or, as in the UK, the party that was formerly the party of the working class, the Labour Party, that did, through most of the twentieth century, pursue social democratic policies, along with pro-capitalist policies, has become transformed, under "New Labour," into another capitalist party, no longer even with a mass working class membership, adopting neoliberal policies that lead to greater inequalities.

The inequalities documented in this paper can be eradicated. Working class consciousness, and class struggles, can and do resist. This can be through resistance by parliamentary reformist means. For example in the social democratic states of northwest Europe. These are not socialist, in the sense that socialism wishes to replace capitalism. Social democrats, however, wish to make capitalism more benign. Social democracy is a contradictory form of resistance to capital—or at least to its wider and wilder depredations—and educational inequalities. Social Democrats seek to advance workers' rights and to reduce inequality—but also to maintain capitalism. As Rosa Luxemburg (1899/1970) explained, the core aim of the revisionist left is the "bettering of the situation of the workers and ... the conservation of the middle classes" (p. 60).

In contrast to social democracy, socialist forms of resistance to capitalism take either revolutionary means (as seen in Russia, Cuba, and China) or evolutionary means, such as through the parliamentary/

democratic processes as witnessed in Nicaragua in the 1980s or Venezuela under Hugo Chavez. Both are responses to the increasing inequalities under capitalism. Both are responses to the choice offered by Rosa Luxemburg, the choice between (capitalist) barbarism on the one hand, or, on the other, socialism.

References

Ahmad, A. (1992). *In Theory: Classes, Nations, Literatures*. London: Verso.

Allman, P. (2001). *Critical Education Against Global Capitalism: Karl Marx and Revolutionary Critical Education*. Westport: Bergin & Garvey.

Allman, P. (1999). *Revolutionary Social Transformation: Democratic Hopes, Political Possibilities and Critical Education*. Westport: Bergin & Garvey.

Althusser, L. (1971). *Ideology and Ideological State Apparatuses - Notes Towards an Investigation*, Lenin and Philosophy and Other Essays. 127-86, New York: Monthly Review Press.

Borg, C., Buttigieg, J. and Mayo, P. (eds.) (2002). *Gramsci and Education*. Lanham Md: Rowman& Littlefield.

Bousted, M. (2006). Education reforms will condemn millions of children to 'ghetto schools', warns ATL's general secretary. Association of Teachers and Lecturers.Accessed 25 April, 2006. Avaliable from: https://www.atl.org.uk/atl_en/news/conferences/ATL_2006/reports/mary_bousted.asp.

Bowles, S. and Gintis, H. (1972). IQ and the Social Class System. *Social Policy* 3(4).

Bowles, S. and Gintis, H. (1976). *Schooling in Capitalist America: Educational Reform and the Contradictions of Economic Life*. New York: Basic Books.

Bowles S. and Gintis, H. (1988). Schooling in Capitalist America: Reply to our Critics. In M. Cole (ed.), *Bowles and Gintis Revisited: Correspondence and Contradiction in Educational Theory*. London: Falmer Press.

Bourdieu, R. (1976). The School as a Conservative Force in Scholastic and Cultural Inequalities. In R. Dale et al., *Schooling and Capitalism*. London: Routledge, Kegan Paul.

Brennan, T. (2003). *Globalization and Its Terrors*. London: Routledge.

Brosio, R. (1994). *A Radical Democratic Critique of Capitalist Education*. New York: Peter Lang.

Brosio, R. (2000). *Philosophical Scaffolding for the Construction of Critical Democratic Education*. New York: Peter Lang.

Callinicos, A. (1991). *Against Postmodernism: a Marxist critique*. Cambridge: Polity Press.

Chitty, C. (1992). *The Education System Transformed*. Tisbury: Baseline.

Cuneo, C.J. (1982). Class Struggle and Measurement of the Rate of Surplus Value, *Canadian Review of Sociology and Anthropology*, 19 (3), 377-426.

D. Morton, and M. Zavarzadeh (eds.), *Texts for Change*. Urbana and Chicago: University of Illinois Press, pp. 1-32.

Dumenil, G. and Levy, D. (2004). *Capital Resurgent: Roots of the Neoliberal Revolution*. London: Harvard University Press.

Eurodad (2006). World Bank and IMF conditionality: A development injustice, June 2006. Online.

Galindo-Rueda, F. and Vignoles, A. (2003). *Class Ridden or Meritocratic?* Centre for the Economics of Education, London: London School of Economics.

Gillborn, D. and Mirza, H. (2000). *Educational Inequality; Mapping race, class and gender: A synthesis of research evidence*. London: Ofsted.

Gimenez, M. (2001). Marxism and Class, Gender and Race: Rethinking the Trilogy, *Race, Gender and Class*, 8 (2), 23–33.

Giroux, H. (1983). Theories of Reproduction and Resistance in the New Sociology of Education: A Critical Analysis. *Harvard Education Review, 55*, 3, pp. 257-293.

Global Policy Forum (2006). *Inequality of Wealth and Income Distribution.*

Glyn, A. (2006, April 5). Marx's Reserve Army of Labour is About to Go Global. *The Guardian* (London).

Gramsci, A. (1971). *Selections from the Prison Notebooks* (edited and translated), Hoare, Q and Smith, G.N. London: Lawrence &Wishart.

Greaves, N.M. (2005). In Search of the 'Real Gramsci': A Historicist Reappraisal of a Marxist Revolutionary. Unpublished doctoral dissertation, University of Northampton, UK.

Harris, K. (1994). *Teachers: Constructing the Future*. London: Falmer Press.

Harvey, D. (2005). *A Brief History of Neoliberalism*. Oxford, England: Oxford University Press.

Hickey, T. (2006). Social Class. In M. Cole (ed.), *Education, Equality and Human Rights* (2nded.). London: Routledge Falmer.

Hill, D. (1997). Equality and primary schooling: The policy context intentions and effects of the conservative "reforms." In M. Cole, D. Hill and S. Shan (eds.) *Equality and the National Curriculum in Primary.*

Hill, D. (1999). Social Class and Education. In Matheson, D. and Grosvenor, I. (eds.) (1999) *An Introduction to the Study of Education*. London: David Fulton.

Hill, D. (2001). State Theory and the Neo-Liberal Reconstruction of Schooling and Teacher Education: A Structuralist Neo-Marxist Critique of Postmodernist, Quasi-Postmodernist, and Culturalist Neo-Marxist Theory. *The British Journal of Sociology of Education*, 22 (1), 137-157.

Hill, D. (2003). Global Neo-Liberalism, the Deformation of Education and Resistance, *Journal for Critical Education Policy Studies,* 1 (1).

Hill, D. (2004). Books, Banks and Bullets: Controlling our minds- the global project of Imperialistic and militaristic neoliberalism and its effect on education policy. *Policy Futures*, 2, 3-4.(Theme: Marxist Futures in Education). Accessed 25 April 2004. Online at http://www.wwwords.co.uk/pfie/content/pdfs/2/issue2_3.asp.

Hill, D. (2005a). State Theory and the Neoliberal Reconstruction of Schooling and Teacher Education. In G. Fischman, P. McLaren, H. Sünker and C. Lankshear (eds.) *Critical Theories, Radical Pedagogies and Global Conflicts*. Boulder, CO, Rowman and Littlefield.

Hill, D. (2005b). Globalization and its educational discontents: Neoliberalization and its impacts on education workers' rights, pay, and conditions. *International Studies in the Sociology of Education*, 15 (3), 257-288.

Hill, D. (2006). New Labour's Education Policy. In D. Kassem, E. Mufti and J. Robinson (eds.) *Education Studies: Issues and Critical Perspectives*. Buckingham: Open University Press.

Hill, D. (2007). Critical Teacher Education, New Labour, and the Global Project of Neoliberal Capital, *Policy Futures,* 5 (2). Online.

Hill, D., Anijar-Appleton, K., Davidson-Harden, A., Fawcett, B., Gabbard, D., Gindin, J., Kuehn, L., Lewis, C., Mukhtar, A., Pardinaz-Solis, R., Quiros, B., Schugurensky, D., Smaller, H. and Templer, B. (2006). Education Services Liberalization. In E. Rosskam (ed.) *Winners or Losers? Liberalizing public services*. Geneva: International Labour Organization.

Hill, D. and Cole, M. (2001). Social Class. In D. Hill and M. Cole (eds.) *Schooling and Equality: Fact, Concept and Policy*. London: Kogan Page.

Hill, D., McLaren, P., Cole, M. and Rikowski, G. (2002). *Marxism Against Postmodernism in Educational Theory.* Lanham, MD, USA: Lexington Books.

Hill, D., Sanders, M. and Hankin, T. (2002). Marxism, Class Analysis and Postmodernism. In D. Hill, P. McLaren, M. Cole and G. Rikowski (eds.), *Marxism Against Postmodernism in Education Theory*. Lanham, MD: Lexington, pp.159-194.

Hirtt, N. (2004). "Three axes of merchandization", in *European Educational Research Journal,* 3, (2). 442-453. Online at http://www.wwwords.co.uk/eerj/.

Hopkin, M. and Blyth, J. (2004). *Worlds of Welfare, Hybrid Systems, and Political Choice: Do Welfare Regimes Constrain Anti-Inequality Programmes?: How Many Varieties of Capitalism?* Structural Reform and Inequality in Western Europe. September 2004, Annual Meeting of American Political Science Association.

Hoxby, C. (2000). Does Competition Among Public Schools Benefit Students and Taxpayers?, *American Economic Review*, 90, 1209-38.

Hoxby, C. (2003a). The Economics of School Choice, Chicago University Press: Chicago.

Hoxby, C. (2003b). School Choice and School Competition: Evidence From the United States, *Swedish Economic Policy Review*, 10, 9-66.

Hursh, D. (2002). Neoliberalism and the Control of Teachers, Students, and Learning: The Rise of Standards, Standardization, and Accountability, in *Cultural Logic* 4 (1). Online at http://www.eserver.org/clogic/4-1/hursh.html.

Hursh, D., and Martina, C. (2003). "Neoliberalism and schooling in the U.S: How state and federal government education policies perpetuate inequality."

Accessed 25 April 2004. Available from http://www.jceps.com/index.php?pageID=article&articleID=12.

International Finance Corporation (IFC). (2001). "IFC and education: Washington, DC, IFC." Accessed 25 April 2004. Available from http://www.ifc.org/ar2001briefs/IFC_and_ Education.pdf.

Johnson and Lynch (2004, March 10). Sponging off the Poor. *The Guardian* (London).

Johnston, D. (2006, April 5). Big Gain for Rich Seen in Tax Cuts For Investments. *The New York Times* (USA).

Kelsh, D. (2006). *The Erasure of Class.*

Kelsh, D. and Hill, D. (2006). The Culturalization of Class and the Occluding of Class Consciousness: The Knowledge Industry in/of Education. *Journal for Critical Education Policy Studies*, 4 (1).

Kimbell, R. and Perry, D. (2001). *Design and Technology in a Knowledge Economy*. London: Engineering Council.

Laclau, E. (1996). *Deconstruction, Pragmatism, Hegemony*, Deconstruction and Pragmatism, (ed.) Mouffe, C.. London: Routledge, pp. 47-67.

Laclau, E. and Mouffe, C. (1985). *Hegemony and Socialist Strategy*, London: NLB.

Luxemburg, R. (1899/1970). *Reform or Revolution. Rosa Luxemburg Speaks.* New York: Pathfinder.

Luxemburg, R. (1916). "The War and the Workers: The Junius Pamphlet."Accessed 25 April 2004. Online at: http://www.fordham.edu/halsall/mod/1916luxemburg-junius.html.

Machin, S. and Vignoles, A. (2006). *Education Policy in the UK.* Centre for the Economics of Education, London: London School of Economics.

Maisuria, A. (2005). "The Turbulent Times of Creativity in the National Curriculum.*Policy Futures in Education,* 3 (2)."Accessed 25 April 2004. Available from http://www.wwwords. co.uk/pdf/viewpdf.asp?j=pfie&vol=3&issue=2&year=2005&article=3_Maisuria_PFIE_3_2_web&id=86.132.99.96.

Marshall, G. (1990). *In Praise of Sociology*. London: Unwin Hyman.

Marx, K. (1867) [1977]. *Capital: A Critique of Political Economy* (Vol. 1). London: Lawrence & Wishart.

Marx, K. (1977). *Selected Writings*. D. McLellan (ed.). Oxford: Oxford University Press.

McLaren, P. (2000). *Che Guevara, Paulo Freire, and the Pedagogy of Revolution*. Lanham Md: Rowman & Littlefield.

McLaren, P. (2005a). *Capitalists and Conquerors: Critical Pedagogy Against Empire*. Lanham, MD: Rowman& Littlefield.

McLaren, P. (2005b). *Red Seminars: Radical Excursions into Educational Theory, Cultural Politics and Pedagogy*. Cresskill, NJ: Hampton Press.

McLaren, P., Martin, G., Farahmandpur, R. and Jaramillo, N. (2004). Teaching in and against empire: Critical Pedagogy as Revolutionary Praxis. *Teacher Education Quarterly*, 31 (3), 131-153.

McLaren, P. and Farahmandpur, R. (2005). *Teaching against Global Capitalism and the New Imperialism: A Critical Pedagogy*. Lanham, MD: Rowman & Littlefield.

McLaren, P. and Scatamburlod'Annibale, V. (2004). Class dismissed? Historical Materialism and the Politics of "difference."*Educational Philosophy and Theory,* 36 (2), 183-199.

McNeil, L. (2000). *Contradictions of School Reform: Educational costs of standardized testing*. New York: Routledge.

Michelle, K. (2006, April 10). School Chief Predicts End of State Education. *Education Guardian.* London. Accessed 25 April 2004. Online at: http://politics.guardian.co.uk/publicservices/story/0,,1750886,00.html.

Neary, M. (1997). *Youth, Training and the Training State*. Basingstoke: Macmillan.

Ollman, B. (2001). *How to Take and Exam ... and Remake the World*. Montreal: Black Rose Books.

Pakulski, J. and Waters, M. (1996). *The Death of Class*. London: Sage.

Paraskeva, J. (2006). Continuities, discontinuities and silences@ a Marxist literary reading of Michael Apple's lines of thought. Paper delivered at the American Educational Research Association Annual Meeting, San Francisco, 7-11 April, 2006. Published in the *Journal for Critical Education Policy Studies*, 4 (2).

Reimers, F. (2000).*Unequal schools, unequal chances: The challenges to equal opportunity in the America*. Cambridge, Massachusetts: Harvard University Press.

Rikowski, G. (1996). Left alone: End time for Marxist educational theory? *British Journal of Sociology of Education* 17 (4), 415–51.

Rikowski, G. (1997). Scorched Earth: Prelude to rebuilding Marxist educational theory. *British Journal of Sociology of Educational Studies*, 18 (4), 551–74.

Rikowski, G. (2001). After the manuscript broke off: Thoughts on Marx, social class and education. Accessed 25 April 2004.Online. http://www.leeds.ac.uk/educol/documents/00001931.html.

Rikowski, G. (2002). Globalization and Education (a paper prepared for the House of Lords Select Committee on Economic Affairs, Report on 'Globalization', HL Paper 5-1, 18th November (on House of Lords CD-ROM)). Accessed 25 April 2004. Available fromhttp://education.portal.dk3.com/article.php?sid=21 and at www.ieps.org.uk.

Rikowski, G. (2003). Schools and the GATS Enigma. *Journal for Critical Education Policy Studies*, 1 (1).

Rikowski, G. (2005). *Silence on the Wolves: What is Absent in New Labour's Five Year Strategy for Education* (Occasional Paper, May). Education Research Centre: University of Brighton.

Rikowski, G. (2006). Marxism and Educational Theory and Research Today. Notes for the Marxism and Education: Renewing Dialogues VIII: Universities Plc? Seminar, 3 May 2006, University of London Institute of Education.

Rose, R., (ed.) (1960). *Must Labour Lose*? Harmondsworth: Penguin.

Rosskam, E. (ed.) (2006). *Winners or Losers? Liberalizing Public Services*. Geneva: ILO

Saltman, K. and Gabbard, D. (2003). *Education as Enforcement: The Militarization and Corporatization of Schools*. London: Routledge Falmer.

Saltman, K. (2005). *The Edison Schools: Corporate Schooling and the Assault on Public Education*. London: Routledge Falmer.

Sarup, M. (1978). *Marxism and Education*. London: Routledge & Kegan Paul.

Schugurensky, D. and Davidson-Harden, A. (2003). From Cordoba to Washington: WTO/GATS and Latin American Education, *Globalization, Societies and Education*, 1 (3), pp. 321-357.

Strass, G. and Hansen, B. (2006). CEO pay soars in 2005 as select group break the $100 mark. *USA Today,* 11 April.

Thomas, V., Wang, Y. and Fan, X. (2000) *Measuring Education Inequality: Gini Coefficients of Education*, World Bank.Accessed 25 April 2004.

Tomasevski, K. (2006a). Six reasons why the World Bank should be debarred from education. Tomasevski, K. (2006b). Both arsonist and fire-fighter: The World Bank on school fees.

Toynbee, P. (2003). *Hard work: Life in low paid Britain*. London: Bloomsbury.

Whitty, G., Power, S. and Halpin, D. (1998). *Devolution and choice in education: The school, the state and the market*. Buckingham, UK: Open University Press.

Willis, P. (1977). *Learning to Labour: How working class kids get working class jobs*. Farnborough: Saxon House.

World Bank (2006). "Economics of Education." Accessed 25 April 2004. Online at http://web.worldbank.org/WBSITE/EXTERNAL/TOPICS/EXTEDUCATION/0, content MDK:20264769~menuPK:613701~pagePK:148956~piPK:216618~theSitePK: 282386,00.html.

7

Immiseration Capitalism, Activism and Education: Resistance, Revolt and Revenge

Dave Hill

Summary

This is a panoptic paper in five parts.

*In **Part One**, Immiseration Capitalism, I examine the current neoliberal cum neoconservative austerity capitalism and its 'class war from above', in particular its resultant relative immiseration and its absolute immiseration, with particular reference to Greece, Ireland, Britain and the USA.*

*In **Part Two**, Anger at, Analysis of and Activism within/against Immiseration Capitalism, I argue that there is a necessity for Anger, (Marxist class-based) Analysis, and Activism, with Programme, Organization and Strategy. Activism, Analysis and Strategy are then addressed in terms both of electoralism and in terms of direct, extra-Parliamentary activism, both being deemed necessary, but with the former having limitations and the latter being deemed essential. Here, I lay a stress on the importance of revolutionary Marxist party.*

*In **Part Three**, I identify the main features of Neoliberalism, Neoconservatism and Education for Austerity Capitalism and Immiseration, contrasting this, in ies, Socialist Education. Here, I summarize key aspects of critical pedagogy and socialist education, and also summarise Marxist critiques*

***Part Four**, with Activism in the Education Arena: Critical Pedagogy of theories that serve to disable class based analysis and activism in education and society: Postmodernism, identity politics, and revisionist/reformist socialism.*

*In **Part Five**, Resistance: Revolt, Revenge and Strategic Activism, I return to Resistance and Revenge and call for them to be strategically focused.*

The paper is also slightly autobiographical, referencing some of my own relevant experiences, blogs and writing. As a panoptic paper it is therefore, inevitable a summary paper, in places, an extended annotated bibliography.

Keywords: *Immiseration, capitalism, socialist education, revolutionary Marxism, activism, critical pedagogy, revenge*

Part 1. Immiseration Capitalism

Across the capitalist world governing capitalist political parties and governments are using Naomi Klein's '*Shock Doctrine*', (2007), to once again wrench back to themselves what David Harvey (in his *A Brief History of Neoliberalism* (2006)) exposed as the increasing concentrations of wealth in a 'class war from above'.

Despite the views of some media pundits, that neoliberalism was dealt mortal blows as an ideology after the Lehman bank demise of September 2008 (e.g. Seamus Milne in *The Guardian*, see Milne, 2008), it is clear that the ruling capitalist classes of many American and European economies, and the international capitalist class as a whole, have not forsaken neoliberalism. Indeed, they are using its nostrums and doctrines with a vengeance to ensure that: firstly, the capitalist system is saved and, secondly, that workers pay for capitalist crisis. The drive to get back to 'normal' capitalist life through pursuing neoliberal policies has recently been made abundantly clear in the case of the UK through Colin Crouch's (2011) detailed account regarding the 'strange non-death' of neoliberalism in overall economic and social policy. And, at a journalistic level, Chang (2012) highlights the similarities between the Structural Adjustment Programmes (SAPs) enforced on governments in Latin America and Africa in the 1980s and 1990s by the IMF and ` European governments inflicting an old IMF-style programme on their own populations (see also Chang, 2010). We see the `explosion of precariousness and the social destructuration in the capitalist metropolises' (International Viewpoint, 2012).

The result is welfare is slashed, the poor live more precariously, more unhealthily, and die earlier. The low paid strata of the working class are duped and failed by the ideological apparatuses of the state, and repressed and kept in line and in prison, and (in some cases) in the ghetto, by the repressive apparatuses of the state. One of the most extreme examples of attacks on the right to organize, and to organize protest is the recent Republican legislation in the US state of Wisconsin to take away public sector workers' rights to collective bargaining (incidentally, occasioning the largest trade union rallying and activism for decades, MacAskill, 2011; Socialist World, 2011).

We are now, in much of the advanced, late capitalist industrialized world, in an era of intensified class struggle, intensified stratification, and intensified resistance. In the words of Karl Marx and Friedrich Engels' of 1847 in *The Communist Manifesto*, 'Society as a whole is more and more splitting up into two great hostile camps, into two great classes directly facing each other: Bourgeoisie and Proletariat' (Marx and Engels, 1847).

The corollary of this intensification of class conflict and resistance, with riots and flames in the streets of Athens, Madrid, London, Lisbon, with millions demonstrating and taking part in general strikes, 'Occupy'/ indignado movements, student protests. Accompanying this is the intensification of repression, together with the rise once again of Nazi and extreme right, racist, anti-trade unionist, anti-Left forces, For example, in Greece, in both the 6 May and the 17 June elections of 2012, the avowedly neo-Nazi Golden Dawn Party won approximately 7% of the votes- including the reported support from 50% of Athens police, and is currently polling over 20% (Smith, 2012). Once again in history, we need to realise that, in Brecht's words (from the final line of his play *The Irresistible Rise of Arturo Ui*) warning us that, even if Hitler is dead, "the bitch that bore him is in heat again". The bitch of capitalism in crisis and under threat.

In what follows, I detail examples of *Austerity Capitalism* and *Immiseration* from states where I have been politically active, attending meetings, taking part in strikes and demonstrations, making speeches at trade union, left activist political and academic meetings, in the last decade: in Greece, Ireland, Britain and the USA.

Greece

Greece, under the heel of the austerity policies of the Troika, (the European Commission (of the European Union), the European Central Bank, and the International Monetary Fund and the 'Memoranda' of Cuts (in salaries, pensions, jobs) and privatisations has become the economic, political and social labouratory for the capitalist onslaught on the pay, workers' rights, and public and welfare services/provision. Greece is where the transnational capitalist class is seeing just how far it can push a national working class before there is social breakdown and revolution (Kloke, 2012a, b). The aim of the transnational capitalist class is clearly to reduce the living standards and lives of Greeks to the levels of other Balkan economies, to the wage levels of •200 per month, from what is the current salary levels of •700 a month (Nikolakai, 2012).

Not since the Nazi occupation, with its mass killings/executions of Greeks and deaths from starvation have Greeks from various strata of the working class suffered such privation, anxiety, terror, impoverishment. This is affecting the so-called 'working class' and the so-called 'middle class'. Both of these strata are, in fact, strata of the working class, those whose labour power is exploited by the capitalist class. I discuss the classic Marxist binary definition of class towards the end of this article). Both strata of the working class suffer. The 'social catastrophe', the 'Catastroika', (Catastroika, 2012; see also Socialist World, 2012) social impoverishment through mass unemployment (with 50 per cent youth unemployment) large cuts in salaries/wages and pensions, the imposition of supplementary taxes, the immiseration that Marx predicted, in *Das Kapital,* (Marx, 1867, Vol. 1, Chapter 25) with real wages falling, and working conditions deteriorating. In recent decades there has been across the capitalist world, the progression of '*relative* immiseration', with the wealth of the working class growing far more slowly than that of the capitalist class. But what we are seeing now, most spectacularly of all in Greece, but also in countries such as Britain, Ireland and the USA, is the progression of '*absolute* immiseration', with an absolute deterioration of income, wealth and living conditions and mass impoverishment (see Hill 2006a; Greaves, Hill and Maisuria, 2007; Hill, Greaves and Maisuria, 2009).

The aim of the Troika is for the Greek wage to be reduced at 150 euro/month. This was said publicly in a hearing at European Parliament after a question of a, Euro-MP EMP Nikos Hountis. Unemployment now (Summer 2012) is 24 per cent whereas in 2008, it was 8 per cent. Among youth, more than half are unemployed. In a population of approximately 11 million, there are now 450,000 families with no wage or any kind of income. In Athens alone there are 25,000 homeless, and the last two years in Greece there have been more than 3,000 suicides (Vatikiotis, 2012). Sotiris (2012a) details the post-June 2012 election demands of 'the Troika' including cutting the number of universities, for a new reduction of the minimum wage (which has already been reduced from 751 to 586 euros), the Troika demands a complete dismantling of whatever has been left of labour market regulation, including abolishing the 5-day working week and re-introducing the 6-day working week.

Sotiris' (2012a) analysis is that

> This process can be described as the "downsizing of a country". In the end Greece will emerge as a poorer country, with a diminished productive base, with reduced sovereignty, with a political class accustomed to almost neo-colonial forms of supervision and with a Greek bourgeoisie ready to accept a subaltern position in the new emerging European division of labour and to see its erstwhile ambition to play a more important economic and political role in the region curtailed in exchange for a violent change in the balance of forces with labour.

But Greece is not alone in facing this capitalist onslaught on the lives, conditions, health and services of the welfare and social state. While the hearts of Greeks burn with anger and misery, the super-rich fiddle—avoiding tax and taking bigger and bigger profits. 'Greece's richest entrepreneurs, the shipping company owners, do not pay any taxes on their earnings, which are exempted from taxation on the grounds that they are international under a rule incorporated into Greece's constitution in 1967, the first year the junta of the colonels was in power'. (Dreier, 2012a).

Britain

This immiseration, both *relative* immiseration and *absolute* immiseration, is also so evident in Britain "The 1,000 richest people in Britain became 30 per cent richer in the last year. That's a £77 billion rise in wealth—enough to wipe out around half the government's budget deficit" (Dorling, 2010a. See also Dorling 2010 b). One banker, Bob Diamond (until recently, head of Barclays Bank) 'earned' £100 million in 6 years. Whereas, for the masses, 'Cuts push UK workers' living standards back 30 years' (Shaoul, 2012), with 'working families struggling to make ends meet are worse off than they were 30 years ago'. Shaoul reports on *All in this together?*, a report by Bristol University's Stewart Lansley, published in January 2012, which shows that 'the share in national output (Gross Domestic Product, GDP) going to workers over the last 30 years has fallen from 58 per cent in 1978 to 53.8 per cent in 2011 ... This is a cumulative wage loss of £1.3 trillion. In 2011, workers lost £60 billion in wages, earning more than £2,000 a year less than in 1978.

Lansley points out that

> Top executives in the UK have been awarding themselves an ever-larger share of the economic cake since the depth of the downturn, even though the cake has been shrinking in size. As a result, the pay gap between executives and their staff has continued to widen, despite the persistence of the economic crisis. In 2000, the ratio of FTSE 100 top executive to typical employee pay stood at 47:1. By 2007 this had nearly doubled to 92:1. By 2011 it has risen again to 102:1. (Lansley, 2012:27).

Whereas for workers,

> In the year to June 2010, average real pay fell by 3.6 per cent, and then by a further 3.8 per cent in the year to June 2011. Fewer than 2 out of every 100 employees enjoyed a pay settlement above the rate of inflation in the year to October 2011. It was a similar story in 2010: while 28 per cent of the workforce enjoyed a nominal pay rise in the first half of 2011, close to three

> in five had their pay frozen and around 6 per cent took a nominal pay cut.
>
> A significant minority of the workforce has suffered a mix of pay cuts and worsening conditions of work, including longer hours, cuts in fringe benefits such as car allowances, and reductions in holiday entitlement and maternity and paternity leave. (Lansley, 2012:29)

Just to take one other example of inequality, in 2010 in London, the top 10 per cent of society had on average a wealth of £933,563 compared to the meagre £3,420 of the poorest 10 per cent—a wealth multiple of 273. This is the multiple of the top 10 per cent. The multiple of the top 1 per cent would be in the thousands. This level of inequality has not been seen since the days of the slave trade. (Ramesh, 2010).

And this increasing impoverishment and immiseration of the poor is set to continue. *Who Gains from Growth?*, drawn up by the Institute for Fiscal Studies (IFS) and the Institute for Economic Research (IER), forecasts that 'even if the economy returns to a "golden scenario" of steady growth, with no further cuts than those already announced' the results will be that 'a household on a middle income of £22,900 will forfeit £800 by 2020, a 3 per cent drop. A low-income couple struggling on £10, 600 (at 2009 prices) can expect a crippling drop of 15 per cent to £9,000' However, in stark contrast, 'those on £50,000 plus a year will enjoy the cream of 1.5 million new jobs and see a rise of 0.2% in their annual income' (*The Observer*, 2012).

These widening gaps in income and wealth will inevitably, accompanied as they are by the decline on welfare service and welfare and labour benefits, result in the poor dying even earlier than the rich. In terms of 'Healthy Life Expectancy' (HLE) at birth, with males in the 'Professional Class' having an HLE of 77.0 years, and males from 'Unskilled' backgrounds having, at birth, an HLE of 65.6 years. (White and Edgar, 2012). According to *The Guardian* newspaper, in 2006, life expectancy in the Glasgow constituency of Shettleston was 63, that is, 13 years less than the UK average (Gillan, 2006).

Ireland

And, as for Ireland, 'The 300 richest people in Ireland are worth almost €57bn or more than the entire Libyan or Croatian economy. They've got much richer too, with close to €6.7bn added to their combined wealth over the last year'. No hard times for them! (*The Independent*, 2011).

In the article 'Ireland: Shock, austerity, Sinn Féin and the United Left Alliance' Derwin (2012) writes that 'the new cohort of young teachers in September will be starting with 30 per cent less pay than they would have had before the cuts'. Derwin continues,

> The "What's Left" tracker index published by the Irish League of Credit Unions in April found that up to 47% of Irish adults have less than €100 to spend by the end of the month once bills are paid (*Irish Times*, April 16, 2012a).

He continues,

> A Central Statistics Office survey on income and living conditions in Ireland in March showed the average income of the top 20% of earners was 5.5 times greater than those in the lowest 20% (*Irish Times*, March 28, 2012b). This inequality ratio—up from 4.3 a year earlier—is the highest figure on record since this measurement was first used in 2004. The survey found that average disposable income for Irish households in 2010 was €22,168, a 5% drop from the 2009 figure of €23,326. This is the lowest figure recorded since 2006. (Derwin, 2012)

The newly elected Fine Gael/Labour Party coalition government in Ireland (in the February 2011 general election) replaced the FiannaFáil government. But, as in other countries, the incoming government adopted austerity policies not dissimilar to their predecessors.

> Instead of getting rid of 30,000 public employees, as Fine Gael wanted, or 17,000, in accordance with the Labour Party's campaign, they reached a compromise and settled for 25,000 to go by 2015. They will cut €9 billion from public spending. They did not increase direct taxes but did increase indirect ones, so the elite will rest easy in their beds. (*Socialist Voice*, 2011).

Socialist Voice continues,

> The privatization of €2 billion of what they call "non-strategic" state assets will only be the start. In the "Programme for Ireland" signed with the EU and IMF there are clear commitments to selling off state assets, including the ESB, An BordGáis, ports, airports, and much more. €2 billion will not be enough (Socialist Voice, 2011).

USA

In the USA, commentators such as Robert Frank, point out that billionaires live in 'Richistan' (Frank, 2007; TimesOnline, 2007) where a particular anxiety appears to be that there is a five year wait for luxury Rolls Royce cars. One CEO (Chief Executive Officer), incoming CEO for Yahoo, has been awarded a pay package of $129 million over five years. (Grey, 2012). As Grey points out,

> This is considerably more than the $102 million the city of Detroit said it would save when, the same week, its Democratic mayor, David Bing, unilaterally imposed an across-the-board 10 per cent cut in city workers'

> pay, along with drastic cuts in health care and hundreds of layoffs. The obscene and absurd compensation package for Mayer—at a time when manufacturing workers are being told their new wage benchmark is $13 an hour or less—is but one more expression of the decay of capitalism and the decadence of the new aristocracy that presides over it. Nowhere are the avarice of the ruling class and its plundering of society more naked than in America.

Millions of workers' main anxiety is the weekly or monthly wait for the next pay cheque to buy the family groceries. Millions in advanced capitalist countries, billions globally, live in 'Pooristan'.

In the USA, 'Inequality in the United States is on the rise, whether measured in terms of wages, family incomes, or wealth and is much higher than that of other advanced countries' (Economic Policy Institute, 2006). And, millions in the USA

> are outraged by a level of class inequality that has taken on obscene proportions not seen since the 1920s, where today 130,000 people have as much wealth as the poorest third of the country. Millions are appalled by rampant corruption, war profiteering, and drastic cuts in desperately needed social services while billions are being spent each week to destroy Iraq. (*International Socialist Review*, 2007).

And, as Yates reminds us, in the USA,

> Over the years 1950 to 1970, for each additional dollar made by those in the bottom 90 per cent of income earners, those in the top 0.01 percent received an additional $162. In contrast, from 1990 to 2002, for every added dollar made by those in the bottom 90 per cent, those in the uppermost 0.01 per cent (today around 14,000 households) made an additional $18,000 (Yates, 2006)

More recently, two reports in Sept 2011 show the shocking growth of social inequality in the United States, with the concentration of wealth in the hands of a few people on a scale not seen since the Great Depression. (Kishore, 2011) (Harvey, 2005, and Dumenil and Levy, 2004 are very clear on this).

Forbes magazine shows that the '400 richest Americans, combined net worth has soared to $1.53 trillion, up 12 per cent since last year'. For the rich, in their apartheid type social segregation, it is party-time, dancing on the graves of those who die early through poverty' Kilshore reports that the 'number of Americans living in poverty—defined as about $22,000 for a family of four—soared to 46.2 million last year, its highest level on record'. And the personal wealth of one man in New York, John Paulson, 'at $15.5 billion was approximately equal to the total net income of the bottom 20 per cent of the New York City Metropolitan area, or about 1.6

million people'. (Kishore, 2011)

At the global level, 'a far-reaching new study suggests a staggering $21tn in assets has been lost to global tax havens. If taxed, that could have been enough to put parts of Africa back on its feet – and even solve the euro crisis' (*The Guardian*, 2012). The article continues, 'the world's super-rich have taken advantage of lax tax rules to siphon off at least $21 trillion, and possibly as much as $32tn, from their home countries and hide it abroad'.

The structure of the rest of this paper, building on an examination of 'Immiseration Capitalism', now moves to: Anger, Analysis (Marxist), Activism, Programme, Organization, Strategy.

Part 2. Anger at, Analysis of and Activism within/against Immiseration Capitalism

In this paper I argue that we need anger, to feel anger, and to display *anger*, at austerity capitalism, at its social class based differential impacts. These impacts are of course, felt differentially within different groups within the working class. Many ethnic minorities, women and the disabled are, in general, not only oppressed, (discriminated against, demeaned, degraded) but are also exploited (in terms of the rewards they gain for selling their labour power) more than other workers).

Anger needs to be accompanied by Marxist class-based *analysis*, of capitalism, of an analysis and understanding of who wins and who loses in capitalism, of who caused the current crisis and who continues to profit by it, and who loses through the crisis and has to pay for it. For me, in my writings and speeches, as a political and trade union activist, and as an academic activist and writer, it is Marxist analysis, of capitalism, the exploitation of the labour power of workers, the capital-labour relation, that best analyses, explains, the current crisis in education and the wider crises in society/politics/economics.

However, anger and the (Marxist) analysis are not enough. This analysis has to lead to *activism*. Activism of a particular type, for the revolutionary transformation of capitalism into democratic socialism/ Marxism. I am using the word 'revolutionary' here to denote major, societal, economic and political change, to denote a transition from the current neoliberal *cum* neoconservative capitalism to democratic socialism/Marxism. Concerning 'democratic socialism', I want to make it clear that here I am *not* talking about parliamentarist social democracy, a social democratic notion of parliamentary "socialism", even of the temporarily benign welfarist redistributionist kind. By democratic socialism, I am trying to express that the goal should be the political power of workers' organizations, that the socialist democracy I, and revolutionary Marxists talk about and work/agitate for, has a revolutionary class content.

By 'the political power of workers' organizations'; I am referring to organizations in Greece that currently exist in embryo, and were apparent and in existence in particular during the 'hot summer' of 2011, and continue in various forms, such as self-help/soup kitchens, 'neighbourhood committees', or 'local assemblies' or 'popular assemblies' together with 'workers' committees' running factories and enterprises that has/have been taken over under workers' control. In other countries in other times such area neighbourhood committees and such factory/enterprise committees might be called 'soviets' or 'workers' councils' (see, for example, Maltby and Thomas, 2012; Catastroika, 2012; Submedia TV, 2012. In this section of the paper I am indebted to Jette Kroman, 2012, for her comments on aspects of political theory/analysis).

Activism is translated into and through a political *programme*, a series of demands/policies. To realize those demands, to progress towards them, requires a means, a vehicle, *organization*. On the question of organization there have been and are considerable debates, between, for example, Anarchists, Anarcho-Syndicalists, the Occupy Movements, social democrats, and various types of Marxist-Leninists, for example about horizontal and vertical organization, vanguardism, democracy from below, and democratic (or, indeed, undemocratic) centralism- about the form of party organization.

I recognize that there are many theoreticians and activists who do not share a preference, an analysis, that leads to privileging the party form of organization. In the November 2012 edition of the *Journal for Critical Education Policy Studies* Issue 10, 2) there are, for example, two articles arguing/exemplifying non-vanguardist and non-vertical forms of organization (Neary, 2012; Neary and Amsler, 2012). Neary (2012) talks of horizontal non-hierarchical sets of perspectives in his education related writing on (and indeed, participation in) *The Edu-Factory Collective* in Britain and the *Universidad Nomada* in Spain.

In Greece in particular, some Anarchist groups have played and continue to play a major historic and contemporary role in anti-fascist/anti-racist/anti-Nazi and anti-capitalist protest, resistance and rebellion. I am not going to rehearse here the considerable debate between the horizontalist form of organization of the Occupy, Indignados, UK Uncut, Tahrir Square organization and their strengths and weaknesses. Instead, I counter pose here the party form of organization. In practice there is and must be cross-dialogue between the different schools of thought on these issues. With Malott (2012) I am in favour of 'building affinity with horizontal, non-hierarchical anarchists and other radicals who do not believe in party politics or any form of working class centralization associated with socialist revolution'. This affinity is, of course, built in side by side struggles against the cuts, against fascists, on the streets, in meetings, in demonstrations.

I do advocate the party form of organization, with internal party pluralism (Mandel, 1970) to put socialist policies into effect, organization to seek and to take power. By internal party pluralism a party comprising/including/embracing forces coming from different experiences and traditions, and welcoming/facilitating the functioning of internal factions and tendencies—but united firmly on the platform of the transitional strategy and 'permanent revolution' (Trotsky, L., 1931).

The notion of programme needs to be linked directly to the notion of strategy— thereby expressing that I am arguing for a system of transitional demands with the aim for the workers to topple the bourgeois state and take power.

On the question of *strategy*, that power may be taken, or won, through direct mass action or, through a combination of both direct mass action on the one hand, and, on the other hand, through electoralism, the 'parliamentary road to socialism'. If we talk about electoralism we have to be clear that we welcome reforms, but from a clear, Marxist, critical position. Thus, in Greece, were Syriza to take office currently (in late 2012) through the electoral system, it would take *office* but not *power*. It might or might not carry out some reforms, some 'dented shield strategy' against the current austerity programme. But it would not be taking *power*. That power would still be held by the national and EU/international capitalist class and their organizations such as The Troika. It would only be taking power if it were to be accompanied by mass action in support of mass nationalizations, workers' control, and control over organs of the state such as the police, armed forces, bureaucracies. One of the criticisms of the major socialist successes of in Venezuela, and one of the lessons to be learned for Europe, is the resilience of national capitalisms and their international alliances and support systems (Denis, 2012; Gomez, 2012). While acknowledging the very major gains by the poor in Venezuela under 14 years of Chavez, this left critique of Chavez notes that 'In the absence of a break with the logic of capital, the main beneficiaries of oil revenues have been the local bourgeoisie and sectors of multinational corporations' (Miranda, 2012).

I want to elabourate on the question of reforms and reformism. In terms of *reformism*, reformist political strategy is one way by which the capitalist class incorporates left forces into capitalism and its institutions and pay-offs and privileges. It is a way for the capitalist class to link the working class to the bourgeois state and capitalist system through parliamentarism. This is clearly a major and century-old bourgeois strategy within the workers movement.

The question of *reform* is a different, though linked, one: in this current period of the intensification of class struggle, and intensification/clarification of class consciousness and organization (to different degrees in different countries) it is one of class struggle by revolutionary means to gain any in fact concessions from the crisis-ridden capitalist class.

As Kelsh and Hill (2006) summarized,

> We support reforms and revisionist political and economic advances that seek to improve the lives of workers, for example, anti-capitalist as well as reformist campaigns and movements such as campaigns for tenants' rights, gender equality, race equality, and campaigns against SATS or the privatization of schools. But, it is crucial to note, we do so *from a critical position*.We believe, along with Marx and Engels (1848/1985), that it is necessary to "fight for the attainment of the immediate aims... of the working class" (p. 119). For, as Marx argues, "by maturing the material conditions, and the combination on a social scale of the processes of production, [the fight for the attainment of immediate aims] matures the contradictions and antagonisms of the capitalist form of production, and thereby provides, along with the elements for the formation of a new society, the forces for exploding the old one" (Marx, 1867/1967a, p. 503; Marx explains this in Chapters 8 and 9 of *Wage-Labour and Capital,* and Chapter 15 of *Capital,* Volume 3).
>
> Yet we also believe, again following Marx and Engels (1985), that it is necessary to "take up a critical position" in relation to reform movements, and to do so in order to educate the proletariat—that class comprised of all who do not own the means of production and are therefore compelled to sell their labour-power to survive—regarding "the hostile antagonism between bourgeoisie and proletariat" (p. 120). In doing so, we aim to provide knowledges that help enable (in relation to various sectional, local, and single-issue campaigns) the development of class consciousness—knowledge of capitalist social relations—and awareness of the need to transform capitalism into socialism.

On the question of strategy, Trotsky clearly differentiated between three types of programme: the *minimum* (reformist) programme; the *transitional* programme (or policy that would break capitalism and which seems feasible for layers of workers to support); and a *maximum* programme, towards which we might move, but would come into force after the demise of capitalism, rather than as a set of immediately realizable aims- (Trotsky, 1938; Hill, 2012a).

For Trotsky (1938, also set out in Hill, 2012a)

> The strategic task of the next period—prerevolutionary period of agitation, propaganda and organization—consists in overcoming the contradiction between the maturity of the objective revolutionary conditions and the immaturity of the proletariat and its vanguard (the confusion and disappointment of the older generation, the inexperience of the younger generation. It is necessary to help the masses in the process of the daily struggle to find the bridge between present demand and the socialist program of the revolution. This bridge should include a system of transitional demands, stemming from today's conditions and from today's consciousness of wide layers of the working class and unalterably leading to one final conclusion: the conquest of power by the proletariat.....
>
> The strategic task of the Fourth International lies not in reforming capitalism but in its overthrow. Its political aim is the conquest of power by the proletariat for the purpose of expropriating the bourgeoisie.....
>
> The Fourth International does not discard the programme of the old "minimal" demands to the degree to which these have preserved at least part of their vital forcefulness. Indefatigably, it defends the democratic rights and social conquests of the workers. But it carries on this day-to-day work within the framework of the correct actual, that is, revolutionary perspective. Insofar as the old, partial, "minimal" demands of the masses clash with the destructive and degrading tendencies of decadent capitalism – and this occurs at each step—the Fourth International advances a system of transitional demands, the essence of which is contained in the fact that ever more openly and decisively they will be directed against the very bases of the bourgeois regime. The old "minimal programme" is superseded by the transitional program, the task of which lies in systematic mobilization of the masses for the proletarian revolution.

Part 3. Neoliberalism, Neoconservatism and Education for Austerity Capitalism and Immiseration

Capitalist education plays a major role in maintaining the social universe of capital. Firstly it not moulds and develops the labour power required by Capital, without which Capital could not profit and survive, it plays a very central role in increasing Malott (2012) summarizes why:

> the productivity of labour. …has been an increasing necessity of the capitalist class due to *the falling rate of profit*. For Marx (1867/1967), the falling rate of profit is one of the central laws of capitalist accumulation—a system based on perpetual growth and thus movement as capitalists, driven by sheer

survival, exist in fierce competition with one another, seek ever higher returns and greater market share. This law stems from "the composition of capital" itself consisting of constant capital (i.e. the means of production such as machinery, land, and buildings) and variable capital (i.e. human labour power) (Marx, 1867/1967, p. 612).

Marx stressed the importance of understanding that these two elements are internally related. That is, when capitalists (at least the small percentage of successful and/or governmentally subsidized ones) enlarge production by reinvesting profits to expand constant capital, an equal increase in variable capital must be realized to set it in motion. If all relevant variables, such as the supply of wage-workers, in a given economy remain constant, the perpetually increasing demand for labourers by the capitalist class will reach a point when "the demand for labourers may exceed the supply, and therefore, wages may rise" (Marx, 1867/1967, p. 613). Of course, as Marx stresses, capitalists, driven by their own insatiable quest for surplus value, have been shown to withdraw their capital from circulation before investing in a situation where wages completely eliminated profitability. The economic cycle therefore ebbs and flows, correcting itself, not in the interests of society as a whole, but in the interests of the capitalist class always.

Toward these ends, capitalism has a long, complex, and often contradictory history of engaging in many practices to counter *the falling rate of profit*. Of these, we might underscore:

Increasing exploitation by driving down the standard of living through dramatically reducing benefits, such as health insurance and public education

War and other forms of wasteful production, but also war to force open markets and gain access to both constant and variable capital

Immigration has long played a central role in increasing the reserve army of workers needed to keep the supply of variable capital up and thus wages and demand down

Financialization, more recently, has played a central role in creating the appearance of growth, when no real productive growth had occurred

Finally, Marx stresses that in the historical development of capital, and even in the business cycle itself, there comes a point when increasing the productivity of labour becomes "the most powerful lever of accumulation" (Marx, 1867/1967, p. 621)—thereby underscoring the significance of education in the historical development of capitalism.

Education also plays the ideological function of normalising death by starvation amidst a sea of plenty, or normalising immiseration and glorifying extreme wealth and exploitation of labour power, of pretending 'we are all in this together'. I summarize the specifically neoliberal developments in education across much of the globe since the Thatcher-Reagan era, noting that they are accompanied by the mailed fist, the use of the repressive state apparatuses.

Neoliberalism and/in Education

In this section I identify, and briefly summarise, ten salient characteristics of neoliberalism in education. These are very well rehearsed in the literature on neoliberalism and education. (e.g. Hill, 2003a, 2004, 2005, 2006a, 2009a, b; Ross and Gibson, 2007; Hill and Kumar, 2009; Hill and Rosskam, 2009; Porfilio and Malott, 2008; Kumar, 2012; Rikowski, 2012). For reasons of space, I will restrict myself here to briefly commenting on the first of these characteristics.

1. Privatization/Pre-Privatization of schooling and higher education. For example, in England, Academies-schools paid for by the state but given over to private control; also, in England, 'Free Schools', schools set up by groups of parents, where the schools are funded by the state. In the USA, some 'Charter Schools' are 'for –profit, run by what Glenn Rikowski calls 'Edubusinesses'—national and international education corporations (Rikowski, 2003a, b). There has also been in the USA and the UK, privatization of national and local para-educational services (cleaning, meals, school inspections). In Britain, where until recently there has been only one private university (all the rest being state universities), a number of private companies and organizations are now being awarded degree awarding powers. Rikowski (2012) writes powerfully on 'the higher education sausage machine' and its ramifications in terms of some of the aspects below, such as intensification of work, commodification, consumerization. (See also, Callinicos, 2006).

2. Cuts in public spending/salaries/pensions/benefits: Mass redundancies/dismissals in universities. The result is a deterioration in provision for those whom use these state/public services, and an increasing gap between those who use state/public services on the one hand, and private services on the other.

3. Marketization, competition between schools and between universities in the name of 'choice' and differentiation. The result is a (racialized/gendered/social class) hierarchy of provision.

4. Vocational education for human capital (except for the ruling class) with differential funding or 'vocational subjects/degrees on the one hand, and for an abolition of government funding for Humanities/Social Science/ Art subjects at universities.

5. Brutalizing management of the workforce: New Public Managerialism as represented in growing and huge differentials in pay/ 'packages' and power between senior management of schools and colleges and universities on the one hand, and the 'shop floor workers', the teachers, administrators, manual staff) on the other. This has signified an end to what there was of democratic participative and collegiate management and decision-making in schools and universities, resulting in 'boss rule'.

6. Competition between workers—performance related pay/payment by results. This is another aspect of the end of collegiality. Teachers and university professors in England and Wales now compete for a restricted range of 'performance related pay'.

7. Casualization/'Precariatization' of public sector workers, with the replacement of full-time and contracted fractional appointment staff being replaced by casual academic labour, hourly paid staff with no security of employment, and staff on short-term contracts.

8. Attacks on trade unions, on workers' rights, on centralized pay-bargaining. Internationally neoliberal governments wish to 'union bust', to break union power, to break national collective bargaining agreements. This can also include derecognizing unions for collective bargaining purposes, withdrawing union facilities, or making union membership illegal.

9. *'Management speak'/Discourse of the market,* e.g. students as 'customers', 'delivering' the curriculum, with the discourse of the market replacing that of social responsibility.

10. Denigration of/ideological attacks on public sector workforce with their pensions, relative job security. In country after country, schools and universities are accused by neoliberals of having suffered 'producer capture', of being run for the benefit of education workers. Public sector workers are depicted as 'lazy', 'feather bedded', with 'gold plated pensions', of being 'the enemy' of prosperity, and of being 'infected with liberal and socialist ideologies'.

Neoconservatism, Repression and Education

Where the ideological state apparatuses (Althusser, 1971) don't work effectively enough, the repressive state apparatuses are brought in. State oppression is increased with intensified use of the repressive state apparatuses and their weapons. One example is that on the Greek General Strike of 15 June 2011 in which I participated-) with tear gas being lobbed by police into Syntagma Metro, clouds of it engulfing Syntagma Aquare, and with Delta Force police, two per motorbike, clubbing demonstrators hospitalizing them. In the USA, in a similar ratcheting up state violence, there was the famous case of a police officer pepper-spraying teargasing seated peaceful protesters at University of California Davis University Occupy encampment, casually strolling along a row of them, and spraying them with pepper spray.

Thus, neoliberalism is not unaccompanied. It is accompanied- and enforced- with laws, guns, gas canisters, tactics such as 'kettling', by neo-conservatism in its repressive and controlling forms. This control is asserted increasingly strongly over education.

These below are some of the characteristics of neo-conservatism in education in various countries.

11. *Neo-Conservatism: Control of Curricula* of schools, teacher education, universities, with the removal of 'dangerous' content. An example is the control of school curriculum in England and Wales, and elsewhere, by a (rigidly policed and surveilled) National Curriculum for schools. Another example is the removal of most sociological, political, and social justice issues from the teacher education curriculum in England and Wales in 1992/1993.

12. *Neo-Conservatism: Control of Pedagogy*: in England and Wales, not only is the curriculum circumscribed, so is pedagogy. The teacher centred methodology of the National Literacy Strategy has come to dominate teacher-student interaction, replacing the student centred methods typical of much primary (elementary) and some secondary (high) school education in the preceding decades, especially during the 'child/student centred, liberal-progressive pedagogy of the 1960s and 1970s.

13. *Neo-Conservatism: Control of Students:* the imposition of heavy university fees, currently up to £9,000 a year, is having the effect of making studying at universities much more instrumental than when there were no university tuition fees. (Fees of up to £1,000 a year, were introduced by the New Labour government in 1998).

14. *Neo-Conservatism: Control of Teachers/Professors*: in schools and universities there is now much more surveillance of teachers/professors, a target culture in schools for assessment and exam results, with penalties for 'underperforming teachers and schools, including school closures and schools being forcibly turned into Academies, with many teachers losing their jobs. These 'high stakes tests' penalize (in the USA and England and Wales) schools in working class areas, those whose exam and test results are not as high as in richer areas. There is also punishment of dissidents and union activists in schools and universities. This is not legal, but managements find ways of discriminating against and even dismissing union and radical activists. (I have, arguably, been 'moved on' from 5 of my 7 jobs in teaching, see Hill, 2003b).

15. *Appeal to a more 'ordered' and hierarchical past, and to 'traditional' values*. This can be and is seen as partially appropriated by Fascist and Nazi parties.

16. *Neo-Conservatism: brute force is applied*, such as riot police breaking up campus demonstrations in the USA and in England and Wales. Other than the University of California, Davis events mentioned above, police in riot gear with dogs attacked a demonstration at Sussex University in March 2010 (Jack, 2010). And on demonstrations in Greece, police use of tear gas, sound/stun grenades, and beatings are common, both in the Hot Summer of 2011 and the Hot Autumn of 2012. And, as Smith (2012) makes clear, there are in some countries deep links between the police and Fascist/Nazi groups. Kostas Tsironis (2012) wrote a savage and damning indictment in *The Guardian* (London) (9 October) about not just the links between the Nazi Golden Dawn part and the Athens police, but the Athens police starting to use Nazi-type brutalizing tactics against detainees:

> Fifteen anti-fascist protesters arrested in Athens during a clash with supporters of the neo-Nazi party Golden Dawn have said they were tortured in the Attica General Police Directorate (GADA)—the Athens equivalent of Scotland Yard—and subjected to what their lawyer describes as an Abu Ghraib-style humiliation.
>
> Some said they were burned on the arms with a cigarette lighter, and they said police officers videoed them on their mobile phones and threatened to post the pictures on the internet and give their home addresses to Golden Dawn, which has a track record of political violence.....
>
> Last month *The Guar*dian reported that victims of crime have been told by police officers to seek help from Golden Dawn, who then felt obliged to make donations to the group....
>
> Dimitris Katsaris, a lawyer for four of the protesters, said .... "This is not just a case of police brutality of the kind you hear about now and then in every European country. This is happening daily. We have the pictures, we have the evidence of what happens to people getting arrested protesting against the rise of the neo-Nazi party in Greece. This is the new face of the police, with the collabouration of the justice system."

Commentators such as Stevens (2012) make similar observations.

The attack on Critical Thinking

An extreme version of the radical right assault on critical thinking is exemplified by a recent state-wide conference of The Republican Party of Texas opposes critical thinking, which passed a resolution opposing critical thinking in education, stating,

> Knowledge-Based Education—We oppose the teaching of Higher Order Thinking Skills (HOTS) (values clarification), critical thinking skills and similar programmes that are simply a relabelling of Outcome-Based

> Education (OBE) (mastery learning) which focus on behaviour modification and have the purpose of challenging the student's fixed beliefs and undermining parental authority. (Austin Chronicle, 2012)

Part 4. Activism in the Education Arena: Critical Pedagogies, Socialist Education

This strengthening of revolutionary, of Marxist theory and practice needs developing within the arena of education, too. Of course, there have been many hundreds of thousands of Marxist and socialist and critical educators throughout the world over the last 150 years, from barefoot Communist teachers in India, through the ranks of the massacred Tudeh (Iranian Communist) and Indonesian Communist teachers and academic workers, through Russia and Europe and the Americas, drawing variously on theoretical versions of Marxism, from Maoism through Leninism, Stalinism, Trotskyism, (Morgan, 2003) through Freirean inspired educators in Latin America and North America. And there are also those drawing radical conclusions, within particular historical-situational circumstances, from the work of Dewey. There is a huge tradition of Marxist and other Left revolutionary educational theory and practice/praxis. This history is sometimes rendered invisible, lost, in the BANA–Britain, Australasia, North America-dominance/hegemony within English language and publications, books, reviews, journals, rendered 'high status' through this Anglophone- and specifically, United States, hegemony. Hence, literature searches for critical pedagogy result in a considerable emphasis on the legacy and interpreters of Freire and of Dewey, rather than of Marx. Glenn Rikowski has charted and analysed the development of Marxist educational thought (in the English-speaking world. See Rikowski 1996, 1997, 2007. A controversial semi-history of Marxist educational thought- and much criticised for its incompleteness- is Anyon, 2011. For debates around this book, see Malott, 2011; McGrew, 2011; Banfield, 2011).

Thus, it does need noting that many other conferences- and books- which self-identify as 'critical pedagogy', especially in the USA- refer to and propagate non-Marxist versions, focussing on more liberal, more democratic-participative, radical democratic versions of critical pedagogy. Some are even less Marxist, and focus on Critical Thinking, developing the ability to think critically, rather than locating such critical thinking within a metanarrative of social justice, let alone a metanarrative of economic justice and equality. It is the task of Marxists to show critical solidarity with such views and their exponents, with the emphasis being on the critical, with a view to informing, influencing, 'winning', radical liberal, and 'Marxian' colleagues to a Marxist analysis.

Some examples of attempts to develop Marxist education, analysis, understanding, praxis, are in the various conferences on Marxist education and critical education and critical pedagogy, such as the International Conference on Critical Education (ICCE) held at the University of Athens in 2011 and 2012, and due to be held in Turkey in July in 2013. Other such radical, Marxist, conferences on education are the long-standing Rouge Forum Conference in the USA, the longstanding Marxism and Education: merd (MERD) held at the London University Institute of Education, and the (new) West Chester Conference on Critical Pedagogy, which commenced in 2012. These are the main Marxist education conferences in the English-speaking world, and there are, doubtless, many dozens, if not hundreds, that that take place outside the English speaking areas known as BANA- Britain, North America and Australasia.

The perspective I take in my own writing is democratic revolutionary Marxist, what I call socialist education (e.g. Hill, 1991; 2007, 2010; Hillcole Group, 1991, 1997; Cole et al 2001, 2006; Hill and Boxley, 2007). Close to this is the Revolutionary Critical Pedagogy of Peter McLaren and his collabourators over the last 15 years. (See, for example, McLaren, 2005, McLaren and Farahmandpur, 2004).

At the educational/sociological theoretical level, Marxist educators need to adopt complementary and mutually supportive analyses and activism, complementary- in fact as part of- the broader socio-economic-political struggles. At this level of ideas, at the level of ideology, I adopt classical Marxist social class analysis, contesting those theoretical analyses that take the focus off of, away from, the analysis of class-based exploitation, the defining feature of capitalism, the capital-labour relation.

I suggest that, in education as in the wider polity, at the political level, we should pursue two developments: Firstly to go *beyond critique* into socialist reconstruction, and secondly, to go *beyond social democratic reformism* into revolutionary anti-capitalist Marxism.

We do need democratically discussed programmes for socialist education, as we do for control of the economy, systems of democratic workers control of the economy. I am not talking of imposing a blue-print, or 'Redprint' for education (examples of socialist education suggestions for discussion rather than imposition, are the Hillcole Group's two books book, *Redprint for Education*' of 1993, Hillcole Group, 1993), and *Rethinking Education and Democracy: a Socialist Alternative for the Twenty-First Century* (Hillcole Group, 1997). I have been, singly and collabouratively publishing on socialist education for 20 years. I deliberately publish most of my work online since I want it to be accessible). (See also the work of Terry Wrigley, e.g. Wrigley 2003, 2006; Wrigley et al., 2011. For different forms of socialist pedagogy, see Malott, 2012; Neary, 2012).

Questions in Educational Theory: Postmodernism, Identity Politics and Revisionist/Reformist Socialism—Social Class and Education

Marxist analysis of the relationships between social class and education has been discussed by British Marxists Dave Hill, Mike Cole and Glenn Rikowski since the mid-1980s, and in the USA by writers of the Red Collective writing in *Red Critique,* by Peter McLaren and his numerous co-writers since the mid-1990s, by Martha Gimenez, and more recently, work by Curry Malott (2011, 2012). I am well aware that I am restricting my references to that privileged group in the political economy of higher education, those in BANA (Britain, Australasia and North America). I attempt in a small way to overcome this linguistic imperialism to an extent by deliberately publishing articles from outside of BANA in JCEPS *(the Journal for Critical Education Policy Studies*) that I edit, and in the composition of the international editorial advisory board.

As a classical Marxist, I hold to a binary analysis of class (see Kelsh, 2001; Gimenez, 2001; Hill, 1999; Kelsh and Hill, 2006; Greaves, Hill and Maisuria, 2007; Hill, Greaves and Maisuria, 2009; Kelsh, Hill and Macrine, 2010) but do recognize, of course, the existence of horizontal different strata (for example, unskilled manual, white collar lower level management and supervisory, professional strata) and vertical segmentation (on the basis of gender, "race' for example) within the working class, which is that class of people who sell their labour power.

While the work of Weberian inspired/lifestyle classifications used in official government statistics can be highly informative concerning patterns and processes of privilege and underpriviledge in the schooling and education (and other) systems, I am not using the official government/ sociological/market research, 'Weberian' definitions of social class.

The effect of the widespread use of Weberian/neo-Weberian/lifestyle/ consumption-based classifications of social class is debilitating and occlusionary. (Hill, 1999; Hill and Cole, 2001; Kelsh and Hill, 2006). Such classifications 'hide' the capitalist class, hide the relations of production—the source of the Marxist definition(s) of class, and serve to segment and divide the working class—that class of workers (and dependents) who sell their labour-power. The Occupy Wall Street slogans about 99% against 1% are an accurate application of the classical Marxist notion/analysis of class—the 1% of the population who are the capitalists, exploiting the rest of the population who, whatever the descriptions applied to them, 'middle class', working class, working middle class, etc. share the major characteristic of Marxist class analysis of the working class—they are all exploited by the capitalist class which makes profit from the surplus value produced by their labour power.

Reformism, Accusations of Economism and Reductionism, and Relative Autonomy

Critics of Classical or revolutionary Marxist analysis within education (and within other social areas) come from a variety of theoretical and political-ideological perspectives. Other than various conservative perspectives, such as neoliberalism and neoconservatism, there are three types of critique that I wish to address here. There share some aspects of criticism of Marxism, but differ on others.

The three types of criticism are, neo-Marxism/revisionist/reformist Marxism; identitarianism; and postmodernism. The connection between education theory and wider social theory is that the principles of each have resonance for, implications for, political action, for questions of organization, programme and strategy.

I will spend time on '*identitarianism*'. Many of the comments critiques I make of identitarianism relate to critiques of the other forms of anti-Marxism.

Firstly, about social class, 'race', gender, sexuality and religion. It is evident that people are harassed, demeaned, violated, spat upon, attacked, killed, raped, because of their sexuality, sex, 'race'/ethnicity, religion. It is also evident that—and this is readily apparent and recognized in academic discourse, in political mobilizations, and in homes and streets and workplaces—we have multiple subjectivities, which come to the fore in our own minds and in the actions of others towards us in particular places at particular times.

In my own writing I focus on social class, which I believe is the salient objective (as opposed to subjective) form of exploitation. But I try always to point out that class segmented in two ways. Social class is stratified horizontally by different social class strata or groups—for example, unskilled workers as the bottom stratum, skilled workers as a stratum above, then 'white collar lower middle class sitting, in diagrammatic terms on top of those two groups and so on with layer upon layer of different social class strata on top. These strata/groups are characterised by different levels of reward, power, autonomy. But social class is also segmented vertically by 'race' and by gender, for example.

This Marxist emphasis on the salience of ('raced' and gendered) class exploitation is represented in/by and leads to vibrant academic and theoretical disputes. In contrast to revolutionary, classical and structuralist Marxists, various analyses see oppressions of class, 'race' and gender as being equivalent. An example is the 'Equivalence' or 'Parallelist' theory of Michael W. Apple. Other theorists go further in their disavowal of social class as the key structuring of exploitation. Thus, in the case of Critical Race Theory, it is argued that 'race' has not just *equivalent*, but actually has *primary*, analytic and explanatory value in analysing oppression.

I critique David Gillborn and his version of Critical Race Theory (CRT) in Britain (Hill, 2010) over the relative salience of class and 'race' in Britain- and in the USA. Gillborn's view is that the most fundamental form and structuring of oppression in Britain, and the most accurate analysis of state policy (for example on education), is that based on 'race'/racism/white superiority, rather than social class exploitation. (Gillborn, 2006, 2008. His reply is Gillborn, 2010. Mike Cole has written very extensively from a Marxist perspective, critiquing Critical Race Theory, as part of a protracted debate between Critical Race Theorists and Marxists (between Gillborn and Cole: e.g. Gillborn, 2008; Cole, 2009; Gillborn, 2009; between Hill and Gillborn: e.g. Hill, 2009c, d, 2012b; Gillborn, 2010; and by Cole and Maisuria, 2007, 2010).

And, the prominent USA radical (neo-Marxist/revisionist) educator, Michael W. Apple, has also, in a thoroughgoing series of revisionist/reformist neo-Marxist essays, criticized the views of Dave Hill, Mike Cole, Glenn Rikowski, Peter McLaren, Deborah Kelsh, Gregory Martin, RaminFarahmandpur, Paula Allman, as economistic, reductionist, deterministic, 'vulgar Marxism' . In this he has support in articles by, for example, Kenneth Saltman and by Ken McGrew. Apple, 2005, 2006. See also Saltman, 2010, 2011; McGrew, 2011. Saltman's online assault (2011) on what he calls 'vulgar Marxists', is very accessible).

This debate is carried out partly in the *Journal for Critical Education Policy Studies*, for example with articles by Farahmandpur, 2004 (see also his 2008); Kelsh and Hill, (2006; Rikowski, (2006; Cole, 2009; Cole and Maisuria, 2007; Hill, 2009c; Banfield, (2011, and Malott (2011) on the one hand, and by Gillborn (2010), and McGrew (2011) on the other.

In particular, Marxists such as Cole and I criticize the *political implications* of what might be termed separatist or non-class based, oppression specific (e.g. gender, 'race'/ethnicity) analyses.

Part 5. The Development of Class Consciousness and Resistance: Revenge, Revolt, and Strategic Activism Revenge

The desire for revenge against those imposing and benefitting from austerity capitalism and immiseration is justified. The political and economic leaders—bankers, financiers, those driving down living conditions, the rich, the capitalist class billionaires and multi-millionaires—get off free in the current crisis- in fact they get richer, they profit from the crisis—as the empirical data evidenced earlier shows. They need to be brought to account. And where found guilty of crimes, punished. And class justice means the introduction of new laws, laws which redefine social irresponsibility and criminality in terms of knowingly causing deterioration to the lives and well-being of the community. ASBOs (anti-social behaviour orders) should be handed out not just to delinquent working class youth as they have been, but need to be redefined so as to target the real, mega-anti-social behaviour.

And where not found guilty of crimes, then, as part of class economic justice and socialization of the economy, the capitalist class should be subject to nationalization, and to expropriation with compensation paid only on the basis of proven need. I am not talking of hanging billionaire tax avoiders from lamp posts, or bringing in the guillotine, and I'm not targeting the small and medium businesses. It's the leading members of the capitalist class who need investigating.

As for the poor, and the not so poor, suicides are increasing, as are early deaths and chronic ill-health, homelessness, hopelessness. Neoliberal capitalist policies deliberately causing immiseration, making the poor die young, with children now fainting at school through lack of food, with hundreds of millions of workers forced into poorer and meaner and less happy and more anxiety-ridden lives.

Such social devastation is not just in Greece. It across cities and ghettoes and suburbs and small towns and villages of all the countries discussed in this article, and many more beside. It is in the schools we and our communities send out children to. This is not just a form of class exploitation, class oppressions, class suppression, it is, at its extremes which we are seeing in Greece already, a form of class genocide.

And it is not an accident. It is the result of deliberate policy. Policy whose initiators and chief beneficiaries and promoters must be held accountable.This is not 'will of God' or 'Act of God'. It is the deliberate and knowing and in some cases gleeful 'Will of the Capitalist Class' and their political placemen/women/servants/collabourators. It is their deliberate, aforethought, weighed up, determined, carefully adjudicated, pontificated on and measured selection of policy and punishment. The poor are to be punished. The disabled to be devastated. The workers in an era of declining wages and increased taxes to have waking nightmares about how to pay the next rent or mortgage, and whether the job will still be there. In contrast, the segregated rich, who do not use our schools, buses, hospitals, pensions, holidays, The rich, the capitalist class, they are rewarded each time they turn the screw on others, on the working classes and our now degraded public services.

Those responsible for and benefitting from these policies—the initiators and chief beneficiaries and promoters—must be held accountable. Revenge and retribution are reasonable and righteous.

The absolute scale of dispossession and depredation by the capitalist class, such as bankers, profiteers from privatization, has been such as to lead to calls for prosecution, for criminal proceedings and for legal punishment. Alongside this is coming a political and economic awareness, with anger and outrage as the soaring levels of inequality and of immiseration and impoverishment, particularly in countries like Greece, are leading to a clamour for redistribution of wealth, power and income, for expropriation of the wealth and assets of the super-rich and of the largest capitalist enterprises such as banks, financial institutions and 'the commanding heights of the economy.

Revolt

The only too evident changes in the material conditions of hundreds of millions of workers- workers from middle as well as lower strata, are, however, leading to widespread changes in class and political consciousness, and to resistance. The concept of 'immiseration' itself. (Marx and Engels 1848; Marx, 1867) was very much derided and dismissed during years of growth (Greaves, Hill and Maisuria, 2007).

Other concepts such as 'proletarianisation' (Braverman, 1974) 'capitalism' and 'anti-capitalism' are far more widely understood and used, in particular 'capitalism and 'ant-capitalism', terms rarely used outside the Left prior to the 2008 onset of the current crisis of Fiscal Capitalism, indeed m of the financialisation of capitalism, of capitalism itself.

The concept of 'the ruling class', that group of mega-rich, socially, politically interconnected, is perfectly encapsulated in the phrase and chant and banners on a thousand demonstrations in different countries, 'We are the 99%'. Banners on the student demonstrations in Britain, 'Strike. Occupy. Shut Down the 1%', and 'Education for the masses, not just the ruling classes (on the various anti-cuts demonstrations in London, of 12

November, 2010, and of 30 November 2011, and the 30 October 2010 demonstration in Brighton, a medium size city of a quarter of a million people). (For my blogspot and photos from these three demonstrations, see Hill, 2010b, c, 2011b).

The neoliberal, pro-austerity orthodoxy mong political parties, all agreeing, in effect, that it is the workers who must pay for the crisis, has delegitimised parliamentary, electoral politics. In Britain, the Labour Party, the Liberal Democratic Party and the Conservative Party are all agree that massive cuts—in services, in the real value of wages/salaries, in pension entitlements, have to be made. Where the conservative New Democracy Party and the traditional social democratic socialist party, PASOK, together with a right split from the (left reformist) Syriza, the Democratic Left, are all united in accepting the 'need' for massive privatisations of public services and massive and unprecedented austerity cuts. And this analysis remains valid in winter 2012, months after the elections.

So there is much more the question, indeed, wide scale questioning, of exactly who does Parliament represent. There is much more understanding that Parliament is 'the executive arm of the ruling class'.

and more interest in 'revolution', in major change in the way society is structured., and in concepts, once deemed highly theoretical, but now deemed more realistic, about the creation of 'dual power', the creation of alternative/oppositional structures of government and administration, from forms of democratic workers' control, to local assemblies, to occupations. And there is resistance on the streets. The spotlight of revolution and of people's assemblies and occupations has turned from Latin America, in particular Bolivia, Argentina and Venezuela, to Europe on terms of anti-austerity capitalism, as well as to North Africa/the Middle East.

Revolt in Britain

In Britain, students are rebelling (Hill, 2010b, c, d). From the 52,000 strong demonstration in Westminster on Nov. 10th 2010 (which went via a student occupation of the Millbank Conservative Party HQ in London, to disciplined and organized student occupations, sit-ins and teach-ins at various universities, through subsequent Days of Action, to student protests across Europe- Paris, Lisbon, Athens, Dublin. Saying, chanting, acting, demanding, 'No to Education Cuts', 'No to (increased) Charges for Education', 'Education should be Free!' The 10 November 2010 demonstration, organized by the National Union of Students and the college lecturers union, UCU, was the biggest student demonstration in

England in a generation. (Englert, 2010; Hill, 2010c; International Socialism, 2011; Robinson, 2011).

This was followed by 130,000 students at universities, further education colleges, Sixth Forms and secondary schools walking out on Weds 24 November, 2010, and demonstrating against cuts and tuition fees, in a national day of action. Some marched on their local Tory party offices, just as 300 students and trade unionists in Barnet marched earlier on the local Tory Party HQ in Finchley. Students were/are saying and chanting 'Students and Workers Unite and Fight', 'We are Part of a Wider Struggle!' Facebook sites such as 'School and FE students Against the Cuts' have basic, bold slogans—'Education for the masses not just for the ruling classes!' Student protests influenced, and were followed by a national public sector workers' strike on November 30, 2011, (Hill, 2011b) the closest Britain has got to a general strike since the 1926 General Strike.

Even closer to a return to the general strike of 1926 is the 20 October 2012 'Anti-Austerity Demonstration' called officially by the TUC, the (national) Trades Union Congress , with potentially a million marchers in London, Glasgow and Belfast. Left unions such as the RMT (The National Union of Rail Maritime and Transport Workers) and the PCS (Public and Commercial Services Union) as well as Marxist and Trotskyist parties/groups such as the SWP (Socialist Workers Party), the SP (Socialist Party) and SR (Socialist Resistance) are urging that the 20 October 2012 demo be the springboard for subsequent 24 hour or 48 hour general strike action by the around 6 and a half million members of trade unions affiliated to the TUC. The SP/placard/slogan for the march, for example, is 'TUC Name Next Strike Day'. (In Britain, the TUC is the only national organization of trade unions. A number of unions are outside the TUC).

Revolt in Ireland

Ireland had five austerity budgets prior to the 2011 general election. But the resistance has been at a markedly lower level than in Greece or Britain. As Derwin writes, 'Whereas the Greeks already had a large militant left, the Irish received this shock on top of 30 years of social partnership that had drained the fight from the trade unions' (Derwin, 2011. See also Keating, Morrison and Corrigan (2010)). There were three large trade union marches (though not in working time) and a one-day public sector strike 'after which the unions entered into the Croke Park Agreement (June 2010), a deal cooperating with the shrinkage of the public service' (Derwin, 2011).

The response was mainly at the local level and on particular issues.

At the level of direct action, there was Occupy Dame Street, the main Irish emulation of Occupy Wall Street. (Sheehan, 2012) Here, though, a phenomenon of various Occupy movements was their inability and hostility to cooperate with trade unions and 'traditional' left parties/organizations. Dublin Trades Council reached out to Occupy Dame Street (ODS), but the ODS refused to join in the trade union protest march DCTU march. (See also Sheehan, 2012, for her comments on the nature of the Occupy Dame Street movement and its hostility to organized forces on the Left. When I spoke at the Occupy London 'Tent City' feeder march on 10 November, 2010 (Marcus, 2011), I was assailed by some of the Occupy demonstrators, objecting to my saying I was representing TUSC (the Trade Unionist and Socialist Coalition) and SR (Socialist Resistance).

The response was also at the ballot box, where, in the 2011 general election, the United Left Alliance, a loose coalition of socialist and Marxist national and local organizations, in a "riot at the ballot box", dealt a near mortal blow to the ruling Fianna Fáil party. Fiana Fáil dominated Irish politics since the 1930s, reducing its seats in the Dáil from 71 to 20. The Labour Party (seen then as an alternative) went from 20 to 37 seats and the Sinn Féin contingent expanded from five to 14 TDs. Five TDs (members of the Irish parliament) were elected for the (avowedly socialist/Marxist) United Left Alliance. Rather like the remarkably successful SSP (Scottish Socialist Party) in Scotland in the early years of the 21st century, and rather like the second coming of Respect Party and George Galloway as an MP in Britain in 2012, the ULA quickly fell foul of aspects of personality politics on the one hand, and the different aims of the broader coalition (in this case, the ULA) and some of its constituent parties) on the other. The ULA basically collapsed in late 2012.

Revolt in Greece

The 'hot summer' in Greece of 2011 saw workers' occupations of ministries, factories, banks, schools, universities, a steel works, a newspaper, together with the operation of around a hundred local assemblies, open, democratic assemblies in the localities, sometimes attended by hundreds of people. Some of these continue, such as the steel strike. In Greece, sacked journalists have taken over a newspaper (*Elifhteria*), doctors and nurses have taken over health centres. In acts of solidarity, there are also popular and social food kitchens, feeding the rapidly increasing numbers of homeless.

The largest 'occupation' was in Syntagma Square, until dispersed by clouds of gas (my blog report is at Hill, 2011a). So, we have seen nascent, early and partial forms of these organizational forms in the Greek resistance of summer 2011, the first in Western Europe for many decades.

The 'quiet period' around and immediately following the two Greek general elections of 2012 ended abruptly with the general strike of 27 September with up to 200,000 on strike and between 70,000 and 100,000 demonstrating in Athens alone, chanting 'We won't submit to the troika!' and 'EU, IMF out!', the start of 'a hot autumn' characterized by tear gas, repression, street battles between police and strikers/protesters. This was followed by the mass protests against the visit to Greece of Angela Merkel on 9 October 2012, with the next general strike being called for 18 October 2012.

What has been happening in Greece since 2008, including its 18 general strikes, has been, arguably, a pre-revolution from below. An outburst of rage and anger and despair and fury coming from the streets and the squares that is without parallel in Europe since the events of 1968. And a situation of intense class polarization, of strengthening of Marxist and socialist organization and understanding among wider and wider layers of the population. So there is the strengthening of revolutionary praxis, the interaction between theory/analysis/understanding on the one hand, and practice, action, organization on the other.

Of course, in a period of social catastrophe, other forces, such as Fascist/Nazi-type parties have also increased their strength, organization, and implantation. The capitalist class, as in the period of the rise of Hitler in Weimar Germany, is willing to hold the Fascists/Nazis in reserve for street violence when 'the reds' get too strong for their liking.

As Sotiris (2012c) notes 'For more than two years Greek society has been the testing ground for aggressive neoliberal social engineering but also a labouratory of struggle, collective experiences, and radical proposals. It has the potential to become not only the symbol of resistance, but also an example of a radical alternative'.

Analysis and Strategic Activism: Electoralism and Direct Action historically and in the current period

In terms of electoralism, in Greece, the Syriza coalition (variously termed 'Far Left', 'Radical Left', though, in my analysis, Hill, 2012a, it is essentially 'left reformist', see also Dreier, 2012b; Kloke, 2012c, d) was close to achieving a Radical Left majority in the 16 June 2012 Greek parliamentary elections. In this same year, Jean-Luc Melenchon polled 11% for the Front de Gauche in the first round of the French Presidential election, and in Portugal, Germany, the Netherlands and Denmark, parties considerably to the left of the current neoliberalized social democratic parties have been polling, on various occasions, more than 10% of the vote. These 'Broad Parties', (see, e.g. Bensaid et al., 2012) and alliances are combinations or coalitions of left social reformist and Marxist revolutionary—often Trotskyist, sometimes Maoist—groups and parties. They are often fissiparous, because of these internal contradictions, but are, with varying degrees of prominence accorded to the electoral process by their various internal components, committed to electoralism, with electoralism taking as great, or greater priority than mobilizing/direct action. And some of these 'Broad Parties' are broader, or narrower, than others, and more, or less, willing to take part in local or regional governments (even where this means voting for cuts, as with Die Linke in Berlin) or for war credits in Afghanistan (as with Rifondazione Comunista) (See Callinicos, 2008).

Indeed, through elections, Social democratic governments throughout the world, after winning elections, have, of course, introduced pro-working class legislation, fiscal policies, labour laws, welfare and social policies. In Britain the (left reformist, social democratic) Labour Party won the 1945 general election and in a period of economic crisis, carried out major pro-working class measures, such as introducing free secondary education for all (high school education), undertaking a series of major nationalisations, and implanting the National Health Service. And Hugo Chavez in Venezuela has been repeatedly elected and re-elected and carried out major reforms, even attempting a sort of dual power/parallel local organizations. Marx and Lenin themselves talked of the necessity for reforms. For example, with respect to 'revisionist', or social democratic reformism/reforms, it is important to note that Marx and Engels in The *Communist Manifesto* recognize that it is necessary to "fight for the attainment of the immediate aims of the working class" (Marx and Engels, 1848/1985, pp. 119).

However, in times of capitalist crisis, when workers' living wages, benefits and standards, are deemed too high and expensive by the capitalist class in general, then a more 'moderate', or 'liberal' or 'labour' party can be brought in, supported by sections of capital and their media, for people to vote for a 'a lesser evil'. It's what millions voted Labour for at the June 2010 general (parliamentary) election in Britain, and why votes for the Irish Labour Party and Sinn Fein leapt in the February 2011 Irish general election. Claiming to speak for workers and minorities these former/quasi social democratic workers' capitalist parties, or liberal versions of the capitalist united front are the more successful in suckering those workers and minorities and disabling their rebellion.

And across Europe, even left social democratic/revisionist/ reformist (pro-capitalist/willing to manage capitalism) parties- such as Syriza in Greece, The Front Gauche/Left Front in France, Die Linke/The Left in Germany, the victory of George Galloway and the Respect Party in a by-election in Bradford, England, in 2012 are proposing heavier taxation on the wealthy and heavier taxes on profits, albeit within a capitalist system.

Such left social democrats, revisionist/reformist parties, and mixtures/ coalitions of revolutionaries with left social democrats, such as Broad Parties of the Left (Bensaid, 2010, Bensaid et al, 2011) propose taxing the wealth and income of top capitalists more heavily, in contrast to Revolutionary Marxist groups and Parties, which call for expropriating, nationalizing that capital and wealth, and calling for the socialist transformation of society/economy/polity (see, for example the blogspot of the Fourth International Revolutionary Marxists, at http:// 4thinternational.blogspot.co.uk/, in particular for revolutionary analysis of the Greek situation).

This division on the Left is expressed in Britain by the neoliberalised Labour Party, the Left social democratic Respect Party, and the revolutionary left parties and groups such as the Socialist Party and the Socialist Workers Party, currently working with leading trade unionists and some members of Socialist Resistance in what might be termed (another) attempt at revolutionary Marxist unity within the Trade Unionist and Socialist Coalition (TUSC). In France the neoliberalized social democratic party is the Parti Socialiste, the left social democratic (i.e. pro- a 'fairer', more redistributive) capitalism, the Parti de Gauche, and the revolutionary Marxist Left represented by groups such as the NPA, the Nouvel Parti Anti Capitaliste. In Greece, the neoliberalized (former) social democratic party is PASOK; the Radical Left Coalition, a Broad Party combining left social democrats and various types of revolutionary Marxist, is Syriza; and the revolutionary anti-capitalist Marxist coalition is Antarsya. In Hill, 2012a, I set out the respective programmes of the Syriza and Antarsya coalitions, the former for example, wishing to renegotiate the debt and (for the time being in the election and immediate post-election period, to have a Parliamentarist strategy, to act as 'a responsible opposition'.

Antarsya differs in both *programme,* urging a Marxist nationalization of the main institutions and companies, together with a refusal to pay, a repudiation of the debt, and leaving the (straightjacket of) the Euro, and the Eurozone. In terms of *strategy*, while (most constituent parts of) Syriza in this current (Autumn 2012) period were staying (for the most part) off the streets, until the October general strike and anti-Merkel demonstrations, anyhow, playing the part of 'a responsible parliamentary opposition'. In contrast, the strategy of Antarsya is to rely on street activism, occupations under workers' control, the development of neighbourhood assemblies, and the gradual development of systems of dual power.

Thus, to talk about direct action, extra-Parliamentary action, there is an argument that workers' power is not possible through the existing state and its organs, that an activist strategy in various circumstances should be won through dual power—the setting up and implantation of alternative and oppositional organizations, while not eschewing elections to the various electoral/representative for a of the bourgeois state.

Sotiris (2012a) summarizes

> That is why must not limit the discussion on power in Greece to electoral politics only. Power is not only about who holds the offices of government. It is mainly about who actually decides about economic policy, about the banking system, about education and health priorities. It is a material balance of forces within society, production, the State, and a question of collective representations, attitudes and everyday practices. In this sense, having a government of the Left only opens the question of power, does not resolve it.
>
> Without a strong social and political movement 'from below', without strong trade unions and student movements, without all forms of popular self-organization and solidarity, any change in the balance of forces at the governmental level will be in constant risk of failure and defeat. A possible victory of the Left in the elections should not be seen as a simple electoral mandate but as the beginning of a new and more intense phase in the struggle.

And this is so, very much so, after the likely collapse of the current government, with the possible election of a Syriza led government in 2014 or 2015, or, indeed with any electoral victory of any anti-austerity coalition/party following the mass demonstrations and strikes across southern Europe and Britain.

'What could be' and 'What should be'

In this current period of Immiseration Capitalism, of Austerity Capitalism, impoverishing and immiserating millions, immiserating in an *absolute* sense, no longer just a *relative* sense, then the gains of historic social democracy, the historic gains of the working class and its organizations, in education as in other sectors, are being stolen away by the capitalist class, which like vultures, are picking at the carcass of the welfare state, free education, as well as free health services, and the dreams hopes and, lives of the working class.

In such a catastrophic situation, the rule, the dictatorship of capital, the nakedness of the rule of capital are opening the eyes of tens of millions to 'what could be' and to 'what should be' in terms of the organisation of human affairs. As alternative dystopias to rapacious capitalism the 'what could be' could be Fascist, or it could be military dictatorial rule. Or it could be the continued exponential increase in inequalities, and the immiserating impacts of neoliberal *cum* neo-conservative/new authoritarian capitalism

But, with the energies, the analysis, the anger, the strategic activism, the organisation, programme and focused strategy of activists, including teachers, professors, students, combining with other workers, the 'what could be' could be the 'what should be'- a democratic Marxist re-ordering, reconstruction of the of the social apparatuses of the state, such as education, within the context of and as part of the wider revolutionary socialist and democratic reconstruction of the economy, society and polity.

Notes

This paper was a plenary paper presented at the International Conference on Critical Education (ICCE) Conference, held at the University of Athens, 10-14 July, 2012.

A version of this article was published as Dave Hill (2012) Resistance, Revolt and Revenge: Austerity Education, Immiseration Capitalism and Strategic Activism, in the Turkish Critical Pedagogy journal, *Ele°tirel Pedagoji,* 23 (September 2012 edition).

References

Althusser, L. (1971). Ideology and State Apparatus. In L. Althusser, *Lenin and Philosophy and Other Essays*. London: New Left Books. Anti-Academies Alliance website, at http://www.antiacademies.org.uk/.

Anyon, J. (2011). *Marx and Education*. New York: Routledge.

Apple, M. (2006). Review Essay: Rhetoric and reality in critical educational studies in the United States. *British Journal of Sociology of Education*, 27(5), pp. 679-687.

Apple, M.W. (2005). "Audit cultures, commodification, and class and race strategies in education", *Policy Futures in Education* 3 (4), pp. 379-399.

Austin Chronicle (2012). The Republican Party of Texas Opposes Critical Thinking. 27 June. *Austin Chronicle*, Texas, USA. Online at http://www.austinchronicle.com/blogs/news/2012-06-27/gop-opposes-critical-thinking/.

Banfield, G. (2011). 'Looking for Marx: A Review of Marx and Education by Jean Anyon'. *Journal for Critical Education Policy Studies* 9 (2). http://www.jceps.com/index.php?pageID= article&articleID=221.

Bensaid, D. (2010). Notes on Recent Developments in the European Radical Left. *International Viewpoint.*Online athttp://www.internationalviewpoint.org/spip.php?article1785

Bensaid, D, Sousa, A., Thornett, A., Leplat, F. et al. (2011). *New Parties of the Left: Experiences from Europe.* International Institute for Research and Education (IIRE), Amsterdam: IMG publications.

Braverman, H. (1974, 1998). *Labor and Monopoly Capital: The Degradation of Work in the Twentieth Century.* New York: Monthly Review Press.

Brecht. B. (1941, 2001). *The Irresistable Rise of Arturo Ui.* New York: Arcade Publishing.

Callinicos, A. (1989). *Against Postmodernism: a Marxist Critique.* Cambridge, UK: Polity.

Callinicos, A. (2006). *Universities in a Neoliberal World.* London: Bookmarks Publications.

Callinicos, A. (2008). Where is the Radical left Going? *International Socialist Review*, Issue 120. Online at http://www.isj.org.uk/?id=484.

Catastroika (2012). *Catastroika: Privatization goes Public.* Written and Directed by Aris Chatzistefanou andKaterinaKitidi and scientific editing by Leonidas Vatikiotis. Online at http://topdocumentaryfilms.com/catastroika/and at http://www.youtube.com/watch?v=RORPpFL21dM.

Chang, H-J. (2010). *23 Things They Don't Tell You About Capitalism.* London: Allen Lane.

Chang, H-J. (2012). The root of Europe's riots. *The Guardian*, 29 September. Online at http://www.guardian.co.uk/commentisfree/2012/sep/28/europe-riots-root-imf-austerity.

Cole, M. (2008). *Marxism and Educational Theory: Origins and Issues*. London: Routledge.

Cole, M. (2009). *Critical Race Theory and Education: a Marxist Response.* New York and London: Palgrave Macmillan.

Cole, M. (2011). *Racism and Education in the UK and the US: Towards a Socialist Alternative.* New York and London: Palgrave Macmillan.

Cole, M., Hill, D., McLaren, P. and Rikowski, G. (2001). *Red Chalk: On Schooling, Capitalism and Politics.*Brighton: Institute for Education Policy Studies. Online at http://www.ieps.org.uk.cwc.net/redchalk.pdf.

Cole, M., Hill, D., McLaren, P. and Rikowski, G. (2006). *Kýzýl Tebeþir* Istanbul, Turkey: Kalkedon Yayinlari.

Cole, M. and Maiuria, A. (2007). Shut the f*** up', 'you have no rights here': Critical Race Theory and Racialization in post-7/7 racist Britain'. *Journal for Critical Education Policy Studies*, 5(1).Online at http://www.jceps.com/index.php?pageID=article&articleID=85.

Cole, M. and Maisuria, A. (2010). Racism and Islamophobia in post 7/7 Britain: Critical Race Theory, (Xeno-) Racialization, Empire and Education: A Marxist

Analysis. In D. Kelsh, D. Hill and S. Macrine (eds.). *Class in Education: Knowledge, Pedagogy, Subjectivity*. New York: Routledge.Corporate European Observatory (2011) *Austerity for Ever.* Online at http://www.corporateeurope.org/publications/austerity-forever.

Crouch, C. (2011). *The Strange Non-Death of Neoliberalism.* Cambridge, England: Polity Press.

Derwin, D. (2012). Ireland: Shock, austerity, Sinn Féin and the United Left Alliance. In *Links International Journal of Socialist Renewal*, June 26. Online at http://links.org.au/node/2931.

Denis, R. (2012). 'Open Horizons' :An interview with Roland Denis. *The Bullet*, Socialist Project • E-Bulletin No. 687 August 24. Online at http://www.socialistproject.ca/bullet/687.php

Dorling, D. (2010a). Divided Britain's Growing Inequality. *Socialist Worker Online,* 29 May Issue 2203. Online at ttp://www.socialistworker.co.uk/art.php?id=21308.

Dorling, D. (2010b). *Inequality: Why Social Inequality Persists.* Bristol: The Policy Press.

Dreier, C. (2012a). Greek government plans further cuts. *World Socialist Website*. Online at http://www.wsws.org/articles/2012/aug2012/gree-a01.shtml.

Dreier, C. (2012b). SYRIZA deepens European Union ties as austerity intensifies in Greece. World Socialist Website, 4 October. Online at http://www.wsws.org/articles/2012/oct2012/gree-o04.shtml

Dumenil, G. and Levy, D. (2004). *Capital Resurgent: Roots of the Neoliberal Revolution*. London: Harvard University Press.

Englert, S. (2010). Student Protest Ignites the Fight. *Socialist Review.* Online at http://www.socialistreview.org.uk/article.php?articlenumber=11468.

Farahmandpur, R. (2004). A Marxist Critique of Michael Apple's Neo-Marxist Approach to Educational Reform. *Journal for Critical Educational Policy Studies,* 2(1), pp. 1-23. http://www.jceps.com/?pageID=articleandarticleID=24.

Farahmandpur, R. (2008). *Class, Ideology, and Hegemony: Rethinking Marxist Educational Theory.* Dusseldorf, Germany: VDM Verlag Dr. Müller.

Fourth International revolutionary Blogspot. (2011/2012). Online at http://4thinternational.blogspot.co.uk/.

Frank, R. (2007). *Richistan: A Journey Through the American Wealth Boom and the Lives of the New Rich.* New York: Crown Business.

Gillan, A (2006). In Iraq, life expectancy is 67. Minutes from Glasgow city centre, it's 54. *The Guardian,* 21 January. Online at http://www.guardian.co.uk/society/2006/jan/21/health.politics.

Gillborn, D. (2006). 'Critical Race Theory and Education: Racism and Antiracism in Educational Theory and Praxis'. *Discourse: Studies in the Cultural Politics of Education* 27 (1), pp. 11–32.

Gillborn, D. (2008). *Racism and Education: Coincidence or Conspiracy?* London: Routledge.

Gillborn, D. (2009). Who's Afraid of Critical Race Theory in Education? A Reply to Mike Cole's 'The Color-Line and the Class Struggle', *Power and Education* 1 (1), pp. 125-131.

Gillborn, D. (2010). Full of sound and fury, signifying nothing?a reply to Dave Hills "Race and Class in Britain: A critique of the statistical basis for critical race theory in Britain". *Journal for Critical Education Policy Studies* 8(1).Online at http://www.jceps.com/index.php? pageID=article &articleID=177.

Gimenez, M. (2001). Marxism and Class, Gender and Race: Rethinking the Trilogy. *Race, Gender and Class* 8(2), pp. 23–33.

Gomez, G. (2012). The Revolution Will Not Be Decreed: An interview with Gonzalo Gómez, *Marea Socialista* (Socialist Tide). *The Bullet*, Socialist Project • E-Bulletin No. 682 August 17, 2012. Online at http://www.socialistproject.ca/bullet/682.php.

Greaves, N., Hill, D. and Maisuria, A. (2007). "Embourgeoisment, Immiseration, Commodification—Marxism Revisited: a Critique of Education in Capitalist Systems." *Journal for Critical Education Policy Studies*, 5(1). Online at http://www.jceps.com/index.php?pageID=article&articleID=83.

Grey, B. (2012). $129 million pay package for new Yahoo CEO . *World Socialist Website*. 24 July. Online at http://www.wsws.org/articles/2012/jul2012/pers-j24.shtml.

Harvey, D. (2005). *A Brief History of Neoliberalism.* Oxford, England: Oxford University Press.

Hill, D. (1991). *What's Left in Teacher Education?* London: Tufnell Press.

Hill, D. (1999). Social Class and Education. In D. Matheson and I. Grosvenor (eds.) *An Introduction to the Study of Education. pp. 84-102.* London: David Fulton. Online at http://www.ieps.org.uk/PDFs/Social%20Class%20by%20dave%20Hill%201999%20 Chapter% 207.pdf.

Hill, D. (2003a). Global Neo-Liberalism, the Deformation of Education and Resistance, *Journal for Critical Education Policy Studies*, 1 (1). Online at http://www.jceps.com/index.php? pageID= article&articleID=7.

Hill, D. (2003b). *Brief Autobiography of a Bolshie Dismissed.* Online at http://www.ieps.org.uk/papersdh.php.

Hill, D. (2004). Books, Banks and Bullets: Controlling our minds—the global project of Imperialistic and militaristic neoliberalism and its effect on education policy. *Policy Futures in Education,* 2 (3-4), pp. 504-522 (Theme: Marxist Futures in Education). Online at http://www.wwwords.co.uk/pdf/viewpdf.asp?j=pfie&vol=2&issue=3&year=2004&article=6_Hill_PFIE_2_3-4_web&id=81.158.104.245.

Hill, D. (2005). Globalisation and its educational discontents: Neoliberalisation and its impacts on education workers' rights, pay, and conditions. *International Studies in the Sociology of Education* 15 (3), pp. 257-288. Online at http://www.ieps.org.uk/papersdh.php.

Hill, D. (2006a). Class, Capital and Education in this Neoliberal/Neoconservative

Period. *Information for Social Change*, 23. Online at http://libr.org/isc/issues/ISC23/B1%20Dave%20Hill.pdf.

Hill, D. (2006b). Education Services Liberalization. In E. Rosskam (ed.) *Winners or Losers? Liberalizing public services,* pp. 3-54. Geneva: International Labour Organisation. Online at http://www.ieps.org.uk/PDFs/DaveHill-2006-EDUCATIONSERVICES LIBERALIZATION.pdf.

Hill, D. (2007). Critical Teacher Education, New Labour in Britain, and the Global Project of Neoliberal Capital. *Policy Futures,* 5 (2), pp. 204-225. Online at http://www.wwwords.co.uk/pfie/content/pdfs/5/issue5_2.asp.

Hill, D. (ed.) (2009a). *The Rich World and the Impoverishment of Education: Diminishing Democracy, Equity and Workers' Rights.* New York: Routledge.

Hill, D. (ed.) (2009b). *Contesting Neoliberal Education: Public Resistance and Collective Advance.* London: New York: Routledge.

Hill, D. (2009c). Race and Class in Britain: A Critique of the statistical basis for Critical Race Theory in Britain, and some political implications. *Journal for Critical Education Policy Studies*, 7 (2). Online at http://www.jceps.com/?pageID=article&articleID=159.

Hill, D. (2010a). A Socialist Manifesto for Education. Online athttp://socialistresistance.org/?p=905 and athttp://rikowski.wordpress.com/2010/04/08/statement-and-education-policy-manifesto-by-dave-hill/.

Hill, D. (2010b). Fantastic Huge Brighton March Against the Cuts Today, Saturday 30 March 2010. Online at BrightonTUSCBlogspot. 30 October. Online at http://brightontusc.blogspot.com/search?updated-min=2010-01-01T00%3A00%3A00-08%3A00&updated-max=2011-01-01T00%3A00%3A00-08%3A00&max-results=47.

Hill, D. (2010c). Massive 52,000 strong march against university fee hikes and abolition of EMAsWEDS 12 November. Online at BrightonTUSCBlogspot. 1 December 2010. Online at http://brightontusc.blogspot.com/search?updated-min=2010-01-01T00%3A00%3A00-08%3A00&updated-max=2011-01-01T00%3A00%3A00-08%3A00&max-results=47.

Hill, D. (2010d). Students are Revolting- and Quite Right Too. *Radical Notes,* online at http://radicalnotes.com/journal/2010/12/03/students-are-revolting-education-cuts-and-resistance/Also in *SocialistResistance*, online athttp://socialistresistance.org/1135/students-are-revolting-education-cuts-and-resistance.

Hill, D. (2011a). Athens general strike (June 2011). Report and photos. 16 June. Online at http://hoverepublic.blogspot.co.uk*/2011_06_01_archive.html.*

Hill, D. (2011b). Brighton TUSC and the November 30 public sector workers strike and march and rally at the Level. Online at *BrightonTUScblogspot*, 30 November. http://brightontusc.blogspot.co.uk/.

Hill, D. (2012a). *Support Antarsya and its Transitional Programme in the June 17 2012 Greek parliamentary elections.* Online at http://4thinternational.blogspot.co.uk/2012/05/vote-in-greece-in-june-17-2012-election.html.

Hill, D. (2012b). Caste, 'Race' and Class Inequality: a Marxist Analysis. In *S.*

Sleeter, S.B. Upadhyay, A.K. Mishra and S. Kumar (eds.) *School Education, Pluralism and Marginality: Comparative Perspectives*. New Delhi: Orient Blackswan.

Hill, D. and Boxley, S. (2007). Critical Teacher Education for Economic, Environmental and Social Justice: an Ecosocialist Manifesto. *Journal for Critical Education Policy Studies*, 5 (2). Online at http://www.jceps.com/index.php?pageID=article&articleID=96.

Hill, D. and Cole, M. (2001). Social Class and Education. In D. Hill and M. Cole (eds.), *Schooling and Equality: Fact, Concept and Policy*. London: Kogan Page.

Hill, D., Greaves, N. and Maisuria, A. (2009). Education, Inequality and Neoliberal Capitalism: a Classical Marxist Analysis. In D. Hill and R. Kumar (eds.) *Global Neoliberalism and Education and its Consequences*. New York: Routledge, pp. 102-126.

Hill, D. and Kumar, R. (eds.) (2009). *Global Neoliberalism and Education and its Consequences*. New York: Routledge.

Hill, D., McLaren, P., Cole, M. and Rikowski, G. (eds.) (2002). *Marxism Against Postmodernism in Educational Theory*. Lanham, MD: Lexington Books.

Hill, D. and Rosskam, E. (eds.) (2009). *The Developing World and State Education: Neoliberal Depredation and Egalitarian Alternatives*. New York: Routledge.

Hillcole Group (1991). *Changing the Future: Redprint for Education*, London: Tufnell Press.

Hillcole Group (1997). *Rethinking education and democracy: a socialist alternative for the twenty-first century*. London: Tufnell Press.

Inal, K. and Akkaymak, G. (eds.) (2012). *Neoliberal Transformation of Education in Turkey: Political and ideological Analysis of Educational Reforms in the Age of the AKP*. London: Palgrave Macmillan.

International,al Socialist Review "Letter from the Editors". *ISR Online*. London: Socialist Workers Party, 2007. Online at http://www.isreview.org/issues/54/editorletter.shtml.

International Viewpoint (2012). *Report on the International Situation*. Online at http://www.internationalviewpoint.org/spip.php?article2568.

Irish Times, (2012a). April 16.

Irish Times, (2012b). March 28.

The Independent, (2011). The rich just got richer—top 300 now have •57bn. Dublin: *The Independent*, 13 March. Online at http://www.independent.ie/business/the-rich-just-got-richer-top-300-now-have-euro57bn-2577762.html.

International Socialism (2011). The student revolt and the crisis, *International Socialism*, Issue 129. 4 January. Online at http://www.isj.org.uk/?id=697.

Jack, M. (2010). University of Sussex cutbacks: Protests, riot police and strike action.*The Independent*, 18 March. Online at http://www.independent.co.uk/life-style/history/university-of-sussex-cutbacks-protests-riot-police-and-strike-action-1923621.html.

Keating, K., Morrison, J. and Corrigan, J. (2010). *Ireland's Credit Crunch: The*

Costs and the Alternative. London: Resistance Press.

Kelsh, D. (2001). (D)evolutionary socialism and the containment of class: For a red theory of class. *The Red Critique: Marxist Theory Critique Pedagogy*, 1(1), pp.9-13. Online at http://www.redcritique.org.

Kelsh, D. and Hill, D. (2006). The Culturalization of Class and the Occluding of Class Consciousness: The Knowledge Industry in/of Education. *Journal for Critical Education Policy Studies,* 4 (1). Online at http://www.jceps.com/index.php?pageID=article& articleID=59.

Kelsh, D., Hill, D. and Macrine, S. (eds.) (2010). *Class in Education: Knowledge, Pedagogy, Subjectivity.* London: Routledge.

Kishore, J. (2011). *Wealth and poverty in America.* 23 September. World Socialist Website. Online at http://www.wsws.org/articles/2011/sep2011/pers-s23.shtml.

Klein, M. (2007). *The Shock Doctrine: The Rise of Disaster Capitalism.* New York: Metropolitan Books. Kloke, A. (2012a). Ruled by the memoranda - dependent or imperialist country? *International Viewpoint, IV Online magazine*: IV446 - March 2012. Online at http://www.internationalview point.org/spip.php?article2526.

Kloke, A. (2012b). The shadow of the Weimar Republic hangs over Greece: The election results of May 6. *International Viewpoint IV Online magazine*: IV448 - May 2012. 16 May. Online at http://www.internationalviewpoint.org/spip.php?article2619.

Kloke, A. (2012c). New Memorandum-Government in Greece. *4th International Revolutionary Marxists Blogspot*, 23 June. Online at http://4thinternational.blogspot.co.uk/.

Kloke, A. (2012d). The Euro, the Greek Crisis, and the Left.*4th International Revolutionary Marxists Blogspot*, 30 September. Online at http://4thinternational.blogspot.co.uk/.

Kroman, J. (2012). Comments on a political theoretical aspects of a Draft of this paper. Unpublished.

Lansley, S. (2012). All in this together? *An audit of the impact of the downturn on the workforce.* London: Trades Union Congress, Touchstone publications. Online at http://www.tuc.org.uk/tucfiles/195/All_In_This_Together.pdf.

MacAskill, E. (2011). US left finds its voice over Wisconsin attack on union rights. *The Guardian*, 24 February. Online at http://www.guardian.co.uk/world/2011/feb/24/wisconsin-union-rights-protest.

Malott, C.S. (2011). Pseudo-Marxism and the Reformist Retreat from Revolution: A Critical Essay Review of JeanAnyon, *Marx and Education. Journal for Critical Education Policy Studies* 9 (1). Online at http://www.jceps.com/index.php?pageID=article&articleID=206.

Malott, C.S. (2012). Rethinking Educational Purpose: The Socialist Challenge. *Journal for Critical Education Policy Studies*, 10 (2) Online at www.jceps.com.

Malott, C., Cole, M. and Elmore, J. (eds.) (2012). *Teaching Marx: The Socialist*

Challenge. Charlotte, NC Information Age Publishing.

Maltby, E. and Thomas, M. (2012). Self-organisation for workers' power? *Workers' Liberty, 15 July.* Online at http://www.workersliberty.org/story/2012/07/15/self-organisation-workers-power.

Mandel, E. (1970). *The Leninist Theory of Organisation: Its relevance for today*. Online at http://www.marxists.org/archive/mandel/196x/leninism/index.html.

Marcus, J. (2011). Occupy London- the 99%. *Dazed Digital.* Online at http://www.dazeddigital.com/artsandculture/article/11967/1/occupy-london-the-99.

Marx, K. and Engels, F. [1848]/(1985). *The Communist Manifesto.* New York: Penguin Books.

Marx, K. [1867] (1999). *Das Kapital*. Chapter Twenty-Five: The General Law of Capitalist Accumulation. Online at http://www.marxists.org/archive/marx/works/1867-c1/.

Marx, K. (1867/1967a). *Capital: A critique of political economy (Vol. 1: The process of capitalist production)*(Samuel Moore & Edward Aveling, Trans.), Frederick Engels (ed.), New York: International Publishers.

McGrew, K. (2011). On Being Holier-Than-Thou: A Critique of Curry Malott's "Pseudo-Marxism and the Reformist Retreat from Revolution. *Journal for Critical Education Policy Studies*, 9 (1). Online at http://www.jceps.com/index.php?pageID=article&articleID=222.

McLaren, P. (2005). *Capitalists and Conquerors: A Critical Pedagogy Against Empire.* Lanham, MD: Rowman and Littlefield.

McLaren, P. and Farahmandpur, R. (2004). *Capitalists and Conquerors: Critical Pedagogy Against Empire.* Lanham, MD: Rowman and Littlefield.

Milne, S. (2008). The political class can't face up to the scale of this crisis, *The Guardian*, 18 September. Online at http://www.guardian.co.uk/commentisfree/2008/sep/18/economy.creditcrunch1.

Miranda, C. (2012). "October 7: Elect Chavez President – October 8: Get rid of the bureaucrats" International Viewpoint - online socialist magazineIV453 - 7 October 2012. Online at http://internationalviewpoint.org/spip.php?article2760.

Morgan, W.J. (2003). *Communists on Education and Culture, 1848-1948.* Basingstoke: Palgrave Macmillan.

Neary, M. (2012). Teaching Politically- Policy, Pedagogy and the New European University *Journal for Critical Education Policy Studies*, 10 (2). October. Online at www.jceps.com.

Neary, M. and Amsler, S. (2012). Occupy: a New Pedagogy of Space and Time. *Journal for Critical Education Policy Studies*, 10 (2).October. Online at www.jceps.com.

Nikolakai, M. (2012). Personal communication. Unpublished.

Pope, C. (2012). Up to 47% of adults have less than €100 a month after bills. *Irish Times*, April 16. Online at http://www.irishtimes.com/newspaper/frontpage/2012/0416/1224314764193.html.

Ramesh, R. (2010). London's richest people worth 273 times more than the poorest.

The Guardian, 21 April. Online at http://www.guardian.co.uk/uk/2010/apr/21/wealth-social-divide-health-inequality.

Resolution Foundation (2012). *Who Gains from Growth? Living Standards in 2020.* London: The Resolution Foundation. Online at http://www.resolutionfoundation.org/media/media/downloads/Who_Gains_from_Growth.pdf.

Richardson, B. (2011). After the Riots. *Socialist Review*, September. Online at http://www.socialistreview.org.uk/article.php?articlenumber=11747.

Rikowski, G. (1996). Left Alone: End time for Marxist educational theory? *British Journal of Sociology of Education*, 17 (4), pp. 415-451.

Rikowski, G. (1997). Scorched Earth: Prelude to Rebuilding Marxist Educational Theory, *British Journal of Sociology of Education*, 18 (4), pp. 551-574.

Rikowski, G. (2003a). The Business Takeover of Schools, *Mediactive: Ideas Knowledge Culture*, Issue 1, pp. 91-108.

Rikowski, G. (2003b). Schools and the GATS Enigma. Journal for Critical Education Policy Studies, 1 (1). Online at http://www.jceps.com/index.php?pageID=article&articleID=8.

Rikowski, G. (2006). In Retro Glide. Journal for Critical Education Policy Studies, 4 (2). Online at http://www.jceps.com/index.php?pageID=article&articleID=81.

Rikowski, G. (2007). Marxist Educational Theory Unplugged. Paper prepared for the Fourth Historical Materialism Annual Conference, 9-11 November 2007, School of Oriental & African Studies, University of London. *The Flow of Ideas.* http://www.flowideas.co.uk ?page=articles&sub=Marxist%20Educational%20Theory%20Unplugged.

Rikowski, G. (2012). *Life in the Higher Sausage Factory*, Guest Lecture to the Teacher Education Research Group, The Cass School of Education and Communities, University of East London, 22 March. The Flow of Ideas. Online at: http://www.flowideas.co.uk/?page=articles&sub=Life%20in%20the%20Higher%20Sausage%20Factory.

Robinson, B. (2011).Young, gifted and striking back: The significance of the student movement. Socialist World, 11 June. Online at http://www.socialistworld.net/mob/doc/5114.

Shaoul, J. (2012). Cuts push UK workers' living standards back 30 years. World Socialist Website, 12 March. Online at http://www.wsws.org/articles/2012/mar2012/wage-m12.shtml

Saltman, K. (2010). *The Gift of Education: Public Education and Venture Philanthropy*. New York: Palgrave Macmillan.

Saltman, K. (2011). Comments on The Pioneers of Marxist Thought in Education: A Review of *Marx and Education* by Jean Anyon, Part One. *Schooling Capitalist America Blog.* Online at http://schoolingincapitalistamerica.wordpress.com/2011/05/24/the-pioneers-of-marxist-thought-in-education-a-review-of-marx-and-education-by-jean-anyon-part-one/.

Shaoul, J. (2012). *Cuts push UK workers' living standards back 30 years*. World Socialist Website, 12 March. Online at http://www.wsws.org/articles/2012/

mar2012/wage-m12.shtml.

Sheehan, H. (2012). Occupying Dublin: Considerations at the Crossroads. 2012. *Irish Left Review,* August 15. Online at http://www.irishleftreview.org/2012/01/19/occupying-dublin-considerations-crossroads/.

Smith, H. (2012). Greek police send crime victims to neo-Nazi 'protectors'. *The Guardiam*, 28 September. Online at http://www.guardian.co.uk/world/2012/sep/28/greek-police-victims-neo-nazi?newsfeed=true.

Socialist Resistance (2012). Democratic Centralism and Broad Left Parties. Online athttp://www.internationalviewpoint.org/spip.php?article1413&var_recherche=Hearse.

Socialist World (2011). Largest protest yet against Wisconsin Governor's anti-union bill. 1 March. *Socialist World.* 1 March. Online at http://www.socialistworld.net/doc/4886.

Stewart, H. (2012). Wealth doesn't trickle down – it just floods offshore, research reveals. *The Guardian,* 21 July. Online at http://www.guardian.co.uk/business/2012/jul/21/offshore-wealth-global-economy-tax-havens.

Socialist Voice (2011). The Election is over but the struggle continues. *Socialist Voice*, March. Dublin: Communist Party of Ireland. Online at http://www.communistpartyofireland.ie/sv2011-03/01-election.html.

Socialist World (2011). Largest protest yet against Wisconsin Governor's anti-union bill. 1 March. *Socialist World.* 1 March. Online at http://www.socialistworld.net/doc/4886.

Socialist World (2012). Greece: Working Class Struggle Returns. *Socialist World.* Online at http://www.socialistworld.net/doc/5968.

Sotiris, P. (2012a). Greece: The Downsizing of a Country. *Greek Left review*, 17 September. Online at https://greekleftreview.wordpress.com/2012/09/17/greece-the-downsizing-of-a-country/#more-3615.

Sotiris, P. (2012b). Greece: On June 18, the war only begins… The Press Project. Online at http://www.thepressproject.net/detailsen.php?id=22267Sotiris, P. (2012c) Greece: the Fight is Far from Over' Online at http://initiativegrecqueaparis.wordpress.com/2012/06/20/greece-the-fight-is-far-from-over-de-panagiotis-sotiris/.

Stevens, R. (2012). Greek police collude with fascist Golden Dawn group. World Socialist Website. Online at http://www.wsws.org/articles/2012/oct2012/dawn-o09.shtml.

SubMediatv (2012). This is Athens, July. Online at http://submedia.tv/stimulator/2012/07/09/this-is-athens.

The Observer (2012). We need to avert this polarisation of Britain. *The Observer*, London, 23 September. Online at http://www.guardian.co.uk/commentisfree/2012/sep/23/editorial-mend-fractured-britain.

TimesOnline (2007). "Welcome to Richistan", 2007. *TimesOnline*, 17 July. Online at http://entertainment.timesonline.co.uk/tol/arts_and_entertainment/books/book_extracts/article1942088.ece.

Trotsky, L. (1922). *The First Five Years of the Communist International: On the*

United Front. Online at http://www.marxists.org/archive/trotsky/1924/ffyci-2/08.html.

Trostsky, L (1931). *The Permanent Revolution.* Trotsky Internet Archive. Online at http://www.marxists.org/archive/trotsky/1931/tpr/pr-index.html.

Trotsky, L. (1938). *The Death Agony of Capitalism and the Tasks of the Fourth International: The Mobilization of the Masses around Transitional Demands to Prepare the Conquest of Power.* Online at http://www.marxists.org/archive/trotsky/1938/tp/index.html.

Tsironis, K, (2012). Greek anti-fascist protesters 'tortured by police' after Golden Dawn clash. *The Guardian* (London), 9 October. Online at http://apps.facebook.com/theguardian/world/2012/oct/09/greek-antifascist-protesters-torture-police.

Vatikiotis, L. (2012). Personal communication, 26 August. Unpublished.

White, C. and Edgar, G. (2010). Inequalities in healthy life expectancy by social class and area type: England, 2001–03 Health Statistics Quarterly, 45. Online athttp://www.google.co.uk/url?sa=t&rct=j&q=&esrc=s&source=web&cd=27&ved=0CFcQFjAGOBQ&url =http%3A%2F%2Fwww.ons.gov.uk%2Fons%2Frel%2Fhsq%2Fhealth-statistics-quarterly%2Fno—45—spring-2010%2Finequalities-in-healthy-life-expectancy-by-social-class-and-area-type—england—2001-03.pdf&ei=ZTApUPrxM4qh4gSHuoHoAg&usg=AFQjCNHmI-dWNI4Zp0lXCJWEa6dRzz6gkA.

Wrigley, T. (2003). *Schools of Hope: A New Agenda for School Improvement.* London: Trentham Books.

Wrigley, T. (2006). *Another School is Possible.* London: Bookmarks. Wrigley, T., Thomson, P. and Lingard, R. (2011) *Changing Schools: Alternative Ways to Make a World of Difference.* London: Routledge.

Yates, M. "Preface to the Turkish Edition of Naming the System". *MRZine*, 2006, 9 September. Online at http://mrzine.monthlyreview.org/yates090906.html.